THE SEPTUAGINT, SEXUALITY,
AND THE NEW TESTAMENT

The Septuagint, Sexuality, and the New Testament

*Case Studies on the Impact of the LXX
in Philo and the New Testament*

WILLIAM LOADER

WILLIAM B. EERDMANS PUBLISHING COMPANY
GRAND RAPIDS, MICHIGAN / CAMBRIDGE, U.K.

© 2004 Wm. B. Eerdmans Publishing Co.
All rights reserved

Wm. B. Eerdmans Publishing Co.
255 Jefferson Ave. S.E., Grand Rapids, Michigan 49503 /
P.O. Box 163, Cambridge CB3 9PU U.K.

Printed in the United States of America

09 08 07 06 05 04   7 6 5 4 3 2 1

ISBN 0-8028-2756-X

www.eerdmans.com

Contents

Acknowledgments

This book had its genesis in the idea of preparing a paper to present to colleagues on an area of special interest. The leaven of those first thoughts produced unexpected growth. By the time I was preparing to present it to the ongoing Seminar, "The Septuagint and the New Testament," which I co-chair, at the *Studiorum Novi Testamenti Societas Meeting* in Montreal, 2001, it had expanded to at least three times a usable length. I am grateful to my colleagues that I was able to present at least sections of it to the group and could make the fuller text available for comment, which I greatly appreciated..

From there the paper expanded to reach its current proportions as a book. I thank my colleagues in Australia for their willingness to read and make comment on the longer form: Professor Michael Lattke of the University of Queensland, Dr John Dunnill and Dr John Olley of Murdoch University, Perth. I am also indebted to Dr Ian Mackay for his careful proofreading.

The research was made possible through the generous support of both Murdoch University, initially through an Australian Research Council Small Grant, and of the Perth Theological Hall of the Uniting Church in Australia. The book took shape during the period in which I was Head of the School of Social Inquiry at Murdoch and had to compete for time with heavy administrative demands.

This specific study belongs within a wider project of research into understandings of sexuality in the New Testament and early Judaism. Beginning before it and finishing after it is another study, *Sexuality and the Jesus Tradition,* which will also appear shortly. I am grateful to William B. Eerdmans Jr for his encouragement and willingness to make both these works available to the reading public.

ix

It is appropriate to the focus of the book, above all, on the Bible's first chapters, that I reflect on my own genesis. In doing so I want to honour my parents who shaped and enriched my life in ways which go far beyond what I can remember or comprehend. My father, Nelson Loader, died in 1987, at the age of 75 after a long struggle with Alzheimers. My mother, Elizabeth Loader, turned 92 in 2003, and takes delight in her children, grandchildren and great grandchildren. The home I cherished then laid a foundation for the family which Gisela, my wife, and I have built together, which has then been a foundation for the lives of our grown up children, Stefanie with her husband, Brendan, and Christopher. I am grateful that Genesis 2 has worked so well for us and am mindful that for many this is not so. May this study contribute to knowledge, but also to a better understanding of what is at stake.

Introduction

The studies in this volume form part of a wider interest in the understanding of sexuality within Judaism and emerging Christianity in the Greco-Roman period. One particular focus of this research is the understanding of sexuality within the early movements of Christianity as reflected primarily in the New Testament. This includes not only the attitudes to sexuality which we find expressed there, but also the possible influences which gave shape to them.

Sexuality was an issue as Judaism sought to come to terms with its identity in the context of a world being increasingly Hellenised. The most important text for Greek speaking Jews of the time was the Greek translation of their sacred writings, commonly designated the Septuagint (LXX), in particular, the Pentateuch. This also holds true for the first Greek speaking Christians who began as a movement within Judaism.

The LXX translation is itself an artefact of the encounter between Judaism and its Hellenistic world. It is at the same time a major source of influence. This book seeks to explore that influence by focussing on three sets of texts: the decalogue, as found in Exodus and Deuteronomy; the first three chapters of Genesis; and the passage about divorce in Deuteronomy. The selection is warranted because these texts, particularly the first two, have undoubted prominence in extant literature, Jewish and Christian, in the period under consideration, but also because they contain important statements pertaining to sexuality.

The approach to the task is beset with some difficulties. What are we talking about when we speak of the LXX? Our focus will be on passages from the Pentateuch. The assumption is that there was a fairly standard Greek translation of the Pentateuch which would have been used in Greek speaking synagogues and churches. "Fairly standard", because, while on the one hand, we know of variants, there is evidence to suggest that a Greek translation of the Pentateuch, in particular, was established and relatively stable, sufficient for us to be able to examine texts and their influence and to take into account occasional variations. We shall take as our starting point the Göttingen edition, an eclectic text with apparatus showing major variants among manuscripts, found in: *Septuaginta. Vetus Testamentum Graecum*, edited by J. W. Wevers (Göttingen: Vandenhoeck und Ruprecht): I *Genesis* (1974); II,1 *Exodus* (1991); III,2 *Deuteronomium* (1977).

A related question is: What are we talking about when we speak of the Hebrew text? Which Hebrew text? For the purposes of this study, unless otherwise indicated, I shall use "the Hebrew (text)" to refer to the *Biblia Hebraica Stuttgartensia*, edited by K. Elliger and W. Rudolph (Stuttgart: Württembergische Bibelgesellschaft, 1983), which reproduces Codex Leningrad, the oldest complete manuscript in the Masoretic tradition. The problem is that there were variant Hebrew texts, so that one cannot assume the LXX translates the text we have in "the Hebrew" nor that the LXX variations necessarily reflect innovations or changes resulting from translation.[1]

The focus of the research is therefore not on the extent to which the LXX adequately translates the Hebrew (where we are confident about what that was), nor with the value of the LXX in reconstructing the Hebrew text which lies behind it and its relation to the textual history, nor with the intention of the translator, including the translator's interpretation in that process, but on the text itself and the way it enabled itself to be read. In other words, the focus is on the influence of a revered text. This may be much the same as the influence of the Hebrew text, but is of particular interest where the Greek translation has introduced new and different possibilities for interpretation which can be shown to have been influential. The extent of influence reaches across many centuries, but the focus here is on emerging Christianity in the first century. The question with which I

---

[1] For recent discussion see E. Tov, *The Greek and Hebrew Bible: Collected Essays on the Septuagint* (Leiden: Brill, 1999), especially the essays in section V; Martin Hengel and Anna-Marie Schwemer (eds.) *Die Septuaginta zwischen Judentum und Christentum* (Tübingen: J. C. B. Mohr, 1994), esp. R. Hanhart, "Textgeschichtliche Probleme der LXX von ihrer Entstehung bis Origenes," 1-19; N. Fernandez Marcos, *The Septuagint in Context: Introduction to the Greek Versions of the Bible* (Leiden: Brill, 2000), esp. Parts 1 and 2; Gilles Dorival, Marguerite Harl, Olivier Munnich, *La Bible Grecque Des Septante: Du judaïsme hellénistique au christianisme ancien* (Éditions du Cerf / Éditions du C.N.R.S., 1994) url: http://www.tradere.com/biblio/lxx/frame.htm., esp. ch. 4; see also Karen H. Jobes and Moises Silva, *Invitation to the Septuagint* (Grand Rapids: Baker; Carlisle: Paternoster, 2000); Folker Siegert, *Zwischen Hebräischer Bibel und Altem Testament: eine Einführung in die Septuaginta* (Münsteraner Judaistische Studien 9; Münster: Lit-Verlag, 2001); Heinz-Josef Fabry, and Ulrich Offerhaus (eds.) *Im Brennpunkt: Die Septuaginta: Studien zur Entstehung und Bedeutung der griechischen Bibel* (BWANT 153; Stuttgart: Kohlhammer, 2001).

approach the Greek text is: to what extent has the way the text deals with matters pertaining to sexuality contributed to the development of attitudes towards sexuality in early Christianity of the New Testament era?

"Early Christianity of the New Testament era" is also a complex phenomenon. Our focus will be on the writings of the New Testament and the traditions which they represent. They originated in predominantly Greek speaking communities where the influence of the Greek text of the Pentateuch would have been present, although some preserve traditions which will have arisen in Aramaic speaking communities.

To speak of "the influence" of the Greek translation of the Pentateuch or of its individual books is in itself problematic. It may be impossible to extract such influence from other factors which played a role in the environment. What constitutes "influence"? At times it may be that we can do little more than identify a common vocabulary used in a common way which may or may not be due to the impact of Septuagintal language. At times one might be able to do no more than identify common values, which may reflect similar influences in the contemporary contexts. "Influence" becomes more specific where the Greek text is cited directly or indirectly, but may also be indicated where particular values expressed in particular terms are present in a text where dependence on the LXX passage under consideration is clearly recognisable.

The following exploration will look at certain passages in the Greek text likely to have been widely known and therefore to have been potentially widely influential. These are: the decalogue (Exod 20:2-17; Deut 5:6-21); the creation narratives (Genesis 1-3, especially 1:26-28; 2:18-25; 3:16-19 and also the related 5:1-3) and the divorce related statement in Deut 24:1-4.

In considering each passage I shall explore the passage itself in the LXX, examining ways in which the text may have been heard. I then turn to Philo to identify ways in which he has read the text and interpreted it. This is a useful study in its own right, but it also provides a sample of one way (sometimes some ways) of hearing the text. It is not done on the assumption that in some way Philo's understanding influences the understanding of New Testament writers. From there I turn to the way in which the text has been heard in early Christianity of the New Testament era.

For reasons dictated by the texts themselves I consider the possible influence of Genesis 1-3 and Deut 24:1-4 on the Christian texts together, because in some key passages they both occur in relation to one another.

This study takes a different direction from most Septuagintal research in not focusing on use of the LXX as a means to reconstruct the original Hebrew text, nor on the LXX itself, nor on its influence on the form of New Testament citations. Instead it focuses on a particular aspect of influence of ideas and in one area in particular: sexuality. I am aware of few comparable studies. Mostly the theme addressed comes incidentally as part of wider considerations. The one that comes closest to the theme and deserves special mention is Klaus Berger's monumental work, announced as Volume 1, but which remained a single volume: *Die Gesetzesauslegung Jesu: Ihr historischer Hintergrund im Judentum und im Alten Testament: Teil I: Markus und Parallelen* (WMANT 40; Neukirchen–Vluyn: Neukirchener Verlag, 1972). He tends to all three sets of texts which form the basis for our investigation. I shall be interacting with his arguments at various points in the study. At times, for instance in relation to the influence of Gen 2:24 LXX, I shall argue that he claims too much, but in the same context I will argue that the context of Gen 2:24 LXX is more influential than he recognises.

As the Göttingen Septuagint provides the starting point for examining the text, so the notes of J. W. Wevers on the text have been an invaluable resource: *Notes on the Greek Text of Genesis* (SBLSCS 35; Atlanta: Scholars, 1993); *Notes on the Greek Text of Exodus* (SBLSCS 30; Atlanta: Scholars, 1990); *Notes on the Greek Text of Deuteronomy* (SBLSCS 39; Atlanta: Scholars, 1995).

Wherever possible I have translated Greek and Hebrew words and passages. In doing so I have take the NRSV as a starting point and then produced a translation which in the case of the LXX reflects the differences and enables them to be easily recognised. At times I have also given more literal translations of the Hebrew or the New Testament Greek for purposes of greater clarity to enable the English-only reader to appreciate the subtleties of the texts.

CHAPTER ONE

The Decalogue

The decalogue, commonly called the ten commandments, is preserved for us in Exod 20:1-17 and in Deut 5:6-21. Appendix A sets out side by side the Göttingen LXX and the Biblical Hebraica Stuttgartensia texts, followed by an English translation of each.

We begin by identifying those aspects of the LXX texts which pertain to sexuality and any distinctive ways that these are represented in the text. We will then examine ways in which Philo read these texts, including where he made particular use of the way they represent aspects of sexuality. From there we turn to New Testament writings to explore possible influences detectable in them which are a result of using the LXX.

1. Distinctive Features of the LXX Versions of the Decalogue (Exod 20:1-17; Deut 5:6-21) in Relation to Sexuality

The major features of note which are relevant for our investigation where the LXX translations differ from the Hebrew are changes in the order in the commandments, and in the tenth, in particular, and in the choice of language.

1.1 Putting adultery first

In the Hebrew of both Exodus and Deuteronomy the commandment לֹא תִּנְאָף ("you shall not commit adultery") comes as the seventh commandment, after the prohibition of murder and before the prohibition of theft. In the LXX translations of Exodus and Deuteronomy as reconstructed by Wevers the commandment οὐ μοιχεύσεις ("you shall not commit adultery") comes as the sixth, before murder and theft. The effect is to make it the first of the second table, thus to elevate its significance for hearers who sense this bipartite division of the decalogue, suggested to hearers by the two tablets of stone (Exod 31:18) and by the changed focus of the content in the second half. Adultery receives, in that sense, greater prominence. The LXX order also differs between Exodus and Deuteronomy with the former having the sequence adultery - theft - murder and the latter the order: adultery - murder - theft, but both agree in giving adultery first place.

This reconstruction is not without difficulty.[1] Codex Alexandrinus of the LXX of Deuteronomy reflects the order, murder - adultery - theft, as in the Hebrew Masoretic Text, 4QDeut[n], the Samaritan Pentateuch and the Peshitta (See Table 1 below). This order is preserved also in Mark (ms. B), Matthew, and the Didache. Wevers, whose text we take as our starting point, follows Codex Vaticanus which preserves the order which places adultery first, which is found also in Romans, Mark (ms. A), Luke and Philo, and also in the Hebrew Nash Papyrus. Mark in 10:19 (MS. B; N.-A.[27]), Matthew in 19:18 and the Didache in 2:2 may reflect an order influenced by the Hebrew; in the case of Mark (and so also of Matthew) this may reflect tradition reaching back to Aramaic speaking contexts. Codex Alexandrinus may well reflect an attempt to restore conformity.[2] Alternatively, different forms of the Greek translation of the decalogue may have been in circulation.[3] For our purposes their existence, reflected already in the New Testament, warrants reflection on the possible impact of such an order in some Greek translations which were obviously in use.

The only extant Hebrew text which gives first place to the prohibition of adultery is the Hebrew Nash papyrus, a liturgical text, dating probably from the 2nd century BCE and containing the decalogue and the *Shema*.[4] Of the latter only Deut

---

[1] See the discussion in Gert J. Steyn, "Pretexts of the second table of the Decalogue and early Christian intertexts," *Neotestamentica* 30 (1966) 451-64. On his evaluation of the diversity among the manuscripts in Mark see the discussion of the New Testament in 1.3 below.

[2] See Wevers, *Notes on the Greek Text of Exodus*, 314: "The majority text which follows the order of MT is undoubtedly a reordering by the hex recension." For discussion of the variations see M. Weinfeld, *Deuteronomy 1-11* (AB 5; New York: Doubleday, 1991) 282; S. A. White, "The all souls Deuteronomy and the decalogue," *JBL* 109 (1990) 193-206, esp. 202-203.

[3] So Steyn, "Pretexts," 457-58, 461-63. See the discussion of the gospel texts below for further comment.

[4] For the linking of the decalogue and the Shema in Jewish worship see *m. Tamid* 5.1 and Weinfeld, *Deuteronomy 1-11*, 264. See also the discussion in D. Sänger, "Torah für die

6:4 and a letter of verse 5 are preserved. The decalogue it records contains a Hebrew text which reflects a mixture of Exod 20:2-17 and Deut 5:6-13. The text conforms generally to Exodus. Its explanation of the sabbath commandment follows the Exodus version, but the enumeration of who is not to work on the sabbath contains the two additional categories present in Deuteronomy (l. 12). Similarly it uses the fuller list in its version of the final commandment (l. 20). Influence from the Deuteronomy text is also reflected in the fuller explanation of the command to honour mother and father, and in the form of the final commandment (the separate, prior mention of the wife and the use of the verbs for desiring). It differs from both Hebrew texts in reordering the commandments to place the prohibition of adultery before the prohibition of murder and theft (as in the LXX of Deuteronomy). The *Shema* includes the introduction otherwise found only in the LXX: Deut 6:4 καὶ ταῦτα τὰ δικαιώματα καὶ τὰ κρίματα, ὅσα ἐνετείλατο κύριος τοῖς υἱοῖς Ισραὴλ ἐν τῇ ἐρήμῳ ἐξελθόντων αὐτῶν ἐκ γῆς Αἰγύπτου ("And these are the ordinances and judgements which the Lord commanded the sons of Israel in the day when they came out from the land of Egypt").

Table 1: The order of the sixth, seventh, and eighth commandments of the decalogue		
murder-adultery-theft	adultery-theft-murder	adultery-murder-theft
Exodus MT	Exodus LXX (ms B)	Nash Papyrus
Deuteronomy MT	(Mark 7:21-22 mss ℵ B)	Deuteronomy LXX (ms B)
4QDeut^n		Philo
Deuteronomy LXX (ms A)		Romans 13:9
Samaritan Pentateuch		Mark 10:19 (ms A)
Peshitta		Luke 18:20
Mark 10:19 (ms B)		James 2:11
Matthew 19:18		
(Matthew 5:21-30)		
Didache 2:2		

The Nash papyrus does not preserve a text that corresponds to what would be a matching Hebrew *Vorlage* (textual base) of either Exodus or Deuteronomy. It reflects the use of the decalogue and *shema* texts for liturgical purposes and is probably conflationary. It may be evidence of a different Hebrew manuscript tradition, but this is far from certain. The presence of the addition in Deut 6:4

Völker - Weisungen der Liebe: Zur Rezeption des Dekalogs im frühen Judentum und Neuen Testament," in *Weisheit, Ethos und Gebot: Weisheits- und Dekalogtraditionen in der Bibel und im frühen Judentum*, ed. H. G. Reventlow (Neukirchen-Vluyn: Neukirchener Verlag, 2000) 97-146, here 110.

would seem to indicate this. It is interesting that the Samaritan Pentateuch also contains within itself evidence of compilation, when it combines Deut 11:29a, 27:2b–3a,4a [Samaritan version], 5–7, and 11:30. The trend towards expansion and harmonisation is also evident elsewhere: in the versions, and in 4QDeut[n], which attaches the grounds given for the sabbath commandment in Exodus onto the commandment in Deuteronomy.

With regard to the particular question of the priority given the prohibition of adultery in the LXX, we may be dealing with faithful translation of the order in the translator's Hebrew originals (as perhaps indicated by the order in the Nash Papyrus) or with innovative translation. At either level it may have been an adjustment in the light of the prominence given to wives in the final prohibition in Deuteronomy, perhaps also drawn forward into proximity with the commandment to honour parents,[5] and perhaps also reflecting a dominant concern with adultery in contemporary society of the time. However it may have come about, the effect is to produce a text which does give it prominence. In what follows I shall speak of the order as a feature of the LXX text and so speak of its influence, but without prejudice to the possibility that it may be preserving an order found already in some Hebrew manuscripts.

1.2   Putting the neighbor's wife first

The second change in order applies only to Exodus. The Hebrew lists coveting one's neighbor's house separately: לֹא תַחְמֹד בֵּית רֵעֶךָ ("Neither shall you covet your neighbor's house"). It then begins afresh, listing wife, male slave, female slave, ox, ass and any other property. All the latter would be deemed to belong to the "house" or "household". The LXX lists desiring one's neighbor's wife separately. It then begins afresh, listing house, field (not in the Hebrew), male slave, female slave, ox, ass, and any other property.

The Hebrew of Deuteronomy, however, also has the wife first. It follows the same structure as the Exodus commandment, but the first separate statement is about the neighbor's wife: וְלֹא תַחְמֹד אֵשֶׁת רֵעֶךָ ("Neither shall you covet your neighbor's wife"). It then begins afresh, as does Exodus, but unlike Exodus, using

---

[5] U. Kellermann, "Der Dekalog in den Schriften des Frühjudentums," in *Weisheit, Ethos und Gebot: Weisheits- und Dekalogtraditionen in der Bibel und im frühen Judentum*, ed. H. G. Reventlow (Neukirchen-Vluyn: Neukirchener Verlag, 2000) 147-226, sees the reordering as the result of an attempt to give structure to the decalogue by bringing together the commandments concerned with protecting the family: sabbath, honouring parents and prohibition of adultery. They would be seen as following the first group of three which are about honouring God and preceding the final group of instructions about the protection of society (153).

waw ("and"; here: "neither") as it has for each commandment,[6] and a different verb (see below). The *waw* is missing before the prohibition of murder in Deuteronomy. The effect is to make all the prohibitions from murder onwards into a single statement. The final prohibition forbids desiring one's neighbor's house, field, male slave, female slave, ox, ass and any other property. The presence of "field" in the Hebrew of Deuteronomy and in the LXX translation of Exodus, where it is missing in the corresponding Hebrew, suggests influence from Deuteronomy on the LXX text of Exodus (or on its Hebrew *Vorlage*) and probably also accounts for the change of order within the commandment.

The Hebrew text of Deuteronomy does not reflect the pattern of Exodus where the household is the head under which the other items are listed, including the wife. Instead its text produces the effect, intended or otherwise, of creating two separate commandments, where we may assume Exodus has one. It does this by singling out the wife, by the use of *waw*, with which each in the list of prohibited actions is introduced, and by the use of a different verb. The first three, murder, adultery, theft, are general; the last three commencing with false witness related specifically to "your neighbor". In addition the final two: coveting one's neighbor's wife and coveting one's neighbor's (other?) property, appear to expand the prohibitions of adultery and theft (understanding what was originally "manstealing" in the broader sense of stealing).

The LXX has not, however, preserved this. It has not preserved the *waw*. Each prohibition stands in its own right. It has the order adultery, murder, theft. Had the translator been seeking to match the acts of adultery and stealing to the desire to do the same, we might have expected the order, adultery-stealing-murder. We do find this in Exodus LXX, but not in Deuteronomy. Nor has the translation in Deuteronomy preserved the difference in verbs in the final two. It has, however, preserved the separate treatment of desiring one's neighbor's wife, which now stands in its own right, and this matches the emphasis now given to adultery in the list.

Overall the effect in the LXX version is to give greater prominence to desiring one's neighbor's wife and to do so in a way which reinforces the impact of the change of the order of the commandments themselves to place the prohibition of adultery first.

---

[6] But note that 4QDeut[n] does not do so. Weinfeld, *Deuteronomy 1-11*, 281. White, "All souls Deuteronomy," 203, argues: "The *waw* conjunctive is not original to the negative commandments".

1.3 Translating תַחְמֹד לֹא by οὐκ ἐπιθυμήσεις in the commandment, "You shall not covet/desire ..".

The third change relates to the choice by the translator in both Exodus and in Deuteronomy to translate לֹא תַחְמֹד by οὐκ ἐπιθυμήσεις. The matter is more complex because Deuteronomy first uses לֹא תַחְמֹד in relation to the neighbor's wife and then uses לֹא תִתְאַוֶּה in relation to the subsequent list. LXX consistently uses οὐκ ἐπιθυμήσεις. The two Hebrew words are almost synonymous.[7] The choice of the different verb may be the effect of parallelism or may reflect sensitivity to different dimensions of desire entailed in desiring one's neighbor's wife. It is somewhat surprising that Deuteronomy does not have the verbs the other way around, since לֹא תִתְאַוֶּה might better suit the passion assumed in adultery,[8] but the choice is indicative of the focus, which, while including passion, is on acquisition of property. Choosing different verbs is, as we have seen, one way in which Deuteronomy separates the two acts of desiring and links them, respectively, to adultery and stealing.[9]

---

[7] L. Koehler, W. Baumgartner and J. J. Stamm, *The Hebrew and Aramaic Lexicon of the Old Testament* (CD-Rom Edition; Leiden: Brill, 1994-2001) on אוה for the *hitp* here in Deut 5:21 and for Num 11:34; Ps 45:12 and Qoh 6:2 give the meaning: "to crave for (usually in an unfavourable sense)". On חמד they give the meaning: "to desire (brings damage upon the thing or person desired) and to try to obtain". See also G. Mayer, "אָוָה" in *TDOT*, 1.134-137, who sees the choice of the verb as "the result of preaching" and "the influence from Wisdom, especially since it has didactic interests and preference for the root 'vh in common with Deuteronomy," with the result that a legal maxim has become a rule for governing conduct (136-37). On חָמַד see also G. Wallis, "חָמַד", *TDOT*, 4.452-61, esp. 459.

[8] "Le verbe *epithuméo* correspond à un terme hébreu qui implique une tentative d'appropriation; il a un sense plus général et convient mieux pour traduire le second verbe hébreu signifiant 'désirer' en Dt 5, 21, où la LXX répète *epithuméo*." (Tr. The verb *epithuméo* corresponds to a Hebrew word which imples a temptation to acquire ownership; it has a more general meaning and suits more for translating the second Hebrew verb signifying "desire" in Deut 5:21, where the LXX repeats *epithuméo*). So Alain Le Boulluec, and Pierre Sandevoir, *La Bible D'Alexandrie: L'Exode* (Paris: Cerf, 1989) 210-11. Cf. Berger, *Gesetzesauslegung Jesu*, 344-45, who argue: the redactor chose a verb which lends itself to the notion of acquisition of property for the household and possessions, but chose the verb closer to ἐπιθυμέω to deal with the neighbor's wife (344).

[9] So Berger, *Gesetzesauslegung*, 344-45: The effect is to group the commandment about adultery with that of taking away the wife of one's neighbor and the commandment about stealing with coveting. He also notes the link between adultery and desire in Prov 6:25-26 LXX. See also Francis Watson, *Agape, Eros, Gender: Towards a Pauline Sexual Ethic* (Cambridge: Cambridge University Press, 2000) 153.

The Hebrew verb, חָמַד, used in both Exodus and Deuteronomy (in relation to the neighbor's wife), has the meaning of desire in response to seeing and being impressed by something or someone. Within the context of the tenth commandment the focus is upon possession of what belongs to another's household, including a wife. The focus is therefore on desire to possess, which includes house, field, slaves and animals. Attention is being given not primarily to theft nor to the act of adultery, but to the response which might lead to both as forms of theft from one's neighbor. The meaning of חָמַד is determined by this context in Exodus.

ἐπιθυμέω is a close translation, but can include a range of meaning beyond חָמַד especially under the influence of much popular Greek philosophy, particularly the Stoics, according to whom passions are either to be eliminated or to be distrusted and held under strict control.[10] Among these sexual passion can be seen as particularly dangerous. Since it now occurs in both LXX translations (of Exodus and Deuteronomy) in a separate statement which precedes the prohibition of coveting the neighbor's possessions, it is more likely to be understood as outlawing sexual desiring of the neighbor's wife.[11] It could lend itself also to the possible interpretation that not only the lustful response is outlawed, but also the sexual passion itself. It need not do so, but it provides a link to value systems which portray passions negatively.

Assuming a LXX text of the decalogue in Exodus and Deuteronomy which gives prominence to adultery, both by listing it first in the second half of the commandments, and which gives separate treatment to desiring a neighbor's wife and uses the verb ἐπιθυμέω ("to desire") in this context, what evidence do we have for the influence of this text on subsequent thought?

In what follows we shall be focusing in particular on the New Testament writings, but we turn first to the writings of Philo.

---

[10] On this see F. Büchsel, "ἐπιθυμέω / ἐπιθυμία," *TDNT*, 3.168-171; H. Hübner, "ἐπιθυμέω," *EWNT*, 2.67-71. On Stoic distrust of passionate desire see Martha C. Nussbaum, *The Therapy of Desire: Theory and Practice in Hellenistic Ethics* (Princeton, N.J.: Princeton Univ. Press, 1994) 359-401.

[11] Watson, *Agape, Eros, Gender*, 154, argues that "the result is that sexual desire is presented as paradigmatic of all desires for prohibited objects".

2   The Influence of the LXX Versions of the Decalogue in Philo in Relation to Sexuality

Philo devotes a treatise to the decalogue, *De decalogo*, and also makes the decalogue the framework within which to expound the Law in detail in *De specialibus legibus* 1-4.[12] Since the latter begins with a treatment of circumcision, it is possible that Philo also envisaged it as a basis for instruction of proselytes. In these writings Philo is clearly using the LXX and even exploits elements which we have noted as distinctive.

In his discourse on the decalogue Philo assumes the order, adultery, murder, theft, false testimony, desire (*Decal.* 36,51) and uses it directly to make the claim: "He [God] begins with adultery, holding this to be the greatest of crimes"[13] (*Decal.* 121). Similarly in *De specialibus legibus*: "It comes first, I think, because pleasure (ἡδονή) is a mighty force felt throughout the whole inhabited world..." (3.8). The prominence is appropriate, Philo argues, because adultery "has its source in the love of pleasure (φιληδονίαν)" (*Decal.* 122), sets up a partnership of wrong and enmity, is destructive both for all three families and for the wider community, and disadvantages children of such relationships (*Decal.* 122-30). "Such being the disasters wrought by illicit intercourse, naturally the abominable and God-detested sin of adultery was placed first in the list of wrongdoing" (*Decal.* 131). Under prohibition of adultery he subsumes: "enactments against seducers and pederasty, against dissolute living and indulgence in lawless and licentious form of intercourse", the aim of such prohibitions being to bring people to shame, "to make them blush" (*Decal.* 168-69). Referring to the final commandment of the second table, he writes: "the fifth blocks that fount of injustice, desire (ἐπιθυμίαν), from which flow the most iniquitous actions, public and private, small and great, dealing with things sacred or things profane, affecting bodies and souls and what are called external things. For nothing escapes desire (ἐπιθυμίαν)", which is "like a flame in the forest" (*Decal.* 173). Philo's railings against passion in expounding the prohibition of adultery are helped by the use of ἐπιθυμέω ("to desire") in the 10th commandment.

Spec. 3.8, cited above, continues with reference to such passion evident among animals, birds, fish. "Now even natural pleasure (ἡ κατὰ φύσιν ἡδονή) is often greatly to blame when the craving for it is immoderate and insatiable, as for instance when it takes the form of voracious gluttony, even though none of the food taken is of the forbidden kind, or again the passionate desire for women

---

[12] On Philo's use of the decalogue see Sänger, "Torah für die Völker," 104-106.

[13] Translations are drawn from *Philo* Loeb Classical Library, 10 vols, 2 suppl. vols, ed. F. H. Colson and G. H. Whitaker et al. (London: Heinemann; Cambridge, Ma; Harvard Univ. Pr., 1961-). I have occasionally inserted the Greek in brackets.

shown by those who in their craze for sexual intercourse behave unchastely, not only with the wives of others, but with their own" (οἱ φιλογύναιοι συνουσίαις ἐπιμεμηνότες καὶ λαγνίστερον ὁμιλοῦντες γυναιξὶν οὐκ ἀλλοτρίαις ἀλλὰ ταῖς ἑαυτῶν)(9). Philo considers the blame as lying in most of these cases not with the soul but with the balance of elements of fire and moisture in the body, when "the moisture is sluiced in a stream through the genital organs, and creates in them irritations, itchings and titilations without ceasing (10). It is not so with men who are mad to possess the wives of others" … where the soul "is incurably diseased" and so should be punished with death (11).

For Philo, not pleasure or desire itself is evil, but excess and misdirection. In *Leg.* 2 he writes: "For the sense and the passions are helpers of the soul and come after the soul" (ἡ γὰρ αἴσθησις καὶ τὰ πάθη τῆς ψυχῆς εἰσι βοηθοὶ νεώτεροι τῆς ψυχῆς)(5). "Moreover, there are, as I have said, helpers of another kind, namely the passions (τὰ πάθη). For pleasure and desire contribute to the permanence of our kind (ἡδονὴ βοηθεῖ πρὸς διαμονὴν τοῦ γένους ἡμῶν καὶ ἐπιθυμία): pain and fear are like bites or stings warning the soul to treat nothing carelessly: anger is a weapon of defence, which has conferred great boons on many: so with the other passions" (8).

Philo's comments about the 10th commandment focus on the word, ἐπιθυμία ("desire").[14] He understands it in a broader sense than desiring what belongs to another. It is a passion of the soul, the hardest of all to deal with (*Decal.* 142). He includes in his exposition a discussion of other passions, drawing on Stoic categories: pleasure, pain, fear, and desire (143-46). He speaks of desire as "when a person conceives an idea of something good which is not present and is eager to get it", like a straining after the unreachable (146). He illustrates the effects of desire by talking about strained eyes and strained ears (147-48). "The person who is mastered by desire (ἐπιθυμία), ever thirsting for what is absent remains unsatisfied, fumbling around his baffled appetite" (149). It is like a disease, which unchecked, will spread (150). "Consider the passion (ἔρως) whether for money or a woman or anything else that produces pleasure; are the evils which it causes small or casual?" (151). He goes on to identify war and associated calamities as "sprung from one source, desire (ἐπιθυμίας), the desire for money or glory or pleasure" (153).

In *Spec.* 4.78 Philo cites the last of the 10 commandments simply as "You shall not covet/desire" (οὐκ ἐπιθυμήσεις) without an object (similarly Paul in Rom 7:7; 13:9; see also 4 Macc 2:6 which begins a discourse on the dangers of desire, ἐπιθυμία). It is interesting that he does not draw attention to the separate mention of "the neighbor's wife", but treats the commandment not to covet as one and not as exclusively sexual. "Every passion (πάθος) is blameworthy" (79).

---

[14] See G. Wallis, "חָמַד", *TDOT* IV, 452-61, here 460.

Passions are to be bridled. "None of the passions is so troublesome as covetousness or desire (ἐπιθυμία - no "or" in the Greek, but just the single word) of what we have not, things which seem good, though they are not truly good" (80). He talks about fierce yearnings, about straining "for money, reputation, government, beautiful women" (82). Desire (ἐπιθυμία) is the fountain of all evils (84) and results in destructive behaviours in each category (87-99). "If the object is bodily beauty they are seducers, adulterers, pederasts, cultivators of incontinence and lewdness, as though these worst of evils were the best of blessings" (89). Philo uses Platonic divisions of the body to locate desire at the navel - a long way from reason (94). Moses "denounced especially desire (ἐπιθυμίαν) as a battery of destruction to the soul" (95). Philo then goes on to show that the food laws illustrate the bridling of passion.

For Philo pleasure in sexual intercourse is appropriate as something which leads to procreation, although even then his approach is very negative. In *Leg.* 2 Philo uses Genesis 2:24 both to illustrate the joining of mind and sense, and to set it in contrast to the image of Levi, who abandons mother and father for God (49-52) and so is a lover of God not of passions. On the other hand in *Quaestiones et solutiones in Genesin*, dealing with Gen 2:24, he writes, "But when Scripture says that the two are one flesh, it indicates something very tangible and sense-perceptive, in which there is suffering and sensual pleasure, that they may rejoice in and be pained by, and feel the same things, and, much more, may think the same things" (29). Aside from doing so for purposes of procreation, seeking such pleasure, even with one's own wife, is excess (*Spec.* 3.9). In this Philo reflects a widespread view of his time in both Jewish and non-Jewish literature. Philo's negativity is also reflected in one of his justifications for circumcision: it is the docking of the penis as the instrument of sexual intercourse with women to curb excessive and superfluous pleasure (*Spec.* 1.9).

While Philo reflects influences from Plato and the Stoics, especially in his treatments of ἐπιθυμία ("desire"), it is also clear that the LXX is the basis for his exposition. This is certainly the case in the prominence he gives to adultery (and sexual sins in general).[15] With the use of ἐπιθυμία / ἐπιθυμέω ("desire"/"to desire") the matter is more complicated. At least the fact that it is used here in the LXX opened for Philo the possibility of bringing a wide range of largely Stoic associations which the word evoked into his interpretation.

---

[15] This is not to prejudge the issue whether the Nash Papyrus is to be taken as evidence that already Hebrew texts of Exodus or Deuteronomy preserved this order. See the discussion above.

3   The Influence of the LXX Versions of the Decalogue on the New Testament in Relation to Sexuality

When we turn to the New Testament, we do find some influence from the LXX versions of the decalogue. This is the case in the matter of order and the prominence it gave to adultery and related sexual immorality.

3.1   *Order and the Prominence of Adultery and Sexual Immorality*

The order of commandments in Matthew 5 in the antitheses of the Sermon on the Mount reflects the order of the Hebrew text (and the LXX text of Codex Alexandrinus): murder, adultery.[16] The same is true of the references to the decalogue in Jesus' encounter with the rich man in Mark 10:19 and Matt 19:18[17] and later of the Didache (2:2-3). In Mark the commandments are formulated simply as: "Do not ...", for example, "Do not kill" etc (μὴ φονεύσῃς). Matthew changes them to conform to the LXX, so that become actual quotations. Thus "Do not kill" (μὴ φονεύσῃς) becomes "You shall not kill" etc (οὐ φονεύσεις).

By contrast, in his version of the encounter with the rich man in Luke 18:20, Luke preserves Mark's form, but, interestingly presents an order of the commandments which matches that of the LXX of Deuteronomy (as preserved in Codex Vaticanus and the text of Wevers), doubtless directly or indirectly under its influence.[18]

---

[16] See also Table 1 on page 7 at the beginning of this chapter.

[17] So Steyn, "Pretexts," who notes that in Mark it is Codex Vaticanus (along with others) which has this order (pp. 455-56). See his discussion of the synoptic texts, 456-58.

[18] Steyn, "Pretext," argues that the differences are probably best explained by Mark and Luke having different versions of the Greek translation of Exodus 20 and Deuteronomy 5, Luke preserving the syntax of Mark, but changing the order to match the order found now in Deuteronomy 5 in Vaticanus (pp. 457-58). Similarly Sänger, "Tora für die Völker," 120-22, who, noting the link between the decalogue and words derived from the stem διδασκ- both here and Rom 2:21-22, argues that the variations will reflect catechetical use both in Judaism and in Christianity. In this respect he draws attention to the allusion to the decalogue in the famous letter of Pliny to Trajan about Christians in Bithynia (*Epistles* 10.96). This is certainly possible; however, in the case of Mark the alternative should also be considered that Mark is drawing on tradition which stands under the impact of the Hebrew.

Table 2: The order of commandments in the meeting of the rich man with Jesus[19]				
Matthew 19:18-19	Mark 10:19	Luke 18:20-21	Hebrew Deut 5:16-20	LXX Deut 5:16-20
τὸ οὐ φονεύσεις, οὐ μοιχεύσεις, οὐ κλέψεις, οὐ ψευδο-μαρτυρήσεις τίμα τὸν πατέρα καὶ τὴν μητέρα, καὶ ἀγαπήσεις τὸν πλησίον σου ὡς σεαυτόν.	μὴ φονεύσῃς, μὴ μοιχεύσῃς, μὴ κλέψῃς, μὴ ψευδο-μαρτυρήσῃς, μὴ ἀποστερήσῃς, τίμα τὸν πατέρα σου καὶ τὴν μητέρα.	μὴ μοιχεύσῃς, μὴ φονεύσῃς, μὴ κλέψῃς, μὴ ψευδο-μαρτυρήσῃς, τίμα τὸν πατέρα σου καὶ τὴν μητέρα.	כַּבֵּד אֶת־אָבִיךָ וְאֶת־אִמֶּךָ ... לֹא תִּרְצָח: וְלֹא תִּנְאָף: וְלֹא תִּגְנֹב: וְלֹא־תַעֲנֶה בְרֵעֲךָ עֵד שָׁוְא:	τίμα τὸν πατέρα σου καὶ τὴν μητέρα σου ... οὐ μοιχεύσεις. οὐ φονεύσεις. οὐ κλέψεις. οὐ ψευδο-μαρτυρήσεις κατὰ τοῦ πλησίον σου μαρτυρίαν ψευδῆ.
You shall not murder; You shall not commit adultery; You shall not steal; You shall not bear false witness; Honor your father and mother; also, You shall love your neighbor as yourself.	Do not murder; Do not commit adultery; Do not steal; Do not bear false witness; Do not defraud; Honor your father and mother.	Do not commit adultery; Do not murder; Do not steal; Do not bear false witness; Honor your father and mother.	Honor your father and your mother ... You shall not murder. Neither shall you commit adultery. Neither shall you steal. Neither shall you bear false witness against your neighbor.	Honor your father and your mother ... You shall not commit adultery. You shall not murder. You shall not steal. You shall not bear witness against your neighbor falsely.

---

[19] For the purpose of the comparison I have used the Deuteronomy text rather than reproduce also the Exodus version, because the order is the same in both. Matthew underlines that the list is a quotation by his introductory article, το, which might be loosely translated: "the ones that say" or "the scripture portion which reads". The table also shows that all placed the commandment about honouring parents last. It also shows that both Matthew and Luke omit Mark's additional prohibition: μὴ ἀποστερήσῃς; "Do not defraud".

Paul similarly follows this order in Rom 13:9. The order, adultery-murder, is reflected in Jas 2:11[20] and possibly behind the tradition in 1 Cor 6:9. Unlike in Philo, no specific mention is made of the prominent position of adultery in the LXX decalogue in any of these texts. Luke does not appear to be drawing attention especially to adultery in the encounter with the rich man. Nor does Paul appear to be making anything of the order. It is probably just the order with which they are most familiar. The influence is incidental.

Mark's summary of what proceeds from the heart reads: πορνεῖαι, κλοπαί, φόνοι, μοιχεῖαι, πλεονεξίαι, πονηρίαι, δόλος, ἀσέλγεια, ὀφθαλμὸς πονηρός, βλασφημία, ὑπερηφανία, ἀφροσύνη ("fornication, theft, murder, adultery, avarice, wickedness, deceit, licentiousness, envy, slander, pride, folly"; 7:21-22).[21] Here prominence is given to πορνεῖαι ("fornication" lit. "acts of sexual immorality"). This may well reflect LXX influence, especially given the tendency to treat the prohibition against adultery as a heading under which to gather all kinds of sexual sins, which we have already noted in Philo. The order of the first three corresponds then to what we find in Exodus LXX. The list, however, continues with direct reference to acts of adultery. The second three appear to relate closely to the first three (πορνεῖαι, "acts of sexual immorality" and μοιχεῖαι, "acts of adultery"; κλοπαί, "acts of stealing" and πλεονεξίαι, "acts of greed"; φόνοι, "murders" and πονηρίαι, "acts of wickedness") and so reinforce the observation that what we have stands under the influence of the LXX order in Exodus.[22]

Mark 7:21	Mark 7:21	Exodus 20:13-15 LXX
πορνεῖαι, κλοπαί, φόνοι	μοιχεῖαι, πλεονεξίαι, πονηρίαι	οὐ μοιχεύσεις. οὐ κλέψεις. οὐ φονεύσεις
acts of sexual immorality acts of stealing acts of murder	acts of adultery acts of greed acts of wickedness	You shall not commit adultery. You shall not steal. You shall not murder.

---

[20] Steyn, "Pretext," 459, notes the correspondence with the order of Deut 5:17 of Codex Vaticanus, but not that it also matches the MT order, there being no mention of adultery, so that we cannot determine whether it might have preceded or followed the two commandments in James' text.

[21] Some mss have μοιχεῖαι ("acts of adultery") as the first of the list followed by the order above. Ms A and most later mss also have this but then reverse κλοπαί ("acts of theft") and φόνοι ("acts of murder"), thus matching the order of Deuteronomy. The order cited above has strong support including ℵ B.

[22] So R. H. Gundry, *Mark: A Commentary on his Apology for the Cross* (Grand Rapids: Eerdmans, 1993) 356.

In his revision of Mark 7:21-22 Matthew, who reduces the list from 13 to 7, corresponding more closely to decalogue categories,[23] also appears conscious of the Hebrew order of the decalogue. He commences the list with διαλογισμοί πονηροί ("evil intentions"), based on Mark's οἱ διαλογισμοὶ οἱ κακοί ("bad intentions"), displaces πορνεῖαι ("sexual immorality"), then returns to the Hebrew order of the decalogue φόνοι, μοιχεῖαι, πορνεῖαι, κλοπαί, ψευδομαρτυρίαι, βλασφημίαι ("murders, acts of adultery, acts of sexual immorality, acts of stealing, false testimonies, slanders" 15:19). It is noteworthy that he retains some emphasis on sexual sins by linking πορνεῖαι ("sexual immorality"), displaced from the head of the list, with μοιχεῖαι ("acts of adultery"). The tendency to use the commandments as a framework of thought for consideration of other related laws was widespread. We have already noted it in Philo. Matthew, himself, illustrates it in the Sermon on the Mount where attached to the exposition about adultery we find sayings about excising offending limbs which offend and about divorce (5:27-32).

Paul, similarly, gives great emphasis to sexual immorality. Thus he places πόρνοι ("people who engage in sexual immorality") at the head of the list of offenders who shall not enter the kingdom (1 Cor 6:9). Sexual offences make up in fact almost the whole first half of the categories: οὔτε πόρνοι οὔτε εἰδωλολάτραι οὔτε μοιχοὶ οὔτε μαλακοὶ οὔτε ἀρσενοκοῖται ("Fornicators, idolaters, adulterers, male prostitutes, sodomites").[24] The focus of the rest is predominantly in the area of theft, thus reflecting the sequence of the prohibitions in Exodus. Paul is possibly dependent on a traditional list, but sexual offences are also a concern in the immediate context of the letter.

While at some points we may trace incidental influence, where the LXX order reappears, the prominence given adultery through its position at the head of the second table of the law is matched at a number of points through a similar prominence given sexual sins, but this may have as much to do with continuing common concerns as it has with the LXX itself. Romans 1 is a typical example of where sexual sins are highlighted as evidence of failure to respond to knowledge of God.

---

[23] D. A. Hagner, *Matthew 14-28* (WBC 33B; Dallas: Word Books, 1995) cautions against the assumption that Matthew was primarily concerned with decalogue categories, noting the omission by Matthew of covetousness (437).

[24] One should not see εἰδωλολάτραι "idolators" as in any sense out of place among these sexual terms, because Hellenistic Judaism linked idolatry and sexual immorality closely together, as is evident in Wisd 14:22-31 and in Paul's great "speech" in Rom 1:18-32.

The attention given to adultery and to sexual immorality in general was by no means a preoccupation only of Greek speaking Jews. The phenomenon was widespread, so that what we see in the order of the decalogue in the LXX is likely to have reflected concerns of its context. The appellation, "adulterous and sinful generation" (Matt 12:39; Mark 8:38; Matt 16:4) doubtless reflects the same emphasis. Adultery was a common metaphor for Israel's unfaithfulness in the prophetic literature (for a similar use see also Jas 2:11).

3.2   *"Do not covet/desire/lust!"*

If we turn to the treatment of the commandment not to desire or lust after one's neighbor's wife, as in Philo we find no particular reference to the prominence created for the adultery theme by the creation of the separate prohibition. On the other hand, the use of ἐπιθυμέω ("to desire") in the commandment may well have played a role.

While a reference to the 10th commandment is missing in the tradition of Jesus' encounter with the rich man,[25] the commandment is cited (simply as "You shall not covet/desire" without an object) directly by Paul in Rom 7:7 and 13:9. In the latter it follows the prohibitions (in the LXX order) to commit adultery, kill, and steal (bearing false witness is missing). The ensuing context then includes the exhortation to make no provision for the "lusts" (ἐπιθυμίας) of the flesh (13:14), clearly referring back to the list in the preceding verse which, as Watson points out, consists of elements either directly sexual or indirectly related to sexual misbehaviours.[26] An allusion to the prohibition is doubtless implied.

---

[25] It may well be present in the narrative in a different form: the challenge not to defraud. It is not to be seen as the one thing that is missing (10:21), because it is Jesus who lists the commandments. What was missing was an attitude towards keeping the commandments for which the challenge to share would not have created a crisis for someone who was keeping them aright.

[26] Watson, *Agape, Eros, Gender*, 154.

Rom 7:7 cites the prohibition as one which will be exploited by sin to produce death. It is both representative of all sins and is suited for the purpose of Paul's argument, since it deals with an inner attitude in a context in which Paul is employing popular psychology of the time to demonstrate human bondage. It has no overtly sexual reference, although it is probable that this is present, given the associations of the word in Paul and especially if the passage alludes to the sin of Eve with some sexual reference.[27] Eve was seduced (2 Cor 11:2-3; Rom 7:11; Gen 3:13). The immediate context has strongly sexual references and themes from 7:1 onwards. There may well be an allusion to Israel's lapse into idolatry and sexual immorality shortly after receiving the Law according to Num 25:1-2 in 7:5 (ὅτε γὰρ ἦμεν ἐν τῇ σαρκί, τὰ παθήματα τῶν ἁμαρτιῶν τὰ διὰ τοῦ νόμου ἐνηργεῖτο ἐν τοῖς μέλεσιν ἡμῶν, εἰς τὸ καρποφορῆσαι τῷ θανάτῳ; While we were living in the flesh, our sinful passions, aroused by the law, were at work in our members to bear fruit for death).[28] Paul reflects on the wilderness generation similarly in 1 Cor 10:6-8.

An allusion to the prohibition in a sexual sense is likely in Matt 5:28, where adultery in the heart equates to looking at a woman (someone else's wife) with a view to sexually desiring her: ἐγὼ δὲ λέγω ὑμῖν ὅτι πᾶς ὁ βλέπων γυναῖκα πρὸς τὸ ἐπιθυμῆσαι αὐτὴν ἤδη ἐμοίχευσεν αὐτὴν ἐν τῇ καρδίᾳ αὐτοῦ ("And I tell you, anyone who looks at [someone's] wife with a view to lusting after her has already committed adultery with her in his heart"). This echoes the prohibition, particularly as it is present in the LXX: οὐκ ἐπιθυμήσεις τὴν γυναῖκα τοῦ πλησίον σου ("You shall desire/lust after your neighbor's wife" Exod 20:17; Deut 5:21). It also reflects the sense of the Hebrew of Deut 5:21. Furthermore, it reflects a widespread theme, present both in Hebrew and Greek Jewish writings and even in non Jewish literature of the time, of warning against the lusting look.[29] Such concerns certainly echo the emphasis preserved in the

---

[27] Taking the words in a sexual sense: R. H. Gundry, "The moral frustration of Paul before his conversion," in *Pauline Studies: FS for F. F. Bruce* ed. D. A. Hagner and M. J. Harris (Exeter: Paternoster, 1980) 228-45; F. Watson. *Paul, Judaism and the Gentiles* (SNTSMS 56; Cambridge: CUP, 1986) 151-56. The problem is that ἐπιθυμέω ("to desire") does not require such a sense, though it may include it. See the discussion in J. A. Ziesler, "The role of the tenth commandment in Romans 7," *JSNT* 33 (1988) 41-56, esp. 45-46. He goes on to draw attention to the link made between the prohibition in the Garden story and in Torah, in particular, the 10th commandment: *b. Shab.* 145b-146a; *b. Yeb.* 103b; *Apoc. Mos.* 19:3; see also Sir 17:7,11-12 as one of the possible backgrounds for understanding Rom 7 (47).

[28] See Watson, *Agape, Eros, Gender*, 167-68.

[29] See Berger, *Gesetzesauslegung* 346-47. "Diese zentrale Bedeutung der ἐπιθυμία macht das 10. Gebot für das hellenistische Judentum zu einem Zentralgebot, da mit der 'Begierde' eben auch alle anderen Gebote übertreten sind." (Tr. This central meaning of

LXX decalogues, but were so widespread that it is debatable whether one can speak specifically of LXX influence here. The context reflects the Hebrew order; the motif is too common; at most the choice of the verb may reflect LXX influence.

On the other hand, both the LXX and this passage in Matthew (like many others) reflect a shift of focus from issues of property and possession to issues of passion. The focus is less on greed for gain than on passion for experience. Certainly the word group, ἐπιθυμέω ("to desire/lust after") helped ingrain these concerns, particularly because of the widely propagated Stoic value systems which called all strong passions into question. This makes it difficult to separate influence from the LXX and its use of the verb (and the prominence it gives to sexual sins) from other influences current at the time. We have seen already in Philo that the matter ·is complex; in his case specific philosophical influences are often more clearly recognisable.

Abrogation of strong desires such as the desire for food and sexual passion or restricting their legitimacy to functional ends, i.e. required nourishment and human reproduction, need not be read into the LXX decalogue, but could easily find support there.[30] "You shall not covet" might translate into: "You shall not lust". This might be so especially where the commandment is cited without the objects which indicate its focus (as in Rom 7:7 and 13:9 and already 4 Macc 2:6) or perhaps primarily with "neighbor's wife" as the object, although I have found no explicit evidence of the latter.

Negative attitudes towards ἐπιθυμία ("desire/lust") with possible sexual connotation are present in a number of texts. As Watson argues, "Like the English 'lust', *epithumia*, can on occasion stand for sexual desire without the need to specify its object."[31] Paul is clearly referring to sexual lusts in the discussion which begins in Romans 1:24: Διὸ παρέδωκεν αὐτοὺς ὁ θεὸς ἐν ταῖς ἐπιθυμίαις τῶν καρδιῶν αὐτῶν εἰς ἀκαθαρσίαν τοῦ ἀτιμάζεσθαι τὰ σώματα αὐτῶν ἐν αὐτοῖς ("Therefore God gave them up to the lusts of their hearts towards impurity to dishonour their bodies among themselves"). In Romans

---

ἐπιθυμία ["desire"] makes the 10th commandment into a central commandment for Hellenistic Judaism, because with covetousness all other commandments are transgressed). Rom 7:7 illustrates this well. Of the "spirits of deceit" enumerated in *T. Reub.* 2, the second is "the spirit of sight, with which desire (ἐπιθυμία) comes". See also *T. Reub.* 3:10-14; 4:1; 6:1; *T. Jud.* 17:1; 12:3; 13:3,5; *T. Benj.* 8:2.

[30] D. Boyarin, *A Radical Jew: Paul and the Politics of Identity* (Berkley, Los Angeles, London: University of California Press, 1994) 163, speaks of the influence of the LXX on Paul.

[31] Watson, *Agape, Eros, Gender*, 155. He argues that while ἐπιθυμία "is not exclusively sexual, it is primarily and paradigmatically sexual".

7:7-8 such a reference is possible, as we have seen; in 6:12 lusts of the body doubtless include sexual lusts. In Rom 13:14, as we have seen, the same connotations are to be assumed. 1 Cor 10:6-8 interprets the lusts to which the wilderness generation fell and to which the Corinthians fell as sexual (linked also with eating and drinking).

In Galatians 5, Paul, in a way reminiscent of Romans 7-8, speaks of conflict between the lusts of the flesh and the life of the Spirit (5:16-17) and the need to shun the "passions and desires" of the flesh (5:24). When he expounds these, sexual immorality heads the list and is prominent, although the list is broader than that. In 1 Thess 4:3-6 Paul uses the word primarily with sexual sins in mind, including adultery:

(3) Τοῦτο γάρ ἐστιν θέλημα τοῦ θεοῦ, ὁ ἁγιασμὸς ὑμῶν, ἀπέχεσθαι ὑμᾶς ἀπὸ τῆς πορνείας, (4) εἰδέναι ἕκαστον ὑμῶν τὸ ἑαυτοῦ σκεῦος κτᾶσθαι ἐν ἁγιασμῷ καὶ τιμῇ, (5) μὴ ἐν πάθει ἐπιθυμίας καθάπερ καὶ τὰ ἔθνη τὰ μὴ εἰδότα τὸν θεόν. (6) τὸ μὴ ὑπερβαίνειν καὶ πλεονεκτεῖν ἐν τῷ πράγματι τὸν ἀδελφὸν αὐτοῦ, διότι ἔκδικος κύριος περὶ πάντων τούτων, καθὼς καὶ προείπαμεν ὑμῖν καὶ διεμαρτυράμεθα

(3) For this is God's will, your sanctification, to abstain from sexual immorality, (4) that each of you may know how to control his vessel in holiness and honour, (5) not in the passion of lust as do the Gentiles who do not know God, (6) not to override or get the better of your brother in the matter,[32] because the Lord is a requiter of all these things, as also we told you earlier and seriously warned you.[33]

Paul may even be disapproving sexual passion towards one's "spouse" (σκεῦος) when not in the context of procreation, like Philo (see above), although this would conflict with his views expressed in 1 Corinthians 7.[34]

---

[32] πράγματι can refer to sexual "affair" and probably does here. So Ronald F. Hock. "God's will at Thessalonica and Greco-Roman Asceticism," in *Asceticism and the New Testament*, ed. Leif E. Vaage and Vincent L. Wimbusch (New York: Routledge, 1999) 159-70, here 161.

[33] Watson, *Agape, Eros, Gender*, 155.

[34] See the renewed argument for reading σκεῦος as wife in Matthias Konradt, "Εἰδέναι ἕκαστον ὑμῶν τὸ ἑαυτοῦ σκεῦος κτᾶσθαι... : Zu Paulus' sexualethischer Weisung in 1 Thess 4,4f," *ZNW* 92 (2001) 128-35, who argues that this makes best sense of the phrase μὴ ἐν πάθει ἐπιθυμίας ("not in the passion of lust"), which does not read well referring to one's treatment of one's own body (133). κτᾶσθαι ("to control") refers then to one's ongoing relationship with one's wife (134). The focus is not that one should have a

Lusts of the flesh in the deuteropaulines similarly appear to include sexual sins, sometimes predominantly (so Col 3:5), but not exclusively so (cf. also Eph 2:3; 4:22; Tit 2:12; 3:3). Doubtless sexual desires are in view in 2 Tim 2:22:

Τὰς δὲ νεωτερικὰς ἐπιθυμίας φεῦγε, δίωκε δὲ δικαιοσύνην πίστιν ἀγάπην εἰρήνην μετὰ τῶν ἐπικαλουμένων τὸν κύριον ἐκ καθαρᾶς καρδίας

Avoid the lusts of youth; but go after goodness, faithfulness, love, peace with those who call on the Lord from a pure heart.

as also in 3:6:

(6) ἐκ τούτων γάρ εἰσιν οἱ ἐνδύνοντες εἰς τὰς οἰκίας καὶ αἰχμαλωτίζοντες γυναικάρια σεσωρευμένα ἁμαρτίαις, ἀγόμενα ἐπιθυμίαις ποικίλαις, (7) πάντοτε μανθάνοντα καὶ μηδέποτε εἰς ἐπίγνωσιν ἀληθείας ἐλθεῖν δυνάμενα.

(6) To these belong people who make their way into households and captivate women laden with sin, driven by various lusts, (7) always learning but never able to arrive at a knowledge of the truth.

James[35] employs the metaphor of reproduction to illustrate the destructiveness of lust and lusting (ἐπιθυμία / ἐπιθυμέω; "desire"/"to desire") generally, but the fact that he uses sexual desire as the paradigm probably reflects a negative assessment of sexual desire: 1:14-15

---

wife instead of engaging in sexual immorality (v3), but that as well as not engaging in sexual immorality one should also treat one's wife properly. He rightly concludes that Paul does not go so far as forbidding sexual intercourse in marriage except for presupposes of procreation (135). See also Hock, "God's will at Thessalonica". Against relating 5:4 and 5 in this way see T. Holtz, *Der erste Brief an die Thessalonicher* (EKKNT XIII Zürich/Neukirchen-Vluyn: Benziger/Neukirchener, 1986) 160. Others take σκεῦος as a reference to one's body, e.g. C. A. Wanamaker, *Commentary on 1 and 2 Thessalonians* (NIGCommNT; Grand Rapids/Exeter: Eerdmans/Paternoster, 1990) 152-53.

[35] See Alicia Batten, "An asceticism of resistance in James," in *Asceticism and the New Testament*, ed. Leif E. Vaage and Vincent L. Wimbusch (New York: Routledge, 1999) 355-70, esp. 359-60.

(14) ἕκαστος δὲ πειράζεται ὑπὸ τῆς ἰδίας ἐπιθυμίας ἐξελκόμενος καὶ δελεαζόμενος· (15) εἶτα ἡ ἐπιθυμία συλλαβοῦσα τίκτει ἁμαρτίαν, ἡ δὲ ἁμαρτία ἀποτελεσθεῖσα ἀποκύει θάνατον

(14) Each is tempted by his own lust, being seduced and enticed, (15) but lust when it has conceived gives birth to sin, and sin when it grows up gives birth to death.

In 4:1-4 he alludes to desire negatively in the context of people having unfulfilled desires and fighting for them, in a way that recalls Philo's linking of lusting with war. James cajoles them as "adulteresses":

(1) Πόθεν πόλεμοι καὶ πόθεν μάχαι ἐν ὑμῖν; οὐκ ἐντεῦθεν, ἐκ τῶν ἡδονῶν ὑμῶν τῶν στρατευομένων ἐν τοῖς μέλεσιν ὑμῶν; (2) ἐπιθυμεῖτε καὶ οὐκ ἔχετε, φονεύετε καὶ ζηλοῦτε καὶ οὐ δύνασθε ἐπιτυχεῖν, μάχεσθε καὶ πολεμεῖτε, οὐκ ἔχετε διὰ τὸ μὴ αἰτεῖσθαι ὑμᾶς, (3) αἰτεῖτε καὶ οὐ λαμβάνετε διότι κακῶς αἰτεῖσθε, ἵνα ἐν ταῖς ἡδοναῖς ὑμῶν δαπανήσητε. (4) μοιχαλίδες, οὐκ οἴδατε ὅτι ἡ φιλία τοῦ κόσμου ἔχθρα τοῦ θεοῦ ἐστιν;

(1) Where do the conflicts and fights come from which you are having? Is it not from within, from the pleasures which are at war in your members? (2) You crave and do not have what you want, you kill and are jealous but you don't get what you want, you fight and battle, but you do not have it because you do not pray; (3) you pray and you not receive because you pray wrongly, so that you might spend on your pleasures. (4) Adulterers, do you not know that love of the world is enmity towards God?"

Other passages which may well have a sexual connotation include 1 Pet 1:14; 2:11; 4:2-3; and 1 John 2:16 (especially the lusts of the eyes). On the other hand, if an allusion to sexual passions is intended in Mark 4:9,

καὶ αἱ μέριμναι τοῦ αἰῶνος καὶ ἡ ἀπάτη τοῦ πλούτου καὶ αἱ περὶ τὰ λοιπὰ ἐπιθυμίαι εἰσπορευόμεναι συμπνίγουσιν τὸν λόγον καὶ ἄκαρπος γίνετα

and the worries of this age and the deceitfulness of wealth and lust after the rest come in and choke the word and it becomes unfruitful

they are scarcely emphasised. In John 8:44 the focus is murderous desires.

Conclusion

Our purpose in this investigation has been neither to reconstruct from the LXX the Hebrew text on which it is based, nor to inquire after the intentions of the translators, but to seek to identify potential influences in relation to sexuality which may flow from the LXX text and to check for evidence of these influences, using Philo and the New Testament writings. We identified three elements in particular in the LXX texts of the decalogue (at least some known versions of it used in the time of Philo and the New Testament). These are the prominence given adultery by moving it to the 6th position and so to the first in the second table (possibly reflecting an order in some Hebrew manuscripts if the Nash Papyrus is to be taken as evidence), the separation of the prohibition of lusting after one's neighbor's wife in the LXX of both Exodus and Deuteronomy, and the use of the word οὐκ ἐπιθυμήσεις ("You shall not desire") in that prohibition.

Philo makes much of the prominence of the prohibition of adultery at the head of the second table and makes it the rallying point for other related prohibitions pertaining to sexuality. He does not make a special point of the separate listing of the prohibition to desire one's neighbor's wife, but does comment extensively on ἐπιθυμία ("desire/lust") and its word group, drawing upon popular Stoic understandings and giving great emphasis to the dangers of passions. He does not go so far as to outlaw passions totally, but reflects an emphasis which goes beyond concern with desire to acquire property to the dangers of passions, themselves.

Among the New Testament writings we found evidence of the order which lists the prohibition against adultery as the sixth commandment in Luke's version of the encounter with the rich man, in Paul (Rom 13:9), and in Mark 7:21-22. While this sometimes led to prominence being given to adultery (and related sexual prohibitions) by its position as first in the list, at no point did we find arguments based on its prominence, as we found in Philo. The fact that sexual sins feature prominently at many points may reflect the prominence given adultery in the LXX decalogue translations being used, but may just as much reflect concerns of the period.

We did not find evidence of arguments from the separation of the prohibition not to desire one's neighbor's wife, but we did find evidence of concern with sexual passion, sometimes directly in relation to the prohibition in the decalogue and its use of ἐπιθυμήσεις ("You shall not desire/lust after"; Rom 13:9-14; Matt 5:28; cf. Rom 7:7). Again, while the formulation of the prohibition may well have influenced other passages where sexual passions are addressed, concern with such passions in popular teaching of the time make attribution of influence of the LXX difficult. It is certainly consistent with what one would expect from such influence, but the translations themselves probably already reflect a growing concern with sexual sins in their time.

CHAPTER TWO

The Creation Stories

The creation stories assume major significance because of their prominence and their theme. Appendix B sets out some of the key verses which relate to sexuality in the Hebrew and Greek with translations of each (Genesis, especially 1:26-28; 2:18-25; 3:16-19; 5:1-3). The discussion which follows will take the broader context into account.

1. Distinctive features of the LXX version of the Creation Stories in relation to sexuality

These texts need to be examined in their narrative context. This entails an act of imagination, as we seek to hear the LXX text as it might have been heard in the period under concern.

1.1 Genesis 1:26-27 LXX. Making "the man" in the likeness of God

In Gen 1:26 the Septuagint renders בְּצַלְמֵנוּ כִּדְמוּתֵנוּ ("in our image according to our likeness") with κατ' εἰκόνα ἡμετέραν καὶ καθ' ὁμοίωσιν ("according to our image and according to [our] likeness"), adding a conjunction,[1] using the double κατά ("according to") construction and removing the possessive from the

---

[1] Also in the Samaritan Pentateuch and the Vulgate. See M. Rösel, *Übersetzung als Vollendung der Auslegung* (BZAW 223; Berlin: de Gruyter, 1994) 48.

second noun to avoid stylistic redundancy.[2] The κατά phrases, between which it is difficult to differentiate in meaning, echo the phrase κατὰ γένος ("according to [its] kind") of the preceding verses, suggesting more strongly than in the Hebrew that humankind belongs to the γένος of God, or, at least, highlighting the contrast with the animals more strongly than in the Hebrew.[3] The Hebrew (followed by the LXX) indicates a contrast by the change to the first person plural verb, נַעֲשֶׂה. ("Let us make"). The phrase κατ' εἰκόνα ("according to the image") would have potential to evoke Platonic use of the term εἰκών ("image").[4] We shall return to this possibility. The rest of the verse in both Hebrew and LXX suggests that the God-like aspect consists in ruling the world of creation.

In 1:27 the translator then offers a slightly abbreviated rendering:

וַיִּבְרָא אֱלֹהִים אֶת־הָאָדָם בְּצַלְמוֹ
בְּצֶלֶם אֱלֹהִים בָּרָא אֹתוֹ
So God created humankind (adam) in his image,
in the image of God he created him.

καὶ ἐποίησεν ὁ θεὸς τὸν ἄνθρωπον
κατ' εἰκόνα θεου ἐποίησεν αὐτόν.
So God created humankind (the man),
in the image of God he created him.

The בְּצַלְמוֹ ("in his image") is omitted from the first line of the LXX, probably because of its presence in the second.[5] The omission results in the

---

[2] On the equivalence of the prepositions and the fact that בְּצַלְמֵנוּ כִּדְמוּתֵנוּ ("in our image according to our likeness") is a single expression, see C. Westermann, *Genesis 1-11: A Commentary* (London: SPCK, 1974) 146-47; G. J. Wenham, *Genesis 1-15* (WBC 1; Waco: Word, 1987) 29-30. Note the double use of κατά ("according to") in 1:11, κατὰ γένος καὶ καθ' ὁμοιότητα ("according to their kind and according to their likeness"). The second has no corresponding Hebrew in the original and probably stands under the influence of Gen 1:26 (so Rösel, *Übersetzung*, 41-43).

[3] William P. Brown, *The Structure, Role, and Ideology in the Hebrew and Greek texts of Genesis 1:1 - 2:3* (SBLDiss 132; Atlanta: Scholars, 1993) emphasises the change from κατὰ γένος ("according to their kind") to κατ' εἰκόνα ("according to the image"). "Whereas all other creatures are organized by their shared characteristics to one another, human beings are set apart by virtue of their resemblance to the divine" (41).

[4] So Rösel, *Übersetzung*, 48-49, with reference to Plato's *Timaeus* 29BC, 92C; see also pp. 73-87. He notes that צלם is consistently translated by εἰκών in the LXX, whereas דמות varies (48).

[5] In relation to the omission J. Cook, "The Exegesis of the Greek Genesis," in *VI Congress of the International Organization for Septuagint and Cognate Studies, Jerusalem*

opening statement of 1:27 placing the emphasis on the creation of humankind, rather than humankind in the image of God. That qualification becomes a second statement. The use, again, of κατ' εἰκόνα ("in the image") would reinforce associations with Platonic categories.

The remainder of the verse stays close to the Hebrew:

זָכָר וּנְקֵבָה בָּרָא אֹתָם

male and female he created them.

ἄρσεν καὶ θῆλυ ἐποίησεν αὐτούς.
male and female he created them.

Like the Hebrew, the LXX rendering leaves open the possibility that hearers might discern a relationship between the references to "male and female" and "the divine image".[6] The text, in both Hebrew and LXX, can just as easily be read as making a transition to the command to be fruitful and multiply in the next verse, a command also shared with the animals. The god-like aspect follows in the command to rule over the creation, echoing 1:26.[7] Being male and female is necessary for the task of being fruitful and multiplying. The statement that God created "them" male and female suggests that in 1:27 both הָאָדָם ("adam, humankind") in Hebrew and τὸν ἄνθρωπον ("man, humankind") in Greek are generic and that the plural, "them", refers to the two kinds of human being, rather

---

1986 (Septuagint and Cognate Studies 23 ed. C. E. Cox; Atlanta: Scholars, 1986) 91-125, notes possible explanations: absence in the Hebrew *Vorlage*; *homoioteleuton* (Fraenkel), but the words are not the same; a deliberate Christian omission, but the text is in Philo; rather he argues it as a result of harmonisation between 1:27 and 5:2, as occurs in the change to the plural in 2:18 to harmonise with 1:26 (107). Against this see Rösel, *Übersetzung*, who argues that 5:2 stands under the influence of 1:27 and so prefers *homoioarkton* or the translator avoiding what he saw as redundancy (50).

[6] See J. C. de Moor, "The duality in God and Man: Gen 1:26-27," in *Intertextuality in Ugarit and Israel: Papers read at the tenth Joint Meeting of the Society for Old Testament Study and Het Oudtestamentisch Werkgezelschap in Nederland en Belgie, held at Oxford, 1977* (OTS XL; Leiden: Brill, 1998) 112-25, who argues that P has an androgynous understanding, concluding that "apparently bisexuality was a sure sign of exalted divinity" (124) and this was true of both male and female deities. Originally 1:27 was in the dual and was replaced by the plural (120-21).

[7] So E. Noort, "The creation of man and woman in biblical and ancient near eastern traditions" in *The Creation of Man and Woman: Interpretations of the Biblical Narratives in Jewish and Christian Traditions* ed. G. P. Luttikhuizen (Themes in Biblical Narrative: Jewish and Christian Traditions I; Leiden: Brill, 2000) 1-18, esp. 8-9.

than to two actual persons or to persons who were bisexual or that the הָאָדָם and
τὸν ἄνθρωπον refer to a bisexual being.[8] But there is some ambiguity, sufficient
to allow such readings. The transition from the singular generic form to the plural
is slightly awkward and would invite some to smooth that out by retaining the
singular and understanding it to refer to an original bisexual human being.[9] A
Platonic reading might understand in 1:26-27 the creation of an archetype, as we
shall see.

Without the reference to male and female most hearers would have assumed
that human beings, like animals, are male and female. The reference to male and
female in relation to humans is in that sense redundant. Its presence therefore gives
special attention to what might otherwise have been assumed and for the informed
hearer, especially in the context of repeated hearing, invites reflection to rebound
from the ensuing narrative where the male-female relationship receives special
attention. This is so both for the Hebrew and the LXX. It also leaves open the
possibility that the הָאָדָם and τὸν ἄνθρωπον is identified directly as Adam, a
single figure. This is more so in the LXX which cannot reproduce the pun which in
Hebrew makes הָאָדָם more than a name. Genesis 2 would then lead to the
assumption that the human being in 1:26-27 is primarily male, as the name, Adam,
which the LXX uses in 2:16, suggests, from whom then the female emerges. God
makes "the man" in his image and likeness. This identification becomes explicit
in the LXX of 5:1, which reworks 1:26-27, as we shall see, and is implied in the
close links which the LXX has forged between 2:18-25 and 1:26-27. With Genesis
2 in mind, where LXX continues to use ἄνθρωπος in speaking of a man, called
Adam, a hearer of 1:27 would take this verse as referring to that Adam, the male,
and understand the shift from singular to plural in 1:27c as prefiguring in summary
the events to follow.

1.2   Genesis 2:4-8, 15-17 LXX - the emerging

2:4b begins the so-called second account of creation. The LXX seems to be aware
of this and has taken measures to smooth some of the difficulties which arise.
These are already evident in the translation of 2:4.

---

[8] For a bisexual reading of Genesis 1:27 see de Moor, "The duality in God and Man:
Gen 1:26-27," 124. See also P. Trible, *God and the rhetoric of sexuality* (Philadelphia:
Fortress, 1978) 17-23, who argues that Genesis should be read as presupposing man and
woman are created from a bisexual or, better, asexual being. Against this Noort, "Creation
of man and woman," argues that P does not elsewhere assume equality, but rather makes the
male-female differentiation in the light of promise of progeny, as comparison with 5:1-3
shows (6-10).

[9] So according to *Gen. Rabb.* 8.1 (more on this in relation to Gen 5:2 below).

אֵלֶּה תוֹלְדוֹת הַשָּׁמַיִם וְהָאָרֶץ בְּהִבָּרְאָם בְּיוֹם עֲשׂוֹת יְהוָה אֱלֹהִים אֶרֶץ וְשָׁמָיִם
These are the generations of the heavens and the earth when they were
created. In the day that the LORD God made the earth and the heavens...

αὕτη ἡ βίβλος γενέσεως οὐρανοῦ καὶ γῆς, ὅτε ἐγένετο. ᾗ ἡμέρᾳ
ἐποίησεν ὁ θεὸς τὸν οὐρανὸν καὶ τὴν γῆν,
This is the book of the origin of heaven and earth when it came about. On the
day on which God made heaven and earth, ...

This will not only give the title to the book, "Genesis", but it sets what follows
under the rubric of γένεσις and γίνομαι, of "becoming". In 2:3, which
concludes the first account, we find another innovation:

וַיְבָרֶךְ אֱלֹהִים אֶת־יוֹם הַשְּׁבִיעִי וַיְקַדֵּשׁ אֹתוֹ כִּי בוֹ שָׁבַת מִכָּל־מְלַאכְתּוֹ
אֲשֶׁר־בָּרָא אֱלֹהִים לַעֲשׂוֹת:
And God blessed the seventh day and hallowed it, because on it God rested
from all the work that he had done in creation

καὶ εὐλόγησεν ὁ θεὸς τὴν ἡμέραν τὴν ἑβδόμην καὶ ἡγίασεν αὐτήν,
ὅτι ἐν αὐτῇ κατέπαυσεν ἀπὸ πάντων τῶν ἔργων αὐτοῦ, ὧν ἤρξατο ὁ
θεὸς ποιῆσαι.

And God blessed the seventh day and consecrated it because on it he rested
from all the works which God began to create

The addition of ἤρξατο ("began") serves to form an inclusio[10] with the
opening words of the book ἐν ἀρχῇ ("in the beginning"), but it may also suggest
or be heard as suggesting that the creating continues in Genesis 2, rather than that
it is being recapitulated. This might fit a Platonic reading which sees here the
beginning of the creation of the material world,[11] but in any case it helps smooth
the difference between the two accounts of creation by the suggestion that the
second is either a continuation or a description of how what was created emerged
or came into being.[12] A similar smoothing occurs in the translation of 2:5. Instead

[10] So Wevers, *Notes on the Greek Text of Genesis*, 21; Brown, *Structure*, 26.
[11] So Rösel, *Übersetzung*, 58-59.
[12] Cf. the attempt at smoothing the difference between the two creation accounts in
Jubilees 3. On this see J. T. A. G. M. van Ruiten, "Eden and the temple: the rewriting of
Genesis 2:4 - 3:24 in the *Book of Jubilees*," in *Paradise Interpreted: Representations of
Biblical Paradise in Judaism and Christianity*, ed G. P. Luttikhuizen (Themes in Biblical
Narrative: Jewish and Christian Traditions II; Leiden: Brill, 1999) 63-94.

of reporting with the Hebrew that there were no plants, the LXX suggests they had just not yet come into being because it had not yet rained. In a similar way the addition of ἔτι in 2:9 and 2:19 relieves the tension by assuming the creation of Genesis 1.[13] Accordingly Genesis 2 describes their emergence not their creation. Genesis 2 in translation is thus in a subtle way more closely attuned to Genesis 1.[14]

1.3   The Hebrew pun and the LXX man called, "Adam"

In relation to the creation of humanity Genesis 2:5-24; 3:1 LXX functions, therefore, as an exposition of 1:26-27. This is especially so with regard to maleness and femaleness. The exposition also relates to issues of being like God and what that can mean, which extend throughout chapter 3. There we will find the human being reminded of the origin in the earth (3:19; Hebrew: dust).

As already noted, the LXX has not been able to reproduce the pun of הָאָדָם on הָאֲדָמָה in 2:7. It has however retained the reference to earth/ground ἀπὸ τῆς γῆς (2:7) and its echo in 3:19: ἕως τοῦ ἀποστρέψαι σε εἰς τὴν γῆν ἐξ ἧς ἐλήμφθης ὅτι γῆ εἶ καὶ εἰς γῆν ἀπελεύσῃ, which thus form an inclusio. When 2:7 in Hebrew tells us that God formed הָאָדָם ("adam/the man") from the dust of הָאֲדָמָה, (adamah/ground), this follows naturally for the reader from 1:26-28 in the sense that it now offers information about how God fashioned (2:7) what he created (1:26-27). Both in Hebrew and in Greek different words are employed for the act of creation in 1:27, בָּרָא ποιέω, and 2:7 יָצַר πλάσσω. Rösel suggests the choice of both ποιέω and πλάσσω reflects the language of Plato's Timaeus.[15] This might evoke a Platonic interpretation of the acts of creation. The translation εἰς ψυχὴν ζῶσαν could also lend itself to a dualistic reading. We shall return to this.

---

[13] So Wevers, *Notes on the Greek Text of Genesis*, 23,26,29.

[14] There are ambiguities in how Genesis 2 LXX might be read in relation to Genesis 1. One could see Genesis 2 as a description of how the creating reported in Genesis 1 was carried out or one could see a genuine sequence of time between Genesis 1 and 2, so that two acts of creation are being referred to. The presence of ἤρξατο ("began") in 2:4 suggests sequence, as does the presence of ἔτι in 2:9 and 2:19. On the other hand, the creation of human kind and of male and female, suggests rather that Genesis 2 describes what Genesis 1 intimates in summary. These ambiguities invite some resolution and popular Platonism provided one way of reading the text; indeed, if Rösel is correct, influenced the text itself.

[15] Rösel, *Übersetzung*, 29-30, 60.

	Hebrew	NRSV	LXX	LXX English
		Table 3: References to "Adam" in Genesis 1-3 and 5:1-4		
1:26	אָדָם	humankind	ἄνθρωπον	humankind/man
1:27	הָאָדָם	humankind	τὸν ἄνθρωπον	humankind/man
2:5	אָדָם אַיִן	no one	ἄνθρωπος οὐκ	no one/man
2:7	הָאָדָם	man (OR: a man)	τὸν ἄνθρωπον	the man
	הָאָדָם	the man	ὁ ἄνθρωπος	the man
2:8	הָאָדָם	the man	τὸν ἄνθρωπον	the man
2:15	הָאָדָם	the man	τὸν ἄνθρωπον	the man
2:16	הָאָדָם	the man	τῷ Αδαμ	Adam
2:18	הָאָדָם	the man	τὸν ἄνθρωπον	the man
2:19	הָאָדָם	the man	τὸν Αδαμ	Adam
2:20	הָאָדָם	the man	Αδαμ	Adam
	לְאָדָם	the man (OR: Adam)	τῷ Αδαμ	Adam
2:21	הָאָדָם	the man	τὸν Αδαμ	Adam
2:22	הָאָדָם	the man	τοῦ Αδαμ	Adam
	הָאָדָם	the man	τὸν Αδαμ	Adam
2:23	הָאָדָם	the man	Αδαμ	Adam
	מֵאִישׁ	Man	τοῦ ἀνδρὸς	husband
2:24	אִישׁ	a man	ἄνθρωπος	man
2:25 (LXX 3:1)	הָאָדָם	the man	ὁ Αδαμ	Adam
3:6	אִישׁ	husband	τῷ ἀνδρὶ	husband
3:8	הָאָדָם	the man	ὁ Αδαμ	Adam
3:9	הָאָדָם	the man	τὸν Αδαμ	Adam
3:12	הָאָדָם	the man	ὁ Αδαμ	Adam
3:16	אִישׁ	husband	τὸν ἄνδρα	husband
3:17	לְאָדָם	the man (OR: Adam)	τῷ Αδαμ	Adam
3:20	הָאָדָם	the man	Αδαμ	Adam
3:21	לְאָדָם	the man (OR: Adam)	τῷ Αδαμ	Adam
3:22	הָאָדָם	the man	Αδαμ	Adam
3:24	הָאָדָם	the man	τὸν Αδαμ	Adam
5:1	אָדָם	Adam	ἀνθρώπων	human beings/men
	אָדָם	humankind	τὸν Αδαμ	Adam
5:2	אָדָם	humankind	Αδαμ	"Adam"
5:3	אָדָם	Adam	Αδαμ	Adam
5:4	אָדָם	Adam	Αδαμ	Adam

The effect on the LXX account, however, of the inability to reproduce the אָדָם / אֲדָמָה ("adam/adamah"; "earthling/earth or ground") pun is that the allusion to the "earth creature" in the word for the human being is lost. Adam is simply a name without the descriptive allusion present in the Hebrew.[16] The knowing hearer of the LXX recognises this act of formation as the creation of the male human being called, Adam, although by retaining the generic term ἄνθρωπος ("man/human being"), the LXX focuses on this man called, Adam, as typical of humankind, rather than on him as an individual. He is the individual male, Adam, nevertheless and this focus is inevitably stronger in the LXX account which lacks the generic playfulness of the pun.

Without the advantage of the pun, the LXX narrative cannot escape an awkward transition from speaking generically to speaking of Adam; the generic ἄνθρωπος ("man/human being") is retained until 2:16, when out of the blue "Adam" appears in the text. Adam is a name for a male, not also a subtle allusion to his origins as "earthling". As already noted it would be natural especially for hearers of the LXX to conclude that in making them male and female, God made the male first and then the female and that the male was called Adam, in other words, that 2:5-25 is explicating 1:26-27 and that 1:26-27 indicates in summary that sequence of events.

We should not however overstress the difference from the Hebrew, which despite the use of aetiology in the name, also assumes God created humankind by forming a male first and ends by reminding this male, now clearly identified as such, that he will serve the ground and ultimately return to it (as the woman will return to her origin and will serve him - on this see the discussion of 3:16-19 below).[17]

The reason for the shift in 2:16 to Ἀδάμ ("Adam") from ἄνθρωπος ("man") in translating הָאָדָם is probably that 2:16 contains the prohibition which the individual figure, Adam, violates in the following chapter. Had the translator retained the generic, one might have gained the impression that humankind, so formed, had been placed in the garden, perhaps many of them. The plural οὐ φάγεσθε ("you shall not eat") in 2:17, replacing the singular in Hebrew (תֹאכַל)

---

[16] It is interesting that LXX does attempt to reserve the word play in the name of Eve. Thus 3:20 reads: καὶ ἐκάλεσεν Ἀδάμ τὸ ὄνομα τῆς γυναικὸς αὐτοῦ Ζωή ὅτι αὕτη μήτηρ πάντων τῶν ζώντων; "And Adam named his wife 'Zoe', because she is the mother of all living", but then returns to the name Εὐα (Eve) in 4:1. There is an awareness of Adam as also a descriptive name in 5:2, but no explanation is attempted.

[17] So Rösel, *Übersetzung*, 68; F. Watson, "Strategies of recovery and resistance: Hermeneutical Reflections on Genesis 1-3 and its Pauline Reception," *JSNT* 45 (1992) 79-103, here 92-93; B. J. Stratton, *Out of Eden. Rhetoric and Ideology in Genesis 2-3* (JSOTSup 208; Sheffield: Sheffield Acad Pr., 1995) 102-103; cf. M. Bal, *Lethal Love: Feminist Literary Readings of Biblical Love Stories* (Bloomington: Indiana Univ. Pr., 1987) 113-16; Trible, *God and the Rhetoric of Sexuality*, 17-21, 97-98. Both argue that man and woman emerge only after the separation in 2:23.

reflects the translator's awareness of the following chapter where the woman (as well as the man) was involved. The return in 2:18 to the generic ἄνθρωπος ("man/human being") reflects the translator's understanding that a general principle was being enunciated, that it was not good for a human being (male) to be alone, although it applied first to this individual figure, this male called, "Adam".

1.4   Genesis 2:18-23 LXX - forming the woman in the likeness of the man

Gen 2:18-23 LXX begins an important new stage in the fulfilment of 1:26-27, whether the latter is understood as summary, genus or archetype. It explains the formation of woman. In 2:18 and in 2:20 we find the Hebrew עֵזֶר כְּנֶגְדּוֹ. The Hebrew means "a helper according to what is before him" (ie. his counterpart).[18] 2:18 translates this as βοηθὸν κατ᾽ αὐτόν. The same Hebrew words in 2:20 are rendered by the translator with βοηθὸς ὅμοιος αὐτῷ. In 2:18 κατ᾽ αὐτόν probably means "according to him, like him", but ὅμοιος αὐτῷ appears stronger; the translator appears to have in mind the fulfilment of God's intention in forming the woman according to 1:26-27. With both κατ᾽ αὐτόν and ὅμοιος αὐτῷ there is an echo in the LXX of 1:26 where the double κατά phrases occur and ὁμοίωσιν is used.[19] The influence of 1:26 is evident also in the change from the singular אֶעֱשֶׂה ("I shall make" in the Hebrew of 2:18 to the plural, ποιήσωμεν ("Let us make") matching 1:26.[20] Gen 1:26-27 will also have influenced the unexpected choice of the generic ἄνθρωπος ("man/human being") instead of ἀνήρ ("man/male/husband") as the translation of אִישׁ ("man/male/husband") in 2:24. This is all part of the attuning of Genesis 2 to Genesis 1 in the LXX, which we have noted earlier, but which is particularly noteworthy in the account of the creation of woman.

The result is that the forming of woman is being set more closely in parallel to the creation of ἄνθρωπος in 1:26. That, in turn, creates an analogy. As ἄνθρωπος, understood as the male, is in the likeness of God (but subordinate), so the woman is in the likeness of the male (and, by implication and analogy, subordinate in the chain of being). This is accordingly how the text was widely read, from Philo to Paul in 1 Corinthians 11, as we shall see below. Similarly because the need is seen as relating to this particular male, LXX uses the name, "Adam", in 2:20, whereas

---

[18] So Wevers, *Notes on the Greek Text of Genesis*, 31.

[19] Rösel, *Übersetzung*, 69.

[20] So Cook, "Genesis," 105; Rösel, *Übersetzung*, 68, who also points out that the use of ποιέω rather than πλάσσω reinforces the connection with Gen 1 (69).

in 2:18 it had used ἄνθρωπος. Adam is the ἄνθρωπος of 1:26 who now has someone in his likeness beside him.

Whereas in Hebrew one may argue that the emphasis of the word עֵזֶר is on the helping companion, the LXX's βοηθός, which is capable of the same meaning, now lends itself to being understood as referring to a helper who is subordinate, especially because of the context which has forged a closer link with 1:26-27.[21] The word βοηθός does not in itself imply inferiority. On the contrary, elsewhere it is used of God (eg. Exod 15:2; 18:4; Deut 33:7,26,29).[22] But within the context of the idea of a chain of being which appears to underlie the LXX translation, the woman is the helper of the man, in the sense that as the man is after the likeness of God, so the woman is after the likeness of the man. Inferior animals did not suffice, but it gave Adam the opportunity to name them. The assumption is that something superior to animals is required, but which is still next after man in the chain of being. 2:22 repeats the phrase used of the animals in 2:19: God brought the woman to Adam. As Adam named the animals, now in 2:23 he names the woman, commonly understood as the action of a superior.[23] Even the joining in 2:24 can be heard in this perspective, since it fulfils God's intention enunciated in 2:20 and 18.

To the extent that the LXX gives more emphasis to subordination than the Hebrew, it opened the possibility that confusion might arise between the curse of domination in 3:16 and its cause, sin, on the one hand, and the subordination implied in 2:20-25, on the other, with the result that sin might be linked with the

---

[21] Cf. Rösel, *Übersetzung*, 69: "Das zur Übersetzung von עֵזֶר hier und in V. 20 benutzte βοηθός bezeichnet eine Hilfe oder Unterstützung im weitesten Sinne und entspricht damit dem Bedeutungsinhalt der Vorlage und des inhaltlichen Zusammenhangs" (Tr. The word, βοηθός, used here and in v.20 to translate עֵזֶר signifies a help or support in the broadest sense and so corresponds to the meaning of the original and the meaning of the context). Noort, "Creation of man and woman," 12, notes that the Hebrew implies mutuality, where the Greek and Vulgate (*ei adiutorium simili sibi*) do not.

[22] So A. J. M. Higgins, "Anastasius Sinaita and the Superiority of Women," *JBL* 97 (1978) 253-56, who argues that the fact that βοηθός nearly always refers to the helper as a superior in the LXX implies that women are pictured as superiors also here in that the man is saved from his solitude. See also *Sir* 36:24LXX which understands βοηθός as indicating a pillar of support. So also Marguerite Harl, *La Bible D'Alexandrie: L'Genèse* (Paris: Cerf, 1986) 104-105; V. P. Hamilton, *The Book of Genesis Chapters 1-17* (Grand Rapids: Eerdmans, 1990) 176. Further on the Hebrew text see Trible, *God and the Rhetoric of Sexuality*, 90-92, and the counter position by D. J. A. Clines, *"What does Eve do to help?" and other Readerly Questions to the Old Testament* (JSOTSup 94; Sheffield: JSOTPr., 1990) 34-35 and Stratton, *Out of Eden*, 96-98.

[23] I appreciate my colleague, John Olley, pointing in conversation to Gen 16:3 where Hagar gives a name to God, clearly an inferior doing the naming, but my point is that the context here in Gen 2 assumes the reverse.

creation of woman and not just with her disobedience (see the discussion of Philo, below).

As God had taken the dust of the ground to fashion the man, so in 2:21 God takes a rib (bone and flesh) from the man and builds a woman.[24] Here the LXX speaks of a spell (ἔκστασιν) rather than deep sleep[25] and speaks of filling up (ἀνεπλήρωσεν) rather than of sewing up, so that the focus is on the filling of a vacant space rather than on joining up and conveys, like the ἔκστασις, a greater sense of mystery.[26] The LXX is unable to render the Hebrew pun in Adam's words in 2:23

וַיֹּאמֶר הָאָדָם זֹאת הַפַּעַם עֶצֶם
מֵעֲצָמַי וּבָשָׂר מִבְּשָׂרִי
לְזֹאת יִקָּרֵא אִשָּׁה
כִּי מֵאִישׁ לֻקֳחָה־זֹּאת:

Then the man said,

"This at last is bone of my bones and flesh of my flesh;

this one shall be called Woman, {Heb [ishshah] } for out of Man {Heb [ish] }

this one was taken."

καὶ εἶπεν Αδάμ Τοῦτο νῦν ὀστοῦν ἐκ τῶν ὀστέων μου

καὶ σὰρξ ἐκ τῆς σαρκός μου·

αὕτη κληθήσεται γυνή,

ὅτι ἐκ τοῦ ἀνδρὸς αὐτῆς ἐλήμφθη.

Then Adam said,

"This is now bone of my bones and flesh of my flesh;

she shall be called Woman,

for she was taken out of her husband."

The final clause no longer focuses on common kind, (as the naming of Adam, the earthling, had focused on the commonness with the earth in the Hebrew), but rather on the man as the woman's husband. Note the addition in the LXX of the possessive genitive ("her") in ἐκ τοῦ ἀνδρὸς αὐτῆς ("out of her husband").[27] She was taken from the man who through this process will become her husband!

---

[24] "The verb *banu* ("to build") is the regular term employed in Akkadian literature to describe the creation of human beings by the gods;" similarly in Ugaritic. So Westermann, *Genesis 1-11*, 230-31, citing U. Cassuto, *A Commentary on the book of Genesis* (Jerusalem: Magnes, 1961-64) 134. It is used of creation also in Amos 9:6.

[25] LXX cannot reproduce the wordplay: תַּרְדֵּמָה/הָאָדָם. For other such word plays see Wenham, *Genesis 1-15*, 59.

[26] So Rösel, *Übersetzung*, 70-71.

[27] The possessive also appears in Targums and Sam Pentateuch.

The reason draws therefore on what is to follow in 2:24. In the LXX it is not at all clear why Adam calls her γυνή ("woman"). The reason, ὅτι ἐκ τοῦ ἀνδρὸς αὐτῆς ἐλήμφθη ("for she was taken out of her husband"), is not enlightening.[28] It may mean nothing more than: because that is what we call the female partner in a marriage. If so, this is rather a lame explanation, but it also has the effect of emphasising 2:24 in a way that gives it even more prominence than in the Hebrew. The shift, however, from focus on commonality through the pun אִשָּׁה אִישׁ מֵ, (ish-ishshah; man-woman) to focus on a wife and her husband, also reflects the chain of being.[29] She, the helper, who is like her husband, has been taken from her husband (and will return to him; 3:16).

---

[28] So also Rösel, *Übersetzung*, "das begründete 'denn' verliert auf diese Weise seinen Sinn" (71). (Tr. The "for", which is based [on the word play], in this way loses its meaning).

[29] By contrast Westermann, *Genesis 1-11*, writes of the Hebrew: "The narrative in Gen 2 reflects a stage in civilization which was aware of the great importance of the role of woman in the existence of humankind." Referring to the words, "a helper fit for him", he writes: "What is meant is the personal community of man and woman in the broadest sense - bodily and spiritual community, mutual help and understanding, joy and contentment in each other." (232). See also B. F. Batto, "The institution of marriage in Genesis 2 and in *Atrahasis*," *CBQ* 62 (2000) 621-31, who argues that Gen 2:18-24 "provides an important hermeneutical tool for understanding the Yahwist's message and Gen. 2:18-24 in particular." The Yahwist follows a source which links marriage and procreation, but by contrast "seems to distance marriage somewhat from procreation. For the Yahwist, the communitarian, affective function of marriage takes precedence over the procreative function of marriage" (631). Batto argues against Gunkel and also Westermann, that 2:24 is about the institution of marriage, as the parallel story indicates (629). The parallel also helps reinforce the understanding of the sexuality in the text according to which sexual intercourse is not the result of sin, but a natural part of creation and so belongs in the garden (630). See also Gordon Paul Hugenberger, *Marriage as a Covenant: A Study of Biblical Law & Ethics Governing Marriage, developed from the perspective of Malachi* (VTSup LII; Leiden: Brill, 1994) who writes: "In view of the literary parallels between Genesis 1-11 and various ancient Near Eastern creation accounts and other myths (e.g., the Sumerian King List, the Sumerian Flood Story or its reconstructed form as the Eridu Genesis, the Memphis creation documents, the Atra-ḫasis Epic Enuma Elis, the Gilgameš Epic, the Adapa meth, etc.), the inclusion of an intentionally paradigmatic marriage in Genesis 2-3 should not be surprising" (154). Probably the creation narrative is deliberately distancing itself from the way sexual intercourse is portrayed in surrounding cultures and their myths (155).

1.5   Genesis 2:24 LXX - becoming "one flesh"

The word play אִישׁ אִשָּׁה (*ish-ishshah*; man-woman) continues in 2:24 but is again lost in the Greek.[30] The Greek even returns to the generic ἄνθρωπος ("man/human").

עַל־כֵּן יַעֲזָב־אִישׁ אֶת־אָבִיו
וְאֶת־אִמּוֹ וְדָבַק בְּאִשְׁתּוֹ וְהָיוּ לְבָשָׂר אֶחָד:

Therefore a man leaves his father and his mother
and clings to his wife, and they become one flesh.

ἕνεκεν τούτου καταλείψει ἄνθρωπος τὸν πατέρα αὐτοῦ
καὶ τὴν μητέρα αὐτοῦ
καὶ προσκολληθήσεται πρὸς τὴν γυναῖκα αὐτοῦ,
καὶ ἔσονται οἱ δύο εἰς σάρκα μίαν.

Therefore a man shall leave his father
and his mother
and be joined to his wife,
and the two shall become one flesh.

One might have expected expected ἀνήρ ("man/male/husband") as the translation of אִישׁ ("man/male/husband"). LXX chooses the generic ἄνθρωπος ("man/human being"). The explanation probably lies in what we have already observed in the preceding verses. The translator has 1:26 in mind, as he has since 2:18, assumes ἄνθρωπος in 1:26 to be male, and sees the formation of woman as the next step after the creation of ἄνθρωπος.[31]

In both Hebrew and Greek 2:24 speaks of the man leaving his family and being joined to his wife, rather than the normal pattern of the woman leaving hers and being joined to the man and his household. It need not however be read as implying a matriarchal societal structure in which males in marriage joined the female family clan.[32] It may reflect that in some circumstances the man would leave his home and establish a new home with his wife. The emphasis is probably not on the detail of who is left nor on marriage as such, nor on the strength of the urge to become one flesh which causes the man to move out from father and

---

[30] Note that the narrative may well go back to a stage where a Sumerian word play on "rib" and "the lady who makes live" played a role (J. B. Pritchard, cited in Westermann, *Genesis 1-11*, 230). Symmachus creates the word, ἀνδρίς.

[31] Cf. Berger, *Gesetzesauslegung*, 529, who speaks about ἄνθρωπος ("man"/"human being") fitting the context better (2:15,18).

[32] See Hugenberger, *Marriage as a Covenant*, 158.

mother (even if not literally) and start afresh in order to be joined to his wife,[33] but on the change of loyalties from parents to one's wife.[34] The focus includes sexual union[35] and living together which would be assumed to entail marriage,[36] but we should not read back our notions of romantic marriage or marriage on the basis of romantic sexual attraction into the text, as though this would have been seen as the basis of marriage then.

With regard to the LXX, 2:23 had already used the language of marriage when it spoke of "her husband". Hearers would understand 2:24 in that context.[37]

---

[33] So Berger, *Gesetzesauslegung*, 528.

[34] So Hugenberger, *Marriage as a Covenant*, 159-160: "the language of 'leave' and 'cleave' appears intended to stress the necessity of a radical change, not of domicile, but of one's preeminent loyalty - a husband is to transfer to his wife the primary familial loyalty which he once owed to his parents."

[35] The focus in Hebrew in 2:23 is on commonality. Noort, "Creation of man and woman," 12, argues that in 2:24 it is on sexual attraction. "Gen 2:18-24 explains in a narrative way what is meant by Cant 8:6 'For love is strong as Death, passion relentless as Sheol'. Where Gen 2:23 celebrated the physical unity of man and woman, 2:24 stresses the physical coupling or sexual contact. In the eyes of the narrator, the creation of man and woman from the one human being explains the real motif: the reason why love breaks social structures. In contrast with the over-all theme of the creation myth, there is no direct reference in V. 24 to the aspect of procreation. Passion is a value in itself." This is in danger of reading through modern romantic perspectives. See also Berger, *Gesetzesauslegung*, 530, who draws attention to the negative sexual interpretation of Gen 2:24 in 1 Esdr 4:20,25 (especially in the context of 14-31 where it warns against sexual drive) and Josephus *A.J.* 11.52. See also his discussion of similar emphases in later rabbinic tradition (531-32).

[36] "The significance of the verse lies in this that in contrast to the established institutions and partly in opposition to them, it points to the basic power of love between man and woman" - so Westermann, *Genesis 1-11*, 233. It includes but is more than sexual intercourse. It is not leaving household, but mother and father. "The primary place is not given to propagation or to the institution of marriage as such. The love of man and woman receives here a unique evaluation" (234). See also Wenham, *Genesis 1-15*, who notes that when 2:22 speaks of bringing the woman to the man, it reflects arranged marriages (70).

[37] Wenham, *Genesis 1-15*, points to the use of covenant language in 2:24, especially the notion of forsaking, not just leaving, though understood in a relative, not absolute sense, and of sticking to (as Gen 34:3; Deut 10:20; 11:22; 13:5) (71). See also W. Brueggemann, "Of the same flesh and bone (GN 2,23a)," *CBQ* 32 (1970) 532-42 and Hamilton, *The Book of Genesis*, 181. This does not appear to be the case in the LXX. The major treatment arguing for an understanding of marriage as covenant here and elsewhere, not least Malachi 2, is Hugenberger's, *Marriage as a Covenant*. He argues that 2:23 is to be understood not just as a statement of welcome but as expressing *verba solemnia* which functioned as an oath before God in marriages. He concludes his discussion (216-39): "from a broad range of biblical and extrabiblical evidence there can be little doubt that marriage in biblical times was, in fact, typically formed with the use of *verba solemnia*. Furthermore, from the many different examples discussed, it is apparent that a wide variety of formulae were

Similarly while nothing is said about procreation, the close link in the LXX with 1:26-28 would doubtless suggest it. The focus however of the LXX, as of the Hebrew, remains on the joining, including sexual union, not on procreation (as if this were its only warrant). The translator has used the word προσκολληθήσεται ("shall be joined/shall join") to translate the Qal, דָּבַק ("join to/stick to"). The range of meaning of both verbs is similar, including "cleave" and "stick".[38] It need not be sexual in reference,[39] but in the context may include sexual union. The future passive form of προσκολλάω opens the possibility, not present in the Hebrew, that the verb be understood not as a deponent passive but as a true passive assuming an agent (eg. God).

In the Hebrew becoming one "flesh" בָּשָׂר is not primarily about sexual intercourse in itself,[40] but about a new relationship which is established through consummation in sexual intercourse[41] and remains. The word, בָּשָׂר ("flesh"), is

---

permissible; hence a case such as Gen. 2:23 cannot be rejected merely because it fails to reproduce the standard formula of the much later (Gaonic) Babylonian *kᵉtubba*" (239). Hugenberger traces the influence of Genesis in the formulations of Mal 2:10-16, which reflect an understanding of marriage as a covenant with oath and attack divorce based on aversion (48-83).

[38] On דָּבַק and προσκολλάω see also the discussion of κολλάω in Renate Kirchhoff, *Die Sünde gegen den eigenen Leib: Studien zu πόρνη und πορνεία in 1 Kor 6,12-20 und dem sozio-kulturellen Kontext der paulinischen Adressaten* (SUNT 18; Göttingen: Vandenhoeck und Ruprecht, 1994) 169-70. She notes that in Philo *Q.G.* 1.29 and 1 Esdr 4:17b-22 the total relationship is in view and that even where sexual intercourse is the focus, such as in Sir 19:2 LXX and 1 Cor 6:12-20, much more is in view than that single act. See also A. C. Thiselton, *The First Epistle to the Corinthians: A commentary on the Greek text* (NIGTC; Grand Rapids: Eerdmans; Carlisle: Paternoster, 2000) 466-67, who notes that "Liddell-Scott-Jones and Moulton Milligan offer a different impression of semantic range and examples from that of Bauer-Arndt-Gingrich-Danker", with a greater emphasis on sexual intimacy.

[39] In *Jubilees* it does not (3:7); in some rabbinic traditions it is taken as explicitly sexual (*Gen. Rab.* 18). See Kirchhoff, *Sünde gegen den eigenen Leib*, 160-63.

[40] So Hugenberger, *Marriage as a Covenant*, 161: "It is doubtful that the reader is to imagine that following the consummation of the marriage in sexual union or following each successive act of intercourse, the couple reverts to their former state of being two separate fleshes!"

[41] On the importance of sexual intercourse as an "oath-sign" which consummates marriage in Israel and surrounding cultures see Hugenberger, *Marriage as a Covenant*, 251-261. He summarises: "Sexual union is the indispensable means for the consummation of marriage both in the Old Testament and elsewhere in the ancient Near East" (279).

being used primarily to refer to this new kin.[42] By contrast the use of σάρξ ("flesh") in the LXX to translate בָּשָׂר ("flesh [kin]") in 2:23-24 puts greater emphasis on the sexual union, because whereas בָּשָׂר can be used metaphorically for one's own kin or family, σάρξ ("flesh") is rarely used in this way in the LXX.[43] In the Hebrew the sexual is more likely to be located in the word דָּבַק ("join to/stick to"), whereas in the LXX both προσκολλάω ("join to") and σάρξ ("flesh") are capable of including sexual connotations.

LXX adds οἱ δύο ("the two") which at one level accurately interprets the sense of the Hebrew, but can also result in greater focus being brought to the fact that from two one results. It opens the possibility which is already implicit in the Hebrew text, that this act in some sense restores to unity what was divided into two. A reference to "the two" in 2:24 also appears in the Peshitta and Vulgate, perhaps under Christian influence, although the Samaritan text also has explicated: "from the two of them".[44] The reference to "the two" appears in the Hebrew of the next verse. This may have also influenced the translator to insert the οἱ δύο ("the two") into 2:24, but the result for the LXX is that an even greater emphasis is placed on the twofoldness by having the reference repeated so close together and on the unity which comes about, rather than on the commonality of being reflected in the Hebrew word play: אִישׁ אִשָּׁה (ish-ishshah; man-woman). 2:25 relates "the two" to the man and the woman in the garden. 2:24 is generic and might be taken as always implying that the proper relationship is exclusively one between two people and not more, in other words, monogamy.[45] It need not do so.[46]

---

[42] So Hugenberger, *Marriage as a Covenant*, 163: "It appears likely that 'they become one flesh' refers to the familial bondedness of marriage which finds its quintessential expression in sexual union."

[43] הַפַּעַם עֶצֶם מֵעֲצָמַי וּבָשָׂר מִבְּשָׂרִי ("bone of my bones and flesh of my flesh") is used similarly in Gen 29:14; Jud 9:2-3; 2 Sam 5:1; 19:13,14 of a permanent relationship (Westermann, *Genesis 1-11*, 232); see also Hugenberger, *Marriage as a Covenant*, 162; Berger, *Gesetzesauslegung*, 528.

[44] See Rösel, *Übersetzung*, 72. He sees the shorter, more difficult text as likely to have been original.

[45] D. Daube, *The New Testament and Rabbinic Judaism* (Peabody: Hendrickson, 1956), writes: "It looks as if the LXX (supported, it is true, by the Samaritan Pentateuch) had inserted 'twain' in order to enjoin monogamy, considered as the more civilized practice by the Greeks" (81). On polygyny see Tal Ilan, *Jewish Women in Greco-Roman Palestine* (Peabody: Hendrickson, 1996; Tübingen: J. C. B. Mohr, 1995) 85. She points to evidence for polygyny in Sir 37:11 and in early rabbinic literature. The Temple Scroll insists on monogyny for the king (57:17-18) and it is implied in CD 4:20 - 5:2, where Gen 1:27 is quoted.

[46] So Berger, *Gesetzesauslegung*, who argues it is not (529).

1.6   *Genesis 2:25 - 3:13 - seduction(?) in the garden*

The transition from 2:25 to 3:1 in Hebrew also includes a play on words.

וַיִּהְיוּ שְׁנֵיהֶם עֲרוּמִּים הָאָדָם וְאִשְׁתּוֹ וְלֹא יִתְבֹּשָׁשׁוּ׃
וְהַנָּחָשׁ הָיָה עָרוּם מִכֹּל חַיַּת הַשָּׂדֶה אֲשֶׁר עָשָׂה יְהוָה אֱלֹהִים

(2:25) And the two of them, the man and his wife, were both naked, and were
not ashamed.

(3:1) Now the serpent was more crafty than any other wild animal that the
LORD God had made.

καὶ ἦσαν οἱ δύο γυμνοί, ὅ τε Αδαμ καὶ ἡ γυνὴ αὐτοῦ, καὶ οὐκ
ἠσχύνοντο.
ὁ δὲ ὄφις ἦν φρονιμώτατος πάντων τῶν θηρίων τῶν ἐπὶ τῆς γῆς,
ὧν ἐποίησεν κύριος ὁ θεός·

Gen 3:1 LXX

And the two, Adam and his wife, were naked, and were not ashamed.
Now the serpent was more crafty than any other wild animal on the earth that
the LORD God had made.

The man and the woman were naked עֲרוּמִּים. (*ʿarummim*). The serpent was
cunning: עָרוּם (*'arum*). This play on words is lost in the LXX translation. The
effect is to bring the statement in LXX 3:1 (Hebrew 2:25) into closer association
with what precedes.[47] Gen 3:1 would be heard as implying that such union,
including sexual union, implied in 2:24, was not a matter of shame.[48]

The serpent's approach to "the woman" in the LXX is to ask why God said
something - then to cite God incorrectly: τί ὅτι εἶπεν ὁ θεός οὐ μὴ φάγητε
ἀπὸ παντὸς ξύλου τοῦ ἐν τῷ παραδείσῳ ("Why did God say, 'You shall not
eat of any tree in the garden'?" 3:1). The Hebrew has לֹא תֹאכְלוּ מִכֹּל עֵץ הַגָּן
אַף כִּי־אָמַר אֱלֹהִים ("Did God say, 'You shall not eat from any tree in the
garden'?"). According to the serpent eating of the tree of knowledge would give
them knowledge of good and evil and they would become "like gods" (so LXX

---

[47] Even though later verse numbering would suggest the opposite! See Wevers, *Notes
on the Greek Text of Genesis*, 36.

[48] Westermann, *Genesis 1-11*, 236, notes that shame "is an extremely puzzling
phenomenon, such as the absence of shame can indicate on the one hand lack of self-
consciousness or innocence, as in 2:25, or on the other hand the way to being inhuman." It
is not here about lack of sexual awareness or of a sense of guilt. I think more
anthropological insights need to be brought in here. The puzzling nature of shame in the
passage invites speculation.

ὡς θεοί; and probably Hebrew: כֵּאלֹהִים). It is interesting that 3:22 indicates that precisely this has happened and that the result echoes 1:26-27, being in the image of God or like God. God was anxious, according to 3:22, that in addition they might eat of the tree of life and live forever. The serpent had promised they would not die, but at that point it was not clear that there were two trees (see 2:9 which in both Greek and Hebrew speaks of the tree of life). The serpent was probably also correct in some sense, therefore, about the tree. This creates a tension in the narrative, because God's warning had been that they would die. As the story reads, God intervened just in time before they ate of the second tree and became immortal. There is no substantial difference here between the Hebrew and the LXX.

The major impact of the act of disobedience was that knowledge of good and evil brought awareness of nakedness. In itself the shame of nakedness did not imply that sexuality was sinful or evil. Rather they recognised wrong or harm ("evil") in being uncovered when and where they should not have been. Shame is not guilt. Sexual parts of the body were simply to be kept covered. Now they knew that; before, they did not. There was a time and place where they could be uncovered. It was shameful for them to be uncovered at the wrong time and place. This view was (and is) very widespread in many cultures. At one level this knowledge is neutral, as awareness of what is shameful and what is not is also neutral.[49] It functions as an aetiology of clothing, especially to cover one's nakedness, sexual organs in particular.

It was also possible to interpret the passage as implying that their naked bodies, in particular, their sexualities were something evil. It seems certain, however, that the reason they hid themselves from God was not to escape notice because they were ashamed of their act, but to withdraw from the divine sight because they were naked. This assumes an incompatibility between nakedness, especially exposure of sexual parts, and divine presence. It reflected an attitude which was widespread among many cultures. It is as though they are naked in the temple, if as it seems, temple values underlie the image of the garden.[50]

The fact that knowing good and evil brought shame about what otherwise was a neutral state of creatureliness, the human body, was bound to lead to the assumption among some that bodiliness, and sexuality in particular, is somehow in

---

[49] Westermann, *Genesis 1-11*, 250-51, sees it as advance in knowledge; it can also be seen as loss of innocence (including positive acceptance of sexuality; certainly not acquisition of awareness of sexuality because that is there in Gen 2). Nakedness, clothing with leaves, then with skins, reflects stages of civilisation (252). Like God, recognising something is not good (Gen 2:8-9) they do something about it (252).

[50] For the notion of the garden as holy like the temple see *Jub.* 3:9-14. On this see Jacques van Ruiten, "The Garden of Eden and Jubilees 3:1-31," *Bijdragen, tijdschrift voor filosofie en theologie* 57 (1996) 305-317.

itself suspect or at least of a nature that does not belong in holy presence. In the interplay of thought about purity (which was amoral) and thought about ethical good and evil, it was almost inevitable that a purity focused on nakedness and sexuality became for some a matter of morality with a resultant devaluing if not bedevilling of sexuality. There is no indication of this in the passage in either the Hebrew or the LXX, but the potential is there in both for such a reading and particularly in the LXX where there are now elements in the narrative which may suggest to hearers a link between the sin and sexuality and thus the shame and sexuality.

3:13 describes Yahweh's confrontation of the woman:

וַיֹּאמֶר יְהוָה אֱלֹהִים לָאִשָּׁה מַה־זֹּאת עָשִׂית וַתֹּאמֶר הָאִשָּׁה הַנָּחָשׁ הִשִּׁיאַנִי וָאֹכֵל:

Then the LORD God said to the woman, "What is this that you have done?" The woman said, "The serpent tricked me, and I ate."

καὶ εἶπεν ὁ θεὸς τῇ γυναικί τί τοῦτο ἐποίησας; καὶ εἶπεν ἡ γυνή ὁ ὄφις ἠπάτησέν με, καὶ ἔφαγον

And God said to the woman, "Why have you done this?" And the woman said, "The serpent deceived me and I ate."

The Hebrew word הִשִּׁיאַנִי has the meaning of "tricked me". Its Greek translation, ἠπάτησεν, includes a range of meaning from "deceive" to "seduce", with sexual connotations (eg. Susanna LXX 56; 2 Cor 11:2-3). This opened the possibility that Eve's sin might be seen as the result of sexual seduction of the woman on the part of the serpent, conveying the impression that the woman (and women in general) are weak and vulnerable to seduction, because they are not able to control their sexuality.[51] This is by no means a necessary conclusion, but where it occurs, the blame given to the woman would focus on her sexuality in particular. It is also of interest that the lure of the fruit and the tree in 3:6 is not portrayed by LXX as something that was also "to be desired to make one wise", as in the Hebrew וְנֶחְמָד הָעֵץ לְהַשְׂכִּיל, but only as something that was physically attractive, the LXX reading instead: ὡραῖόν ἐστιν τοῦ κατανοῆσαι ("beautiful to look at"). Seduction by beauty was a common theme in warnings against sin, especially sexual sin. From such indicators it would not be difficult for a reader to make further links which would sexualise the whole episode: primary sin is sexual sin; shame at nakedness is appropriate as guilt about sexuality; sexuality is a primary

---

[51] The change in 3:6 from the attractiveness of acquiring wisdom to visual attraction might contribute to this emphasis. Seduction by beauty was a common theme in warnings against sin, especially sexual sin.

human flaw. Something was wrong in the patent. Philo will explain that it lies with the junior partners of God in creation.

1.7   Genesis 3:16-19 LXX - the punishment

The result of this deception, potentially read as seduction of the woman and then persuasion of the man, is the curse on all three. Adam will return to the ground and toil over it all his life. Similarly the woman returns to her husband. She will be ruled by him (he shall rule over her: κυριεύσει). As the man toils for the earth, she toils for him and does so with increased pain in childbearing. The serpent is reduced to living on the ground/earth and eating it (3:14; cf. Hebrew has "dust" עָפָר; LXX has "earth" γῆν)![52] Gen 3:16 reads:

אֶל־הָאִשָּׁה אָמַר הַרְבָּה אַרְבֶּה
עִצְּבוֹנֵךְ וְהֵרֹנֵךְ בְּעֶצֶב תֵּלְדִי בָנִים וְאֶל־אִישֵׁךְ
תְּשׁוּקָתֵךְ וְהוּא יִמְשָׁל־בָּךְ: ס

> To the woman he said,
> "I will greatly increase your pangs in childbearing;
>   in pain you shall bring forth children,
>   yet your desire shall be for your husband,
>   and he shall rule over you."

καὶ τῇ γυναικὶ εἶπεν Πληθύνων πληθυνῶ τὰς λύπας σου καὶ τὸν στεναγμόν σου,
ἐν λύπαις τέξῃ τέκνα·
καὶ πρὸς τὸν ἄνδρα σου ἡ ἀποστροφή σου, καὶ αὐτός σου κυριεύσει.
And to the woman he said,
"I will greatly increase your pains and your groaning;
in pain you shall bring forth children,
yet your return shall be to your husband,
and he shall rule over you."

The woman's curse has a strongly sexual component: she will be plagued by desire for her husband. This is clearly so in the Hebrew which reads: תְּשׁוּקָתֵךְ וְאֶל־אִישֵׁךְ ("and your desire will be for your husband"; 3:16).[53] Strikingly the

---

[52] Note translation of "watch carefully" in LXX, not "pierce" or "bruise".

[53] Cf. Wenham, *Genesis 1-15*, 81, who refers to Susan Foh, "What is the woman's desire?" *WTJ* 37 (1974/75) 376-383, for the view that the word תְּשׁוּקָתֵךְ ("your desire")

LXX translates this with καὶ πρὸς τὸν ἄνδρα σου ἡ ἀποστροφή σου ("Yet your return shall be to your husband"). The sense may be similar in that it indicates that the woman will keep returning to her husband and so becoming pregnant again and again, as the context suggests.[54] Thus while unlike the Hebrew the LXX is not explicitly sexual, it doubtless intends it and would convey that intention. In the choice of ἡ ἀποστροφή σου ("your return") the translator may well be making a connection with ἕως τοῦ ἀποστρέψαι σε εἰς τὴν γῆν ἐξ ἧς ἐλήμφθη ("until you return to the earth, from which you were taken"). Or, at least, the effect is to highlight this connection for the hearers.[55]

(17)

וּלְאָדָם אָמַר כִּי־שָׁמַעְתָּ לְקוֹל אִשְׁתֶּךָ
וַתֹּאכַל מִן־הָעֵץ אֲשֶׁר צִוִּיתִיךָ לֵאמֹר לֹא
תֹאכַל מִמֶּנּוּ אֲרוּרָה הָאֲדָמָה
בַּעֲבוּרֶךָ בְּעִצָּבוֹן תֹּאכֲלֶנָּה כֹּל יְמֵי חַיֶּיךָ:
(18)

וְקוֹץ וְדַרְדַּר תַּצְמִיחַ לָךְ
וְאָכַלְתָּ אֶת־עֵשֶׂב הַשָּׂדֶה:
(19)

בְּזֵעַת אַפֶּיךָ תֹּאכַל לֶחֶם עַד שׁוּבְךָ
אֶל־הָאֲדָמָה כִּי מִמֶּנָּה לֻקָּחְתָּ
כִּי־עָפָר אַתָּה וְאֶל־עָפָר תָּשׁוּב:

(17) And to the man {Or [to Adam] } he said, "Because you have listened to the voice of your wife, and have eaten of the tree about which I commanded you, 'You shall not eat of it,' cursed is the ground because of you; in toil you shall eat of it all the days of your life; (18) thorns and thistles it shall bring

---

implies that women will seek to dominate men; see also Hamilton, *The Book of Genesis*, 201.

[54] "The Hebrew word refers to sexual desire, but the Greek avoids this (as it does at 4:7). What the translator probably meant was that though 'in pains you will bear children,' yet 'your return will be to your husband,' i.e. you will keep coming back to him." So Wevers, *Notes on the Greek Text of Genesis*, 45; cf. Rösel, *Übersetzung*, who speaks of finding protection "Zuflucht," (95), pointing to the use of the noun in 4:7. Cf. R. Bergmeier, "Zur Septuaginta-Übersetzung von Gen. 3:16," *ZAW* 79 (1967) 77-79.

[55] Gen 4:7 also contains the word תְּשׁוּקָה ("desire"), referring to sin lurking like an animal at the door. Here, too, LXX translates ἡ ἀποστροφή ("return"), where probably with reference to sin it refers to sin returning and to Cain's needing to rule over it. The formulation in both the Hebrew and the LXX of the second part of the verse is very close. By association one might then read the woman's "return" as something negative, even if not as "sin". תְּשׁוּקָה ("desire") is clearly used of sexual desire in Cant 7:11.

forth for you; and you shall eat the plants of the field. (19) By the sweat of
your face you shall eat bread until you return to the ground, for out of it you
were taken; you are dust, and to dust you shall return."

(17) τῷ δὲ Αδὰμ εἶπεν ῞Οτι ἤκουσας τῆς φωνῆς τῆς γυναικός σου
καὶ ἔφαγες ἀπὸ τοῦ ξύλου, οὗ ἐνετειλάμην σοι τούτου μόνου μὴ
φαγεῖν ἀπ' αὐτοῦ, ἐπικατάρατος ἡ γῆ ἐν τοῖς ἔργοις σου· ἐν λύπαις
φάγῃ αὐτὴν πάσας τὰς ἡμέρας τῆς ζωῆς σου. (18) ἀκάνθας καὶ
τριβόλους ἀνατελεῖ σοι, καὶ φάγῃ τὸν χόρτον τοῦ ἀγροῦ. (19) ἐν
ἱδρῶτι τοῦ προσώπου σου φάγῃ τὸν ἄρτον σου ἕως τοῦ ἀποστρέψαι
σε εἰς τὴν γῆν, ἐξ ἧς ἐλήμφθης ὅτι γῆ εἶ καὶ εἰς γῆν ἀπελεύσῃ.
(17) And to Adam he said, "Because you have listened to the voice of your
wife, and have eaten of the tree about which I commanded you only of this
one not to eat from it, cursed is the ground in your toils; in pain you shall eat
of it all the days of your life; (18) thorns and thistles it shall bring forth for
you; and you shall eat the grass of the field. (19) By the sweat of your face
you shall eat your bread until you return to the earth, from which you were
taken; because you are earth and to earth you shall return."

In its own way the LXX highlights the reversal more strongly than the
Hebrew: as the man derives from the earth, and the woman from the man, so
disobedience will bring the man back to earth to serve it and the woman back to
the man to serve him. LXX also reinforces this by the use of γῆ ("earth") in 3:19
where Hebrew has עָפָר ("dust"). This echoes the use of γῆ in 2:7 and so forms a
more effective inclusio or bracket.

These curses come as punishment or at least as consequences of the
disobedience and come in addition to expulsion from the garden which follows in
3:24. There is a certain tension in the narrative between the curses in 3:14-19 and
the creation of woman in 2:21-25. If sexual attraction, at least of the man for the
woman in 2:24, is a fruit of God's creation and positive, in 3:16 it has become a
curse, unless we are to assume the sexual passion belonged originally with the
male and the curse gave sexual passion also to women. Then as men became like
God, "knowing good and evil" (3:22), so women became like men, having sexual
passion. Alternatively the difference is between controlled and uncontrolled sexual
drive. In the Hellenistic environment of the LXX this would be heard as reflecting
the widespread view that women are not able to control their sexuality. That would
be the curse, rather than sexual attraction, itself,[56] although 3:13 may read as

---

[56] For instance in the *Testaments of the Twelve Patriarchs* see *T. Reub.* 5; on Philo see
D. Sly, *Philo's Perception of Women* (BJS 209; Atlanta: Scholars, 1990) 108. She writes in
relation to the biting serpent and to the eating of forbidden fruit: "There is little doubt that in

indicating that such lack of control was the reason why the woman was seduced in the first place and will be read by some as an original flaw. For this reason they need to be ruled by their husbands, an element not present in 2:20-25, but echoing rather what was said of the animals.

As the man must now toil for the earth and return to it, so the woman must toil for (keep returning to) the man. The role of "helper", already in its context in the LXX implying some inferiority, now becomes a kind of enslavement because of her own sexual passions. Part of the curse is also the increased pain in childbirth. The sexual relationship which included reproduction has now been injected with pain, just as the happy tending of the ground has become for the man a grind and a battle. Such an understanding of the text, whether Hebrew or Greek, sat well in the prevailing values of the world of the time and would help reinforce them.

The use of ἠπάτησέν, to translate הִשִּׁיאַ֫נִי in 3:13, however, which could be heard as referring to sexual seduction, and the potential for confusion between what are now statements of subordination in both the curse (3:16) and the creation (2:18-25) opened the possibility that the scene as a whole might be read as referring to sexual sins and sexual shame as guilt and as implying sexuality as a flaw in creation.

1.8   Genesis 5:1-3 LXX - human beings, Adam and origins

It is important to consider this passage not only because it reiterates the thought of Gen 1:26-28, but also because the LXX has translated it in a way which may reflect its special interests and assumptions.

זֶה סֵ֫פֶר תּוֹלְדֹת אָדָם ("This is the list of the descendants of Adam") becomes αὕτη ἡ βίβλος γενέσεως ἀνθρώπων ("This is the book of the origin of human beings"). Here the LXX not only reads אָדָם ("Adam") in a generic way, but indicates this by the plural ἀνθρώπων ("human beings"). This may well indicate sensitivity on the translator's part that he has been using the singular to mean the male (eg. in 2:24) and Adam, in particular. What follows in 5:1b-2 represents a summary in which key elements of 1:26-28 are taken up.

---

both cases Philo sees the 'fall' as sexual. The serpent represents pleasure, and the most intense pleasure Philo knows is that experienced by a man in intercourse" (109).

(1b)

בְּיוֹם בְּרֹא אֱלֹהִים אָדָם

בִּדְמוּת אֱלֹהִים עָשָׂה אֹתוֹ

(2)

זָכָר וּנְקֵבָה בְּרָאָם

וַיְבָרֶךְ אֹתָם

וַיִּקְרָא אֶת־שְׁמָם אָדָם

בְּיוֹם הִבָּרְאָם׃

(1b) When God created *adam*,

he made him in the likeness of God.

(2) Male and female he created them,

and he blessed them

and named them *adam* when they were created.

(1b) ᾗ ἡμέρᾳ ἐποίησεν ὁ θεὸς τὸν Αδάμ,

κατ᾽ εἰκόνα θεοῦ ἐποίησεν αὐτόν·

(2) ἄρσεν καὶ θῆλυ ἐποίησεν αὐτούς.

καὶ εὐλόγησεν αὐτούς.

καὶ ἐπωνόμασεν τὸ ὄνομα αὐτῶν Αδάμ,

ᾗ ἡμέρᾳ ἐποίησεν αὐτούς.

(1b) When God created Adam,

he created him according to the image of God.

(2) Male and female he created them,

and he blessed them

and named them Adam,

when he created them.

Having translated אָדָם by ἀνθρώπων in the opening statement of 5:1a, LXX shifts to the individual figure "Adam", even though it had used ἄνθρωπον ("man/human") in both 1:26 and 1:27 (and 2:24) which are echoed here. In 5:1-2 the translator is clearly reading 1:26-27 as a reference to the creation of Adam. As in the Hebrew, 5:2 returns to the plural, following 1:27, but compounds the alternation of plural to singular to plural in 5:1-2 by concluding that God named them "Adam" on the day he created them.[57] This would give added impulse to interpretations which might see the original male Adam as incorporating a male and a female.[58]

---

[57] Rösel, *Übersetzung,* 124, rightly notes that the use of Adam here probably indicates that the translator and his community were still aware of the collective use of the word.

[58] Given the even more striking change of persons here in 5:2 than in 1:27c it is not surprising that it is especially in relation to this text, that interpretations arose which drew

The Hebrew of 5:1 produces a statement which uses only כִּדְמוּתֵנוּ ("in our likeness") from 1:26 (so בִּדְמוּת 5:1 "in the likeness") and not בְּצֶלֶם ("in his image") which is present in both 1:26 and 1:27 ("in the image" 1:27; also בְּצַלְמֵנוּ "in our image" 1:26 and בְּצַלְמוֹ "in his image" 1:27). In 5:1 the LXX translator chooses not καθ' ὁμοίωσιν ("in the likeness") to translate בִּדְמוּת ("in the likeness") as he had for כִּדְמוּתֵנוּ ("according to his likeness") in 1:26, but κατ' εἰκόνα ("according to the image"), which he had used to translate בְּצֶלֶם ("in the image") in both 1:26 and 27. This may reflect the philosophical framework of the translator in which εἰκών ("image") is a fundamental term or at least would resonate with hearers who had such a philosophical framework. Significantly in 5:3 the words בִּדְמוּתוֹ כְּצַלְמוֹ, ("in his likeness according to his image"), an allusion to בְּצַלְמֵנוּ כִּדְמוּתֵנוּ ("in his image according to his likeness") in 1:26, are translated by κατὰ τὴν ἰδέαν αὐτοῦ καὶ κατὰ τὴν εἰκόνα αὐτοῦ ("according to his appearance and according to his image"). Here, too, we find terms which would resonate with Platonic philosophy.[59] Such words are being used now to describe Adam begetting his children in his likeness.

זָכָר וּנְקֵבָה בְּרָאָם ("male and female he created them" 5:2) repeats בָּרָא אֹתָם זָכָר וּנְקֵבָה 1:27c almost word for word, in the LXX exactly so.[60] *Gen. Rab.* 8.11 appears to know a LXX text which changed the pronominal plural ("them") to a

---

selectively upon speculation about androgyny, first found on the lips of Aristophanes in Plato's *Symposium* 189C-193D. See the recent discussion of *Gen. Rab.* 8.1 and related passages in L. Teugels, "The creation of the human in rabbinic interpretation," in *The Creation of Man and Woman*, 107-127, esp. 108-109. See also Berger, *Gesetzesauslegung*, 526, who cites interpretation of Gen 1:27, reflected in *Midr. Ps.* 139:5, which explains the shift in number from 27b to c on the basis that Adam was created two sided, with two faces, two fronts, and was then sawn in two, commenting on צַרְתָּנִי אָחוֹר וָקֶדֶם

"You hem me in, behind and before" Ps 139:5. *Gen. Rab.* 14.7 also interprets Gen 2:7 as bisexual, dust representing the male and ground, the female. See Teugels, "Creation," 113.

[59] So Rösel, *Übersetzung*, 124, who notes the avoidance of ὁμοίωσις ("likeness") which he suggests may have been seen as unsuitable to describe relations among human beings. We noted above however that it was used of woman's relation to man, but then that probably reflects the chain of being. Seth's relation to Adam is a different order.

[60] Rösel, *Übersetzung*, 123: "So wird insgesamt als Ergebnis der oben beschriebenen Arbeitsweise des Übersetzers mit 5,1b-2bα ein Text erreicht, der sich wie ein Zitat von Gen 1,27-28aα liest, auch wenn die zugrundeliegenden hebräischen Texte gerade im ersten Teil nicht völlig deckungsgleich miteinander sind." (Tr. So overall the outcome of the way described above of how the translator worked with 5:1b-2 bα is such, that it reads like a citation of Gen 1:27-28aα, even though the Hebrew texts which lie behind them, especially for the first section, are not fully identical).

singular ("him"): "This is one of the things which they altered for King Ptolemy",[61] but no extant manuscripts attest this reading. Only the opening words of 1:28, וַיְבָרֶךְ אֹתָם אֱלֹהִים ("And God blessed them"), are cited in 5:2 (אֹתָם וַיְבָרֶךְ), similarly in the LXX. The substance of the blessing in 1:28: multiplying, is implied in the genealogy which follows in 5:3.

1.9   Conclusion

Platonism?

In our overview of the relevant texts we noted some terminology which could connect readers with the philosophical world of Platonism. In a world of thought informed by popular Platonism the so called second account of creation could also be understood as making the visible on the basis of the invisible or archetypal created in Genesis 1. This could be seen as a way of explaining both the formation of the human and the formation of animal life in 2:18-20 and so would provide a way of reconciling the tension between two accounts. A Platonic reading would recognise the materiality of the created man in 2:7 and might contrast this with the man in Gen 1:26-27, which would provide the model after which the material human being was shaped.

In his treatment of Genesis 1-2 Rösel makes a strong case that the translator stands under the influence of the *Timaeus*. He concludes: "An verschiedenen Stellen war die Vermutung geäussert worden, dass bestimmte Elemente der Übersetzung, besonders die Wahl von Äquivalenten, mit dem platonischen Dialog *Timaios* in Verbindung zu bringen sind." [62] He argues that Genesis 1-2 and the

---

[61] On this see E. Tov, "The rabbinic tradition concerning the 'alterations' inserted into the Greek translation of the Torah and their relation to the original text of the Septuagint," in *The Greek and Hebrew Bible*, 1-20, esp. 11, 17-18. See also Rösel, *Übersetzung,* 123.

[62] Rösel, *Übersetzung,* 73. (Tr. At various points the suspicion was expressed that certain elements of the translation, especially the choice of equivalents, are to be brought into connexion with Plato's *Timaeus*). Of Genesis 1-2 as a whole he writes: "Der Schöpfungsbericht Gen 1+2 erscheint in der Version der Septuaginta als eine in sich geschlossene Einheit, die vom Beginn der zwei wesentlichen Aspekte der Wirklichkeit berichtet, dem der immateriellen Welt und dem der sichtbaren Schöpfung. . . . Durch die Aufnahme der platonischen Schöpfungsvorstellungen wurde erreicht, dass die biblische Kosmogonie mit dem Wissen der Zeit im Einklang stand, zugleich bleibt jedoch unstrittig, dass der vom Judentum verehrte Gott Israels Grund der Schöpfung und Bürge für ihren Bestand ist" (251). (Tr. The account of creation in Gen 1+2 in the Septuagint version appears as a single, coherent unit, which reports the beginning of the two different aspects of reality, the one relating to the immaterial and the other to the visible creation ... The

Timaeus assume a creation in two stages and share a common order in describing the events: heavenly bodies (1:6-8/33Bff), stars and time (1:14-19/38Bff), sea creatures, birds and animals (1:20-25/40A), humankind (1:26-28/41Dff); and beginning afresh: the formation of the human being (2:7/69Aff), mention of plants (2:8/77Aff) and concluding with formation of animals (2:18-20/97Aff). In both the creator assesses his work as very good (1:31/37C), before resting (2:3/42E).[63] Common terminology includes ἀόρατος καὶ ἀκατασκεύαστος in Gen 1:1;[64] the use of ποιέω for בָּרָא as for עָשָׂה and πλάσσω for יָצַר, στερέωμα in 1:6, γένος and ὁμοιότης in 1:11, τετράποδος in 1:24, εἰκών in 1:26-27; 5:1,3 (see also ἰδέα in 5:2-3), κόσμος and συντελέω in 2:1.[65] "Vor dem Hintergrund dieser Überlegungen werden die wesentlichen Abweichungen der LXX vom MT verständlich: Aus dem kaum verbundenen Nebeneinander der beiden biblischen Schöpfungsberichte entsteht ein Bericht, der sinnvoll in zwei Teile unterschieden ist, dabei gibt es vor allem im zweiten Teil Verweise auf den ersten. Der Anfang des Berichts ist als Schilderung des Schaffens der immateriellen Welt zu verstehen, analog zu dem durch die Vernunft Hervorgebrachten in *Timaios*. Erst der zweite Teil berichtet die Entstehung der sichtbaren Schöpfung."[66] While acknowledging that Genesis 1-2 is not to be interpreted solely against this background and that at some points the translator remains bound to the original, nevertheless the effect is to encourage speculation such as we find in Aristobulus that Plato was dependent upon Moses.[67]

---

effect of taking up Platonic ideas of creation is that the biblical cosmogony coheres with contemporary knowledge, while at the same time it remains beyond dispute that the God of Israel revered in Judaism is the reason for the creation and guarantor of its continuing existence). Of Gen 1:26 he writes: "dass schon der hebräische Text von Gen 1,26 der Grund dafür war, Elemente der platonischen Philosophie zur Interpretation zu benutzen" (43). (Tr. that already the Hebrew text of Gen 1:26 was ground for using elements of Platonic philosophy for interpretation). He notes that the idea of the heavenly pattern is already suggested in Daniel and in Exodus 25:9 (40).

[63] Rösel, *Übersetzung*, 81

[64] Rösel, *Übersetzung*, 31-33

[65] Rösel, *Übersetzung*, 82-83

[66] Rösel, *Übersetzung*, 84. (Tr. Against the background of these considerations the main deviations of the LXX from the MT can be understood: from the two biblical accounts of creation which are hardly connected an account has emerged which meaningfully comprises two parts. There is cross-referencing especially in the second part to the first. The beginning of the account is to be understood as depicting the creation of the immaterial world, analogous to what is brought about by Reason in the *Timaeus*. It is only the second part that reports the origin of the visible creation).

[67] Rösel, *Übersetzung*, 85.

Rösel may be correct about the translator. An alternative could be that the translator works with this philosophical background but in a different way. Gen 1:1-2 or 1:1-5 could be understood as referring to the creation of incorporeal forms (uncreated in Plato, created in Genesis), while the remainder refers either to actual creation of the material world or, as a second level, to creation of various kinds, intellectual constructs, followed by creation of actual species in Genesis 2.[68]

In the context of our discussion, whether intended by the translator or not, the fact that philosophical language is present or can be heard to be present in his work would invite attempts to explain Genesis 1-2 in a philosophical framework.[69] Gen 1:26-28 could then refer to the invisible idea, Gen 2:5-25 to its material realisation. There would be difficulties for this reading of the text, especially with the command to multiply in 1:28, but this too need not have proved an obstacle. Alternatively Gen 1:1-2 might be seen as the creation of the invisible and the rest as creation is the *genera* and species.

Where Gen 1:27 was interpreted as a statement about heavenly realities in a Platonic sense, the union, including sexual union, of 2:24 would be understood as

---

[68] So Richard A. Baer, *Philo's Use of the Categories Male and Female* (ALGHJ III; Leiden: Brill, 1970) who points out on the basis of interpreting Philo, there is another possibility: to see everything after the first day as the creation of the genera on the basis of which then the specific are created in Genesis 2, so that one would have to reckon with a 3 stage process: creation of ideas, then *genera*, then specific forms. Similarly Brown, *Structure*, who argues that while Gen 1:1-2 remain outside the act of creation in the six days and find their echo in 2:1-2 as an inclusion, "the LXX construes the first verse as an initial step in the creative process, but a step that remains apart from the formal creation reported in 1:3-31. It is a creation that lacks form (1:2)" (31). "What is implied, then, in Gen 1:1-3 of the LXX is a 'double creation': Heaven and earth are the created 'aformal' substances from which the entities *named* 'heaven' and 'earth' are fashioned in vv 6-8 and 9-10, respectively, within the formal creation account of six days" (35). See also David T. Runia, *Philo of Alexandria and the Timaeus of Plato* (Philosophia Antiqua XLIV; Leiden: Brill, 1986) 92-94, 169-70, 418, and on the "double creation of man": 334-36.

[69] Johann Cook, "Greek Philosophy and the Septuagint," *JNSL* 24 (1998) 177-91, vigorously denies Platonic influence in Genesis 1 and 2. He begins by disputing Philo's Platonic reading of Genesis. He goes on to argue: "the only indications in Gen 1 of possible Greek philosophical influence seems (sic) to be the phrase ἀόρατος καὶ ἀκατασκεύαστος. The mistake made by scholars in the past is that they concentrated too much on this single phrase, searching for possible parallels without taking the rest of the chapter and the book for that matter into account" (182-83). This is far too sweeping as the detailed argument of Rösel shows. It remains a question however whether we are talking about direct or indirect influence and about translators' intentions or hearers' perceptions. In relation to the translation of Genesis Cook does, however, acknowledge: "By the time this rendering took place there would have been Jews who had become hellenised; however, whether this happened to the extent that was the case with Philo Judaeus remains an open question" (182).

restoring an original unity, perhaps in the sense that in marriage the heavenly archetype of humankind embodying male and female was truly reflected.[70] The joining of male and female need not have been seen as restoring brokenness, especially since the separation was a divine initiative, but rather as reaching for and reflecting the ideal (as the human seeks oneness with God). Inevitably the LXX narrative would be heard as portraying the original or ideal humankind as male which embodied female within it, especially since Adam and the generic ἄνθρωπος ("man/human being") of 2:7 was clearly male.[71] It would not have been far from that to conclude that Gen 1:27 implied the ideal or heavenly archetype is an androgynous male, but that was far from a necessary conclusion.[72] This is still a long way from Plato's notion that the creation of woman was the result of failure and that sexual union is relief from the distress.[73]

---

[70] On the notion of man and woman becoming see Plato's *Symposium* 189C-193D. "I propose to fuse and weld you into a single piece, so that from being two you may become one" (*Symp.* 192E). See also *Diod. Sic.* 4, 6; *Ovid Met.* 4.285ff; Pliny *Natural History* 7, 2. 3.

[71] See Helen Schüngel-Straumann, "On the creation of man and woman in Genesis 1-3: the history and reception of the texts reconsidered," in *A Feminist Companion to Genesis* ed. A. Brenner (Sheffield: Sheffield Academic Pr., 1993) 53-76, who argues that there developed a reading of Gen 1 in both Hebrew and Greek of man as a male and so εἰκών ("image") referred to male, exemplified by Paul (61), enhanced further by the fact that the new Adam, Christ, is male (63).

[72] For the rabbinic interpretation which links Gen 1:27 and 5:2 to marriage see Berger, *Gesetzesauslegung*, 527.

[73] "The men of the first generation who lived cowardly or immoral lives were, it is reasonable to suppose, reborn in the second generation as women; and it was therefore at that point in time that the gods produced sexual love, constructing in us and in women a living creature itself instinct with life" (Plato *Timaeus* 90E - 91A). See the discussion in Watson, *Agape, Eros, Gender*, 63, who writes: "As in Genesis, man is formed first and then woman. But in Genesis, woman is formed in order to remedy the not-goodness of man's solitary state; in the *Timaeus*, she incarnates the not-goodness of his moral choices, so that - as in the Pandora myth - her being is his punishment" (63). "The erotic union of man and woman engulfs them in the disorder of passion, and, like woman's very existence, is an unfortunate side-effect of the original male's lapse from virtue and philosophy" (64). By contrast male-male relations reflect a higher order (65-67). See also E. Cantarella, *Bisexuality in the Ancient World* (New Haven, London: Yale University Press, 1992) 58-62. Runia, *Philo of Alexandria*, 283-87; 345-46. Watson argues that Paul's claim that woman is "the glory of man" reflects a much more positive, even though still androcentric, appreciation of eros derived from Genesis. "She is created from and for man, but her secondariness is not that of the inferior whose being represents the decline from original perfection towards the maternal abyss, but that of the counterpart whose being contradicts and overcomes the imperfection of an original being that is not-good in its abstract solitude"

Inevitably there would be attempts to explain some link between the human beings of Genesis 2 and creation in Genesis 1. Thus the distance of image and its reflection invites itself to be transcended by positing a link between the soul or mind of the Genesis 2 being and the heavenly image.[74] Nothing in the translation requires such a conclusion.

While there is sufficient in the translation to indicate the translator's philosophical framework as at least influenced by Platonism and to evoke Platonic connections among hearers, the translation is still substantially controlled by the original. It is the one God who is at work in both creation narratives. It is still easy to hear Genesis 1 as creation of the material world and to see Genesis 2 as further elaboration. The translator adds ἤρξατο in 2:3, so that God rested now from all he had begun to do - and so was soon to do more! The translation in 2:4, instead of reporting with the Hebrew that were no plants, suggests they had just not yet appeared because it had not yet rained. Adding ἔτι in 2:9 and 2:19 relieves the tension between Genesis 1 and Genesis 2 by assuming the former describes creation and the latter, emergence. This does not, however, relieve the tension between 1:26-27 and 2:7, but this did not require the assumption that two separate acts of creation are being narrated, as some Platonic models assume.

5:1-3 LXX sheds light on how 1:26-28 LXX might have been understood. It assumes 1:26-27 was describing the creation of the male, Adam. And Adam was made after the εἰκών of God and, in turn, reproduced others according to his ἰδέα and εἰκών

(5:3). While the choice of language reflects Platonic terminology, the fact that 5:1-3 speaks of the creation of Adam in 5:1 and goes on to speak of Adam begetting Cain and Abel suggests that the translator made no distinction between the creation in Genesis 1 and the formation in Genesis 2. Both referred to the one man. This would fit more easily into a Platonic model of interpretation which saw 1:1-5 or 1:1-2 as the creation of the images and the rest as either a summary of creation with Genesis 2 recapitulating and providing an explanation of how it happened or of the rest of Genesis 1 as the creation of *genera* followed by creation of species, such as we find in Philo.

(68; similarly 58-61). This probably sits more easily with the Hebrew text, but remains substantially so also in the LXX except, as we have seen for the inferiority it assumes.

[74] Rösel, *Übersetzung*, points to the interpretative translation πᾶσαν ψυχὴν ζῴων ἑρπετῶν ("every life/soul of living reptile") in 1:21 as opening the possibility that creation in Gen should be seen as referring to the soul as separate from the body (46-48).

Special features

Aside from the particular issue of the extent of Platonic influence on the text or able to be brought to the text by a hearer, we can note the following significant features in the translation which are of potential relevance for understanding the impact of the text on understandings of sexuality.

The use of Adam as a name without the descriptive element preserved in the Hebrew pun, הָאָדָם (*adam*; "earthling") on הָאֲדָמָה (*adamah*; "ground/earth"), results in a (or a stronger?) focus on ἄνθρωπος ("man/human") primarily as male. This is but one of the word plays which could not be reproduced in the Greek. It produced an awkward transition in 2:16, but more significantly a reinforcing of maleness in human origins. A hearer familiar with what follows would most naturally interpret Genesis 1:26-27 as a reference to the creation of Adam, the male, and as foreshadowing how from this male the female emerged. Genesis 5:1-3 confirms that the translator would have been aware of the generic use of אָדָם (*adam*) in 1:26-27. Gen 2:5-25 would be understood as explaining how the man was formed and how the female emerged from him.

While this may also be a way of hearing the Hebrew, Gen 2:18-25 in the LXX contains more allusive echoes of 1:26-27 than does its Hebrew counterpart. These include the different translation of the identical Hebrew, עֵזֶר כְּנֶגְדּוֹ ("a helper as his partner") in 2:18 and 20 by the two expressions, βοηθὸν κατ᾽ αὐτόν ("a helper according to him/like him") and βοηθὸς ὅμοιος αὐτῷ ("a helper like him/in his likeness") the latter echoing the use of the double κατὰ-phrase in 1:26, especially καθ᾽ ὁμοίωσιν ("accord to our likeness"); in 2:18 the use of the plural verb, ποιήσωμεν ("let us make") matching 1:26, instead of the Hebrew singular אֶעֱשֶׂה ("I shall make"); and the use of ἄνθρωπος ("man/human") as the translation of אִישׁ ("man/male/husband") in 2:24 under the influence of 1:27, instead of ἀνήρ ("man/male/husband"). The effect of the closer links with 1:26-27 is to set up a parallel between the male being made in the image of God in 1:26-27 and the formation of woman in 2:18-25, so that what results is a chain of being in which as the man is in the image of God, so the woman is in the image of the man and her role as helper is now read as the role of a subordinate, including her role as "helper", a term otherwise not suggesting subordination.

There are also associated implications, some of which arise in part from the inability of the LXX to reproduce the word play, אִישׁ אִשָּׁה (*ish-ishshah*; man-woman). In 2:24 it leads to the emphasis falling not on commonality of being, celebrated in the pun, but in unity of two into one, reinforced perhaps by the addition οἱ δύο ("the two"), or at least by its presence now in the text, whatever its origin, which invites a parallel with the oneness to be sought by the man with God. The links developed between 2:20-25 and 1:26-28 invite speculation that in some way what is described in 2:24 also fulfils 1:27, restoring an original and desired state (of marriage? sexual union? maleness? androgyny?). Some of these possibilities will appear in texts discussed below.

At the same time the use of σάρξ ("flesh") in 2:23-24 to translate בָּשָׂר ("flesh/kin") which emphasises kinship and its establishment through sexual intercourse, brings the focus more strongly on sexual union itself. The use of the passive form, προσκολληθήσεται ("shall be joined") in 2:24 also allows for hearing the text as explaining something which God effects, ie. as a true passive.

The pattern of subordination implied in the chain of being opens the possibility for confusion in relation to the curse of the woman, which in the LXX is constructed in the context of a similar chain of relationships, reflecting origins. Using the word, ἡ ἀποστροφή ("the return") in the curse of the woman, καὶ πρὸς τὸν ἄνδρα σου ἡ ἀποστροφή σου ("your return shall be to your husband"; 3:16) has the effect of forming a link with the use of τοῦ ἀποστρέψαι ("to return") in the curse of the man: ἕως τοῦ ἀποστρέψαι σε εἰς τὴν γῆν ἐξ ἧς ἐλήμφθη ("until you return to the earth from which you were taken"; 3:19). The result is a reverse sequence in which the curse of the woman is to return to the man and the curse of the man is to return to the earth. In both cases the text speaks of painful subservience, the man toiling at the land and returning to it, the woman returning to her husband again and again and bearing children in pain. The LXX thus reinforces this parallel and underlines it by the more explicit inclusio created between 2:7 and 3:19 by the use of γῆ ("earth"; cf. 3:19 where Hebrew has עָפָר; "dust").

As a consequence of these developments through the translation there is a potential ambiguity in the text in relation to sexual intercourse or the desire for it on the part of the woman: is it part of the curse or part of the creative purpose? Has it now become the woman's lust whereas before it was the man's acceptable desire which unites two to one? This allows for the possibility that in 3:13 the woman's sin is also explained by her seduction by the serpent, in other words, her failure to control her sexuality and in 3:9 her susceptibility to sensual attraction.

The overall effect of the narrative in 2:5-25 is to portray the real outcome of God's creation of human kind, male and female, in Gen 1:27. That outcome according to the LXX is a twofoldness, of differentiated male and female, with the female the likeness of the male as the male is in the likeness of God, a chain of being, and a unity in flesh of the two without shame. Within this framework of thought the role for the woman is defined as helper of the ἄνθρωπος, "the man/human", who is "her husband". The additional allusions in the LXX bring 2:18-25 into relation with Genesis 1:26-28 more strongly than the Hebrew, so that it would have been natural to hear the text as implying that union, including marriage, is the context in which this helping takes place. There is no explicit reference to marriage, though it is doubtless to be assumed in the background. Nor is a connection made between sexual union and reproduction, but this may be assumed, especially given the links the LXX builds with 1:26-28 and the interpretation of the curse in 3:16. Unlike in the *Timaeus* woman is not a sign of failure. There remains however a cloud of ambiguity around her sexuality which will open the text to diverse readings and pose major questions for male self understanding. At best the unities can be affirmed: with God and between man and woman, including sexual union. Its dark side is a cursed subservience in which sexuality is ambiguously implicated. The confusion of shame with guilt, purity with morality, can turn the Eden story into something which involves sexuality.

2. Influence of the LXX version of the Creation Stories in Philo in relation to sexuality

Philo's use of Genesis 1-3 is extensive. The discussion will remain focused on those parts which pertain to his understanding of sexuality. As in his treatment of the decalogue and the prominence given to adultery in the LXX, so we find features peculiar to the LXX translation reflected in Philo's expositions. These include, for instance the use of ποιήσωμεν ("let us make") in 2:18 (*Opif.* 75), ἀνεπλήρωσεν ("filled up") in 2:21 (*Leg.* 2.20), νῦν ("now") in 2:23 (*Leg.* 2.41), γυνή ("woman") in 2:23 (*Q.G.* 1.28) and προσκολληθήσεται ("shall be joined" in 2:24 (*Leg.* 2.49).

He notes the sudden shift to "Adam" in 2:16, where he also demonstrates knowledge of its etymology:

> We must raise the question what Adam He commands and who this is; for the writer has not mentioned him before, but has named him now for the first time. Perchance, then, he means to give us the name of the man that was moulded. "Call him earth" he says, for that is the meaning of "Adam," so that when you hear the word "Adam," you must make up your mind that it is the earthly and perishable mind; for the mind that was made after the image is not earthly but heavenly. *Leg.* 1.90

More significant and indicative is Philo's focus on the use of εἰκών ("image") and related Platonic terms, which enable him to read the Genesis 1-3 LXX within the framework of popular Platonism.[75] According to Philo on day one God created the incorporeal world through the Word, who is the εἰκών ("image") of God (*Opif.* 29-35).

---

[75] On the influence of the *Timaeus* on Philo see the major treatment of Runia, *Philo of Alexandria*.

The incorporeal world, then, was now finished and firmly settled in the Divine Reason, and the world patent to sense was ripe for birth after the pattern of the incorporeal. *Opif.* 36; see also 62, 76.

This has created problems for interpreters, particularly in relation to the interpretation of Gen 1:26-27 and Gen 2:7. Days two to six represent the creation of the *genera* not of the incorporeal ideas.[76] Philo has, therefore, three levels: the incorporeal (1:1-5; 2:4-5), the *genera* created after their pattern (1:6-31; 2:6) and the species (Gen 2:7-25).[77]

In *Creation* Philo explains that the climax is the creation of the ἄνθρωπος ("man/human being") in 1:26. He is in the image of God, not with respect to his body, but in respect of his *nous*. Thus in *Creation* he can write:

No, it is in respect of the Mind, the sovereign element of the soul, that the word, "image" (εἰκών) is used; for after the pattern of a single Mind, even the Mind of the Universe as an archetype, the mind of each of those who successively came into being was moulded. It is in a fashion a god to him who carries and enshrines it as an object of reverence; for the human mind evidently occupies a position in men precisely answering to that which the great Ruler occupies in the world (69).

Philo appears to exclude other aspects of the *genus* from that quality. Later, in interpreting Gen 2:7, he makes a similar point interpreting the divine breathing as the gift of the rational soul.[78] The formed man is thus the temple of the soul (*Opif.*

---

[76] On this see Baer, *Male and Female*, 26-27; similarly Brown, *Structure*, 31,35,56 n.107. Generally on Philo's understanding of the creation of man and woman in a Platonic frame see A. van den Hoek, "Endowed with Reason or Glued to the Senses: Philo's Thought on Adam and Eve," in *The Creation of Man and Woman: Interpretations of the Biblical Narratives in Jewish and Christian Traditions* ed. G. P. Luttikhuizen (Themes in Biblical Narrative: Jewish and Christian Traditions I; Leiden: Brill, 2000) 63-75, esp. 65-69. See the discussions in T. H. Tobin, *The Creation of Man: Philo and the History of Interpretation* (CBQMS 14; Washington: CBA, 1983), who argues that some of the inconsistencies in Philo reflect traditions he has used; but see the critique in Runia, *Philo of Alexandria*, 556-57.

[77] So Baer, *Male and Female* , "Thus Philo takes Gen. 2:4-5 to refer to the creation of the incorporeal ideas (*Op. Mund.* 129-30), Gen. 2:6 to the creation of the visible *genera* but not including man (*Op. Mund.* 131-33), and Gen. 2:7 to the creation of man (*Op. Mund.* 134ff)" (29).

[78] So Baer, *Male and Female*, who points out that also 2:7 serves similarly to indicate the divine spirit in *Q.G.* 1.50 and *Her.* 56-57. So Philo finds the mind in both 1:27 and 2:7 (24-25). "Philo generally uses both Gen. 1:27 and 2:7 to establish the essential kinship

137). When Philo speaks of the heavenly man, referring to 1:26 (-27), he is speaking substantially of that aspect of the human *genus* which is the image of God. The *genus* is formed into a species in Gen 2:7 where now the material aspect has been realised and so may be described as the earthly man.[79] That earthly man still has a soul, just as the man of 1:26-27 still has deficiencies, not yet realised. Thus Philo speculates that the plural, "Let us make" (ποιήσωμεν) of 1:26 reflects that God had co-workers and that these will have been responsible for the deficiencies in humankind (72-75).[80] There are potential flaws from the beginning.

These distinctions appear also to hold in Philo's allegories which are notoriously difficult to systematise. Thus in *Leg.* 1.31 in interpreting Gen 2:7 he writes:

> There are two types of men; the one a heavenly man, the other an earthly. The heavenly man, being made after the image of God (κατ' εἰκόνα θεοῦ), is altogether without part or lot in corruptible and terrestrial substance; but the earthly one was compacted out of the matter scattered here and there, which Moses calls "clay".
> (similarly *Q.G.* 1.4)

With reference to Gen 2:15 he writes:

> It would seem then that this is a different man, the one that was made after his image and archetype, so that two men are introduced into the garden, the one a moulded being, the other "after the image" (τὸν μὲν πεπλασμένον, τὸν δὲ κατ' εἰκόνα). The one then that was made according to the original has his sphere not only in the planting of virtues but is also their tiller and guardian, and that means that he is mindful of all that he heard and practised in his

---

between the rational soul of man and God. With respect to Gen. 1:27 he argues on the basis of the assertion that man was created κατ' εἰκόνα θεοῦ ("according the image of God"). In Gen 2:7 he refers to the divine inbreathing of πνεῦμα (or πνοὴ) ζωῆς ("spirit" or "[breath] of life"). In a number of passage he quotes both texts together as his authority" (25-26).

[79] Of the heavenly and earthly man, Baer, *Male and Female*, writes that "because man is a composite (συνθήτον, σύνκριμα) however, consisting of both a heavenly and an earthly part, in the case of man God first forms the *genus* of each part of man, which only 'afterwards' together form the first empirical man, the species Adam. Neither of these 'men', the earthly or the heavenly (i.e. the man created after the image of God), is to be thought of as an actually existing man but only as a generic component part of the first empirical man" (28). "Philo interprets Gen. 2:4-7 not as recording a new creation but rather as a summary recapitulation of what has already been described in Gen. 1:1 - 2:3" (29).

[80] On this see Runia, *Philo of Alexandria*, 242-49.

training; but the "moulded" man neither tills the virtues nor guards them, but is only introduced to the truths by the rich bounty of God, presently to be an exile from virtue. *Leg.* 1.53-54.

A little later, again on Gen 2:15, he writes:

"The man whom God made" (ὃν ἐποίησεν ὁ θεὸς ἄνθρωπον)[81] differs, as I have said before from the one that was "moulded" (πλασθέντος); for the one that was moulded is the more earthly mind, the one that was made the less material, having no part in perishable matter, endowed with a constitution of a purer and clearer kind (88).

For there are two races of men, the one made after the (Divine) Image (τό δὲ κατὰ τὴν εἰκόνα) and the one moulded out of the earth (τό πεπλασμένον). For the man made after the Image it is not good to be alone, because he yearns after the Image. For the image of God is a pattern of which copies are made, and every copy longs for that of which it is a copy, and its station is by its side. Far less good is it for the man moulded of the earth to be alone. *Leg.* 2.4.

Elsewhere he explains:

And when Moses called the genus "man", (ἄνθρωπον) quite admirably did he distinguish its species, adding that it had been created "male and female", and this though the individual members had not yet taken shape. *Opif.* 76.

For Philo male and female are as appropriate as odd and even numbers (part of his argument for the appropriateness of the number six used in identifying the order in creation in *Opif.* 13). It is interesting that Philo includes male and female within the *genus* not as indicating an original androgyny or bisexuality, but as reflecting the two different kinds yet to be realised. Thus he writes:

Before the species He completes the genera (πρὸ γὰρ τῶ εἰδῶν ἀποτελεῖ τὰ γένη). He does so in the case of man. Having first fashioned man as a genus (γένος) in which the prophet says that there is the male and the female genus (γένος). He afterwards makes Adam, the finished form or species (εἶδος). *Leg.* 2.13.

---

[81] Philo reads ἐποίησεν ("made") not ἔπλασεν ("formed") in Gen 2:15.

Similarly in *Creation* he writes:

> And when Moses called the genus (γένος) "man", quite admirably did he distinguish its species (εἶδος), adding that it had been created "male and female," and this though its individual members had not yet taken shape. (76).

Also:

> Both man and woman, being sections of Nature, become equal in one harmony of genus, which is called man. *Q.G.* 1.25.

The *genus* (γένος), as we have seen, is the work of God and his co-workers, indicating the potential for deficiency. The male and female is not in itself indicated to be a deficiency in 1:27 by Philo and, as we have seen, belong together, as in the number 6, as something appropriate and desirable. In the materialisation of the *genus* the deficiencies emerge. Identifying two kinds of human being, heavenly and earthly, inevitably implies some fault in the earthly. The earthly, unlike the heavenly, is not instinctively virtuous:

> Now it is to this being, and not to the being created after His image and after the original idea (οὐχί τῷ κατ᾽ εἰκόνα καὶ κατὰ τὴν ἰδέαν) that God gives the command. For the latter, even without urging, possesses virtue instinctively; but the former, independently of instruction, could have no part in wisdom. *Leg.* 1.92.

> Quite naturally, then, does God give the commandments and exhortations before us to the earthly man, who is neither bad nor good but midway between these. *Leg.* 1.95.

There is the additional problem of male and female. The chain of being implicit in the LXX account of creation of woman appears in various forms in Philo.[82] Sometimes he appears almost to ignore that male and female also belonged to the archetypal, as in the following:

> By this he shows very clearly that there is a vast difference between the man thus formed (τοῦ πλασθέντος ἀνθρώπου) and the man that came into existence earlier after the image of God (κατὰ τὴν εἰκόνα τοῦ θεοῦ): for the man so formed is an object of sense-perception, partaking already of such

---

[82] See also Sly, *Philo's Perception of Women*, 105, on the role the chain of being in Philo which sees women as lower than men.

or such quality, consisting of body and soul, man or woman, by nature mortal; while he that was after the (Divine) image was an idea or type or seal, an object of thought (only), incorporeal, neither male nor female, by nature incorruptible. (ὁ δὲ κατὰ τὴν εἰκόνα ἰδέα τις ἢ γένος ἢ σφραγίς, νοητός, ἀσώματος, οὔτ' ἄρρεν οὔτε θῆλυ, ἄφθαρτος φύσει). *Opif.* 134.[83]

The *genus* had to be male and female, because the species would be male and female, but the male and female is realised only in the species. That does not, therefore, assume androgyny or bisexuality, because we are dealing with a *genus*.[84] That aspect of the *genus* which is after the image of God, which may be called the

---

[83] On this see Runia, *Philo of Alexandria*, 336-38; Baer, *Male and Female*, 29; van den Hoek, "Endowed with Reason," 68-69; Berger, *Gesetzesauslegung*, 523.

[84] So Baer, *Male and Female*, who writes of this passage that it "is probably to be identified with the rational soul of man, the nous, and is not androgynous - even in the sense of a pre-differentiated combination of male and female - but rather asexual" (65) and should not be identified with *Leg.* 2:13. He refers to the dissertation of Basil A. Stegmann, *Christ, The "Man from Heaven": A Study of I Cor. 15:45-47 in the Light of the Anthropology of Philo Judaeus* (Washington, 1927) 19-49, who disputed the usual interpretation of Gen 2:7 and 1:27 in Philo. Baer notes that Philo also uses male and female to describe the rational soul as male and the irrational soul as female. Male in that context is asexual, but female "points to the sexual realm, the sphere of male female polarity" (65). For detailed discussion see 19-26. See also Sly, *Philo's Perception of Women*, 98-103. "Thus, in his summary recapitulation of the story of creation, Philo interprets Gen. 2:7, in conjunction with Gen. 1:27, to refer to the creation of the generic component parts of man and their combination in the individual, sense-perceptible, composite man, i.e. the first empirical man, the species Adam. In his usual fashion he interprets both the creation of man after the image of God and the inbreathing of the divine spirit to refer to the essential similarity between man's rational soul and the divine Logos (cf. especially *Op. Mund.* 139,144,146)." So Baer, *Male and Female*, 31. He argues that even in *Leg.* 2:13 we should not read the *genus* as equivalent to the Platonic idea, which was created on Day One. So the neither male nor female of *Opif.* 134 refers to the *genus*, not as bisexual, but as embodying the potential. "The generic earthly man is said to contain within himself the male and the female sexes in so far as he is potentially either male or female" (34). He does argue that while androgynous ideas are not present here, nevertheless they appear behind *Opif.* 151-52 (echoing Plato *Symposium* 189C-193D), otherwise scorned in *Contemp.* 63 (38). See also van den Hoek, "Endowed with Reason," 70-71. See also Runia, *Philo of Alexandria*, 337-38, who points out that in contrast to elsewhere where he tends to merge the rational part in Gen 2:7 and the creation in 1:27 Philo differentiates between them in *Opif.* 134-35: "The reason for this, we must surmise, is the recognition that, when man's god-like part is stationed in the body, it is so distracted by its corporeal entanglements that it becomes a shadow of its true self" (337).

heavenly man,[85] does not include the physical aspects which would materialise in the formed bodies. It is therefore in that sense not male and female.

This is not to say that the male and female or the body is in itself evil. It was God's creation or formation, even though with co-workers. Thus there are passages in which the male-female relationship, including sexuality is idealised by Philo. On Gen 2:21-22 he writes:

> The harmonious coming together of man and woman and their consummation is figuratively a house. And everything which is without a woman is imperfect and homeless. For to man are entrusted the public affairs of state; while to a woman the affairs of the home are proper. The lack of her is ruin, but her being near at hand constitutes household management. *Q.G.* 1.26.

She is clearly a "helper", even though she is of inferior being, as Philo explains in the earlier part of *Q.G.* 1.26, where he argues from the days of uncleanness after childbirth (40 and 80 - cf. also *Jub.* 3:9-11) that the male is worth double the female. On Gen 2:21, he points out that woman was not formed from earth, and so cannot be equal in honour with the man, and should not in marriage be equal in age. Of God's purpose he writes that a man should care for his wife as a daughter and she, treat him as a father and "that man should take care of woman as a very necessary part of him; but woman, in return, should serve him as a whole." (*Q.G.* 1.27). The hierarchy of male over female implicit in the LXX finds its echo in Philo. It also reflected prevailing values of his time.

Within this framework of subordination Philo can sometimes speak very positively of women. Giving birth is a primary function: Philo salvages something from the failure of the LXX to reproduce the אִשָּׁה אִישׁ (*ish-ishshah*; man-woman) pun of 2:23 by interpreting the LXX's γυνή ("woman") as deriving from γεννάω, ("to give birth"): "And the woman is called the power of giving birth." (*Q.G.* 1:28). Reflecting the emphases of the LXX version of 2:24 on oneness and union of flesh he writes:

> But when Scripture says that the two are one flesh, it indicates something very tangible and sense-perceptive, in which there is suffering and sensual pleasure, that they may rejoice in and be pained by, and feel the same things, and, much more, may think the same things. *Q.G.* 1.29.

---

[85] According to Baer, *Male and Female*, 1:27 is taken in Philo as describing the *nous* of created man, which was created after the image of God; 1:26 is taken to mean the composite; 1:27a to mean the rational; and 1:27b to mean the composite as potentially male and female (28-29).

Sexual desire has its place, as Philo explains, but its role is reproduction:

> And certainly the first approaches of the male to the female have pleasure
> (ἡδονήν) to guide and conduct them, and it is through pleasure that begetting
> and the coming of life is brought about (*Opif.* 161).

In allegorical allusion to the word, "helper" βοηθός, Philo explains:

> For the sense and the passions are helpers of the soul and come after the soul.
> ἡ γὰρ αἴσθησις καὶ τὰ πάθη τῆς ψυχης εἰσι βοηθοὶ νεώτεροι τῆς
> ψυχῆς. *Leg.* 2.5.

> Moreover, there are, as I have said, helpers of another kind, namely the
> passions (τὰ πάθη). For pleasure and desire contribute to the permanence of
> our kind (ἡδονὴ βοηθεῖ πρὸς διαμονὴν τοῦ γένους ἡμῶν καὶ
> ἐπιθυμία): pain and fear are like bites or stings warning the soul to treat
> nothing carelessly: anger is a weapon of defence, which has conferred great
> boons on many: so with the other passions. *Leg.* 2.8.

The function of sexual passion in bringing about the union of man and woman
is procreation. Thus Philo can affirm femaleness and affirm sexual relations - all in
their proper place.

Philo explains, however, that passions are dangerous like wild beasts (*Leg.*
2.11-13). Philo sees the creation of woman as a disastrous turn of events in this
regard because of the potential it created. It was an act for which God is not
directly responsible. Thus he cites the plural ποιήσωμεν ("let us make") of the
LXX of Gen 2:18 (Hebrew has the singular, but the plural in 1:26 to which Gen
2:18 LXX alludes) in order to explain that: "others from the humbler of His
subordinates are held responsible for thoughts and deeds of a contrary sort" (*Opif.*
75; see also *Fug.* 68-70).[86] Through creation from the man "Woman becomes for
him the beginning of a blameworthy life" (*Opif.* 151) because of her negative
potential. He continues:

> But when woman too had been made, beholding a figure like his own and a
> kindred form, he was gladdened by the sight, and approached and greeted her.
> She, seeing no living thing more like herself than he, is filled with glee and
> shamefastly returns the greeting. Love (ἔρως) supervenes, brings together and
> fits into one the divided halves, as it were, of a single living creature, and sets

---

[86] See already C. H. Dodd, *The Bible and the Greeks* (London: Hodder and Stoughton,
1935) 155, who points to the background of this thought in the *Timaeus*.

up in each of them a desire (πόθον) for fellowship with the other with a view to the production of their like. And this desire (πόθος) begat likewise bodily pleasure (τὴν τῶν σωμάτων ἡδονὴν), that pleasure which is the beginning of wrongs and violation of law, the pleasure for the sake of which men bring on themselves the life of mortality and wretchedness in lieu of that of immortality and bliss. *Opif.* 151-52.

We see here a positive evaluation of sexual attraction, especially for the purposes of reproduction, but otherwise a negative assessment. Passion not for procreation is spurned, even when it is present in marriage. He speaks of "the passionate desire for women shewn by those who in their craze for sexual intercourse behave unchastely, not only with the wives of others, but with their own" (*Leg.* 3.9). Philo has not waited for an act of disobedience which will issue in a curse which will make the woman uncontrollable and needing to be ruled; he already faults her formation. This is in tension with his positive affirmations of woman and sexual relations. The woman fails because she is "prompted by a mind devoid of steadfastness and firm foundations", and so consented to the serpent (*Opif.* 156).[87] The LXX invited such a reading.

He explains:

Pleasure (ἡδονὴ) does not venture to bring her wiles and deceptions to bear on the man, but on the woman, and by her means on him. This is a telling and well-made point: for in us mind corresponds to man, the senses (αἴσθησις) to woman. *Opif.* 165.

In his allegorical treatment of 2:24 and the connecting of mind with the passions, Philo writes quite negatively:

For the sake of sense-perception (ἕνεκα τῆς αἰσθήσεως) the Mind (ὁ νοῦς), when it has become her slave, abandons both God the Father of the universe, and God's excellence and wisdom, the Mother of all things, and cleaves to and becomes one with sense-perception (καί προσκολλᾶται καὶ ἑνοῦται

---

[87] See also Sly, *Philo's Perception of Women*, 106-108: "According to Philo the whole problem presented by sexual desire does not affect man until woman is created. then she gives rise to it, unwittingly, and simply by virtue of being woman. Philo sees sexual control as a man's responsibility. Woman's lust .. is a feature of her womanhood, which not she, but the men in her life, her father and her husband, must control by controlling her" (108). Philo links Adam's sin with sexual desire (109). So *Opif.* 152. See also van den Hoek, "Endowed with Reason," 73-74, on the way what begins as positive attraction becomes symbolic of perilous passion.

τῇ αἰσθήσει) so that the two become one flesh and one experience (ἵνα γένωνται μία σὰρξ καὶ ἓν πάθος οἱ δύο). Observe that it is not the woman that cleaves to the man, but conversely the man to the woman, Mind to Sense-perception. *Leg.* 2.49-50; similarly *Gig.* 65.

He prefers the love of his passions to the love of God. *Leg.* 2.51.

Here Philo uses προσκολλάω ("join to, become stuck to") very negatively. The man who joins himself to the woman, or at least allegorically, the mind joined to the senses is stuck. The allegorical use will not be without significance for the literal coming together, which, apart from its advantage for reproduction, Philo views so negatively. Gen 2:24 becomes bad news. He then goes on to speak of Levi who makes a different choice, citing Deut 33:9.

This man forsakes father and mother, his mind and material body, for the sake of having as his portion the one God, "or the Lord Himself is his portion": (Deut x.9). Passion (τὸ πάθος) becomes the portion of the lover of passion, but the portion of Levi the lover of God is God. *Leg.* 2.52.

Elsewhere Philo will speak of the need to leave the female behind.[88] It is interesting that in his exposition of Gen 3:13 in *Leg.* 59-67 (see also *Q.G.* 1.46) that Philo appears not to take up ἠπάτησεν ("deceived/seduced") of Gen 3:13 in a sexual sense, preferring to expound more broadly in relation to the passions (including sexual seduction and gluttony). In other words he does not appear to read Gen 3:13 in terms of sexual seduction.

Much of what Philo has written in relation to Genesis 1-3 stems from influences which lie beyond the LXX or which flow from aspects which the LXX and Hebrew texts share. The latter must be taken into account in speaking of the influence of the LXX.

If we focus on the influence of what is distinctive in the LXX, we can identify a number of points where Philo expounds words or ideas which are distinctive to the LXX. Some give rise to particular arguments, such as ποιήσωμεν ("let us make") in 2:18, and γυνή ("woman") in 2:23. More important is the use of Adam

---

[88] On use of woman to represent the irrational see Baer, *Male and Female*, 40-44. Thus the religious life means becoming male (45-49), becoming one by negating the irrational (49-51), becoming a virgin (51-53); divine impregnation of the soul by Sophia and Arete (as male, though they are pictured as passive/female before God) (62). See also van den Hoek, "Endowed with Reason," who writes: "The answer to the question whether there is any hope for Eve in Philo is clear: basically there is none. Her only hope is to change, either to become a man, or to become a virgin, no matter how much offspring she may have had" (74).

only as a name, the emphasis on fleshly union and oneness (2:24) and generally the chain of being reflected in 2:20-25, including its understanding of helper and its subordination of woman. Of great importance is the presence of Platonic language like εἰκών ("image") which encouraged a reading of the creation accounts within a Platonic frame of reference. Philo has effectively made woman a curse not so much on the basis of the judgement which followed the sin in Eden, namely, 3:16, but on the basis of her creation or co-creation in 2:21-25 and ultimately 1:26. This, as we have seen, was a possibility created by the links and potential confusion in the LXX between the curse and creation of woman, and in particular of sexual desire. By shifting the blame to faulty co-workers in God's creation factory, Philo necessarily portrays human beings, but especially women, as flawed by nature, particularly because of their sexuality. The LXX both lent itself to such conclusions and to some extent enabled them.

The influence of the Septuagint version of the creation stories on the New Testament in relation to sexuality will be considered at the end of Part Three after the consideration of Deut 24:1-4 because of those instances where both the Genesis and Deuteronomy texts appear in the same context.

CHAPTER THREE

Divorce

Deuteronomy 24:1-4

The third passage to be considered is Deut 24:1-4, which contains reference to divorce. The Hebrew and Greek with English translations are set out in Appendix C.

1. Distinctive features of the LXX version of the passage relating to divorce (Deut 24:1-4)

The complex protasis of the Hebrew of Deut 24:1-3 is retained in the LXX with minor variations. In both Hebrew and LXX Deut 24:1-4 constitutes a single conditional sentence with 24:4 as the apodosis.[1] In both, what might especially interest us is therefore incidental. The main point is the prohibition of remarriage to the former husband. Important incidental details are: the grounds for divorce, the bill of divorce and the fact that the woman has been defiled.

Is there a distinctiveness in the LXX text which might possibly lead to distinctive influence? It is possible to read καὶ ἔσται in a jussive sense: "and it shall be" in the sense of "this is what should apply", and to read καὶ ("and") in καὶ γράψει ("and he shall write") as redundant or as "also".[2] Then writing the

---

[1] On this see Wevers, *Notes on the Greek Text of Deuteronomy*, 377 and Berger, *Gesetzesauslegung*, 513.

[2] Berger, *Gesetzesauslegung*, notes the awkwardness created by translating *waw* as καί, arguing that the effect of the LXX construction is to turn καὶ γράψει αὐτῇ βιβλίον ἀποστασίου καὶ δώσει εἰς τὰς χεῖρας αὐτῆς καὶ ἐξαποστελεῖ αὐτὴν ἐκ τῆς οἰκίας αὐτοῦ ("and so he writes her a certificate of divorce, puts it in her hand, and sends

certificate of divorce becomes an instruction or command, rather than an incidental.[3] Such a construction would be difficult, because one would expect an indication of a new protasis in 24:2. The same however applies equally to the Hebrew, where וְהָיָה might be understood in a jussive sense ("and let it be").[4] One would not, however, have had to read the detail about issuing a certificate of divorce as part of an apodosis in order to reach the conclusion that it was something commanded.[5]

Distinctive elements in the LXX which were potentially of consequence are: the translation of עֶרְוַת דָּבָר (lit. "shame of a matter"; "a shameful matter") by ἄσχημον πρᾶγμα ("shameful matter"); and of סֵפֶר כְּרִיתֻת ("certificate of divorce/lit. cutting off") by βιβλίον ἀποστασίου ("document of separation/ divorce"). In Deut 23:15 עֶרְוַת דָּבָר (lit. "shame of a matter") is translated by ἀσχημοσύνη πράγματος (lit. "shamefulness of a matter"). There the context is the requirement that people go outside the camp to relieve themselves of their faeces, dig a hole and then cover it before returning. God must not see. The LXX turns this into a passive: οὐκ ὀφθήσεται ἐν σοὶ ἀσχημοσύνη πράγματος ("a shameful thing shall not be seen among you"). Nakedness and human excretion are to be hidden, covered up, in the presence of the holy. In Deut 24:1-4 the דָּבָר עֶרְוַת ("shameful matter") is being used to describe not something that is to be hidden or covered before God, but something which is intolerable to the husband. The structure of thought, however, is not dissimilar. The עֶרְוַת דָּבָר ("shameful matter") is something which must be put outside the camp, as it were, of the man's house or household. The translation ἄσχημον πρᾶγμα ("shameful matter") preserves the Hebrew sense, but uses the Greek adjectival rather than the genitive construct form.

---

her out of his house") into an instruction which can stand on its own and be understood as a commandment about divorce procedure (513). This will have understood וְהָיָה ("and it happens that") as jussive ("and let it be that").

[3] So, for instance, Josephus, *A.J.* 4.253.

[4] So Berger, *Gesetzesauslegung*: "Freilich kann man auch aus dem hebräischen Text ein eigenständiges Gebot herauslesen, wenn man diesen Satz isoliert sieht" (514). (Tr. One can of course read a separate commandment also from the Hebrew text, if one looks at the sentence in isolation). For a reading of the Hebrew text in this way where 24:1b is a first apodosis see Andrew Warren, "Did Moses permit divorce? Modal *weqatal* as key to New Testament readings of Deuteronomy 24:1-4," *TynBul* 49 (1998) 39-56; see also David I. Brewer, "Deuteronomy 24:1-4 and the Origin of the Jewish Divorce Certificate," *JJS* 49 (1998) 230-43, here 230-31.

[5] Brewer, "Deuteronomy 24:1-4," 235 n. 25 notes that כתב may be read as "he may write ..." or "he must write ...", citing Mishnaic interpretation for the latter (*m. Sot.* 4.1-5) and Matt 19:7-8 for the former.

The question arises whether עֶרְוַת דָּבָר ("shameful matter") refers to a pollution in a general sense (not just in relation to the husband) and also whether it would be understood as remaining a pollution (at least, in relation to him). If the עֶרְוַת דָּבָר ("shameful matter") here were referring to a permanent pollution in the woman, then the woman would be permanently banned. This is not the case. The סֵפֶר כְּרִיתֻת ("certificate of divorce") frees the woman to marry another. There is a pollution, therefore, in relation to the first husband - the cause of the divorce. 24:4 also speaks of pollution: She has been defiled: אַחֲרֵי אֲשֶׁר הֻטַּמָּאָה μετὰ τὸ μιανθῆναι αὐτήν. ("after she has been defiled"). This is also related in some way to the first husband. Is it the same pollution or is it something in addition to the first pollution?

If it were the latter it would be referring to the fact that she has in the interim married another. The remarriage to the first husband would therefore not be an "abomination" תּוֹעֵבָה and a sin against the land וְלֹא תַחֲטִיא אֶת־הָאָרֶץ ("and you shall not bring guilt on the land"; or more neatly in the LXX καὶ οὐ μιανεῖτε τὴν γῆν; "you shall not defile the land"; echoing μετὰ τὸ μιανθῆναι αὐτήν; "after she has been defiled") because of the first pollution, but because she married another man and thereafter the first marriage was reconstituted. In this case no explanation would be given why the bill of divorce from the second husband should not make her free to marry not only another man, but also her first husband again. The assumption would be that sexual intercourse with another established a barrier to sexual intercourse with the original husband.[6] This appears to be so in cases of illegitimate sexual intercourse intended or otherwise (i.e. cohabitation is not to be resumed), but our passage does not assume anything illegitimate about the second marriage. It does not assume, for instance, that the second marriage is the result of an adulterous relationship, even though Philo appears to read it this way, as we shall see below.

More probably the Hebrew אַחֲרֵי אֲשֶׁר הֻטַּמָּאָה ("after she has been defiled") is referring to the woman being made to declare herself unclean by the first husband. [7] It would then be referring to the same delict as עֶרְוַת דָּבָר / ἄσχημον

---

[6] So Wevers, *Notes on the Greek Text of Deuteronomy*, 379: "The point is that as far as the first husband is concerned, his former wife is now defiled by remarriage. Such a marriage is by definition a βδέλυγμα before the Lord." C. Carmichael, *The Laws of Deuteronomy* (Ithaca: Cornell Univ. Pr., 1974) 203-207, suggests that people found the idea of taking back a wife repulsive, citing the example of Abraham and Abimelech. Brewer, "Deuteronomy 24:1-4," 232, rejects this example, following Hugenberger, *Marriage as a Covenant*. Brewer cites David's willingness to receive back Michal (2 Sam 3:14; cf. 1 Sam 18:27; 25:44).

[7] So John H. Walton, "The Place of the *hutqattel* within the D-stem Group and its Implications in Deuteronomy 24:4," *HS* 32 (1991) 7-17; see also Brewer, "Deuteronomy 24:1-4," 233.

πρᾶγμα ("shameful matter"), which was something shameful in relation to the first husband and remained so. The abomination consists in the fact that the husband would be going back on what he then instituted, probably with a divine oath. For he would have profited at the initial divorce by retaining the dowry and now would be seeking double profit by remarrying her after she had received back her dowry from the second marriage which ended in divorce through aversion[8] in which she was an innocent party or ended in the death of the second husband. This was scandalous profiteering. It would have been an abomination especially because it would have entailed going back on a divine oath,[9] effectively taking the Lord's name in vain.

What was the delict, described as עֶרְוַת דָּבָר / ἄσχημον πρᾶγμα ("shameful matter")? If it meant sexual intercourse with another man, the reason would be clear and reflect a widespread belief that adultery requires divorce and so necessarily makes return to the marriage an offence. The problem with such an interpretation is that Deuteronomy states the penalty for adultery as death (Deut. 22:22-27).[10] The עֶרְוַת דָּבָר / ἄσχημον πρᾶγμα ("shameful matter") would therefore have to be something other than adultery. Alternatively, with Otto, one could argue "that Deut. 22.22a,23-27 only deals with the special case of adultery proved by detection in flagranti delecto, whereas other cases of adultery, which are not proven in court, are a matter of divorce". In relation to עֶרְוַת דָּבָר ("shameful matter") in Deut 24:1 he continues, "then there is no reason to exclude adultery from the semantic spectrum".[11] The borderline case is being cited, he

---

[8] This negative interpretation of "hate" is argued by R. Westbrook, "Prohibition of Restoration of Marriage in Deuteronomy 24:1-4," in *Studies in Bible 1986: Scripta Hierosolymitana* 31 ed. S. Japhet (Jerusalem: Magnes, 1986) 387-405. See also Hugenberger, *Marriage as a Covenant*, who argues that the position taken in Mal 2:16 coheres with Deuteronomy 24 in condemning divorce on the basis of aversion (83). He translates: "if one hates and divorces [that is, if one divorces merely on the ground of aversion], says Yahweh, God of Israel, he covers his garment with violence [i.e. such a man visibly defiles himself with violence], says Yahweh of hosts. Therefore take heed to yourselves and do not be faithless [against your wife]" (76).

[9] So Brewer, "Deuteronomy 24:1-4," 231-34, who bases his understanding on the interpretation of Westbrook, "Prohibition of Restoration of Marriage," 387-405, but expanding it by emphasising the abomination of the abrogated oath (234-35). See also Hugenberger, *Marriage as a Covenant*, 79-81, who argues for a rejection of divorce on the basis of aversion in Mal 2:16 (83).

[10] Brewer, "Deuteronomy 24:1-4," 235.

[11] E. Otto, "False weights in the Scales of Biblical Justice? Different Views of Women from Patriarchal Hierarchy to religious Equality in the Book of Deuteronomy" in *Gender and Law in the Hebrew Bible and the Ancient Near East* ed. Victor H. Matthews, Bernhard M. Levison and Tikva Frymer-Kensky, (JSOTSup 262; Sheffield: Sheffield Academic Pr., 1998) 128-47, here 138.

argues, to show that the first husband must stay by his declaration of pollution. "The man's title to his wife was restricted not in order to preserve the patriarchal family, but to limit male titles of disposal and to give women the dignity of being legal subjects of their own, independent of titles and the decisions of men."[12] The problem with this interpretation would be if אַחֲרֵי אֲשֶׁר הֻטַּמָּאָה μετὰ τὸ μιανθῆναι αὐτήν ("after she has been defiled") refers to something other than and subsequent to עֶרְוַת דָּבָר / ἄσχημον πρᾶγμα ("shameful matter"), but that, as we have noted may not be so. It may alternatively have referred to infertility or a matter of ritual impurity.[13]

The matter is far from clear[14] and gave rise, in part, to the famous controversy between the houses of Hillel and Shammai (*m. Git* 9:10; *b. Git* 90a). It is no more clear in the LXX. In Susanna 63 ἄσχημον πρᾶγμα clearly refers to adultery, probably reflecting the author's reading of our passage.[15] The LXX has dealt with the unusual expression תַחֲטִיא אֶת־הָאָרֶץ ("sin against/bring guilt upon") in ולֹא ("and you shall not bring guilt on the land") by translating μιανεῖτε ("you shall not defile") and so also turning it to the plural (also used in the Samaritan Pentateuch) and using the same verb which earlier in the verse translated הֻטַּמָּאָה ("she has been defiled"), referring to the woman's defilement. If anything this keeps the focus on ritual defilement and so perhaps less on what might have been the original concern: dishonest greed and abrogation of an oath. Aside from this it is difficult to speak of the LXX as distinctive in substance or emphasis. The only other element of note is the choice of βιβλίον ἀποστασίου ("document of separation/divorce") to translate סֵפֶר כְּרִיתֻת ("certificate of divorce"), i.e. use of a word which emphasises abandonment and dismissal whereas the Hebrew belongs

---

[12] Otto, "False Weights," 138.

[13] So P. C. Craigie, *The Book of Deuteronomy* (Grand Rapids: Eerdmans, 1976) 304-305.

[14] See the extended discussion of alternatives in Brewer, "Deuteronomy 24:1-4," 231-34, where he argues that the focus of the passage is on a man who seeks financial gain by divorcing his wife, retaining her dowry, then remarrying her after a subsequent divorce where she as an innocent party and so had retained her dowry, thus bringing a twofold gain to the man. The use of sacred oaths also played a role, thus accounting for the strong term, abomination for what the man did.

[15] ἄσχημον refers to illicit sexual intercourse also in Gen 34:7. ἀσχημοσύνη regularly refers to physical nakedness (like עֶרְוַת) particularly with reference to sexual parts. As such it is a constant feature of the incest prohibitions in Leviticus 18 and 20. It can also refer to human faeces as in Deut 23:14-15, but can be much broader referring to shame through loss of face, humiliation (ἀσχημονήσει Deut 25:3).

to the idea of cutting off or cutting away.[16] It will probably reflect actual terminology in use at the time of translation.[17]

2. The Influence of LXX version of the passage concerning Divorce in Philo

Within the context of expounding laws concerning marriage, Philo alludes to Deut 24:1-4 in *Leg.* 3.30-31. In his loose paraphrase he states:

> If a woman after parting from her husband for any cause whatever (καθ'ἣν ἃ τύχῃ προφάσιν) marries another and then again becomes a widow (χηρεύσῃ), whether this second husband is alive or dead, she must not return to her first husband but ally herself with any other rather than him, because she has broken with the rules that bound her in the past and cast them into oblivion when she chose new love-ties in preference to the old (θεσμοὺς παραβᾶσα τοὺς ἀρχαίους, ὧν ἐξελάθετο φίλτρα καινὰ πρὸ τῶν παλαιῶν ἑλομένη) (30).

It is interesting that Philo speaks of the woman's initiative in parting from her husband, making no mention of divorce by the husband. In fact, he assumes she has broken rules and gone after another man, ie. committed adultery. One could find an allusion to ἄσχημον πρᾶγμα ("something shameful") in the phrase "for any cause whatever", as if Philo had interpreted it as meaning: "whatever excuse *she* had for doing so".[18] It is more likely however that he assumes ἄσχημον πρᾶγμα ("something shameful") means adultery. Philo also suppresses the divorce from the second husband by using the verb, χηρεύσῃ ("becomes a widow"), ie. she is no longer bound to a husband, because he is dead or she has left him. Philo is happy for her to marry yet another, but not to marry the first husband. He says nothing of defilement of the woman or the land. Instead his argument seems to be that she must not return because she has violated the rules which bound her to him. Other unspoken assumptions lie behind these comments.

---

[16] On the origins of the *get* and its wording see Brewer, "Deuteronomy 24:1-4," 235-43.

[17] So C. Dogniez and Marguerite Harl, *La Bible D'Alexandrie: Le Deutéronome* (Paris: Cerf, 1992) 265; J. B. Bauer, "ἀποστάσιον," *EWNT*, 1.339-40.

[18] Josephus, *A.J.* 4.253, speaks of a man divorcing his wife "for whatsoever cause" (καθ' ἀσδηποτοῦν αἰτίας), probably reflecting the liberal approach espoused by Hillel according to *m. Git.* 9:10 and probably his own: cf. *Vita* 426 (his wife's behaviour did not please him); cf. Matt 19:3.

Does the translation ἄσχημον πρᾶγμα ("something shameful") make it easier for Philo to ignore the pollution issues, in favour of the moral issues? At most we could say that they allow Philo to disregard the issues of pollution altogether and the divorce which they justify, in favour of simply assuming the woman is adulterous. This would explain why he can pass over the matter of divorcing, which is assumed, because his focus is on the adultery which lay behind it and which on his reading prevents the return. As we have seen the language of pollution is, if anything, slightly stronger in the LXX version, but it is not Philo's emphasis.

It is interesting that Philo goes on to condemn the husband who would be willing to take back such a woman:

> And if a man is willing to contract himself with such a woman, he must be saddled with a character for degeneracy and loss of manhood. He has eliminated from his soul the hatred of evil, that emotion by which our life is so well served and the affairs of houses and cities are conducted as they should be, and has lightly taken upon him the stamp of two heinous crimes, adultery and pandering. For such subsequent reconciliations are proofs of both. the proper punishment for him is death and for the woman also. *Leg.* 3.31.

In doing so he would make himself guilty of adultery and of procuring an immoral relationship. Apparently Philo sees such a man as effectively condoning rather than condemning his wife's adultery and therefore declares his taking her back as the equivalent of procuring a prostitute. The man would also be undermining his manhood and abandoning hatred which according to Philo should play its role in household and state management. Both he and the woman should die. So, in effect, Philo understands both as worthy of the punishment for adultery.

Philo might have said all of this also with the Hebrew text before him. Perhaps the words ἄσχημον πρᾶγμα ("something shameful") have contributed to the shift of focus away from pollution to morality, but such influence would be incidental compared with other values which are playing a role here, including Roman law, which in the Lex Julia declares "that a husband who does not at once dismiss his wife whom he has taken in adultery can be prosecuted as a panderer".[19] In the broadest sense such prohibition is informed by purity assumptions which were present in many cultures of the time in relation to adultery and had been for

---

[19] The *Lex Iulia de adulteriis* cited from Paulus, *Opiniones* 2.26, in M. R. Lefkowitz and M. B. Fant *Women's life in Greece and Rome* (London: Duckworth, 1982) 182. A similar stricture on remaining married to a wife who has committed adultery was also an aspect of Greek law (see the citation from Apollodorus in the same collection, pp. 50-57).

centuries, so that the *Lex Julia* might be seen as giving expression to a value already playing a role in Deut 24. It probably also indicates that Philo would have read Deut 24:1-4 in this context and not as one concerned with marriage, divorce and remarriage for greed and through abrogation of sacred oaths.

CHAPTER FOUR

Creation and Divorce

The Impact of the LXX Creation Stories and
Deuteronomy 24:1-4 LXX in the New Testament

1.   The Gospels

Mark 10:2-9

Three of the texts we have considered appear in Mark's anecdote about Jesus and divorce: Deut 24:1-4; Gen 1:27 and Gen 2:24. The latter two are quoted directly. The passageas are set out side by side in the Appendix D.

While in the earliest form of the anecdote Jesus' response may have been only the typically bipartite punchline: "What God has yoked, let no human being separate" (9:9),[1] Jesus' reply now contains a counter question alluding to Deut 24 and a biblical argument supplied by linking Gen 1:27 and 2:24.

There is a textual difficulty in Mark 10:7 because some manuscripts, including ℵ B and Ψ omit the words, καὶ προσκολληθήσεται πρὸς τὴν γυναῖκα αὐτοῦ ("and be joined to his wife").[2]

---

[1] See William Loader, *Jesus' Attitude towards the Law: A study of the Gospels* (WUNT 2.97; Tübingen: Mohr Siebeck, 1997; Grand Rapids: Eerdmans, 2002) 89-90 n. 165, 130-131.

[2] On determining the original Gundry, *Mark*, wisely notes: *non liquet* 531. See also B. M. Metzger, *A Textual Commentary on the Greek New Testament* (2d ed.; Stuttgart: Deutsche Bibelgesellschaft; New York: United Bible Societies, 1994) 88-89. A scribe's eye may have slipped over one καί. Alternatively the text has been supplemented to bring it into line with the Matthean parallel and the text of Gen 2:24. I shall argue below that internal considerations favour its retention.

It is not possible in the context of this paper to consider the full range of exegetical issues which the passage raises. Our question is what, if any, influence the LXX passages might have had on the anecdote in its present form. Berger argues that Mark 10:3-8 is possible only on the basis of the LXX text.[3] He points to the treatment of divorce as an instruction, to οἱ δύο ("the two"), which links Gen 2:24 to 1:27, and to the use of ἄνθρωπος ("man").

Clearly the allusion to Deut 24:1-4 and the quotations from Genesis assume a text identical to what we know as the LXX. βιβλίον ἀποστασίου ("certificate of divorce" Mark 10:4) is the term which the LXX uses. The single line from Gen 1:27 matches the LXX exactly. The same is true of the quotation from Gen 2:24.[4] Thus it includes the addition οἱ δύο ("the two") over against the Hebrew text and has the tell-tale LXX use of ἄνθρωπος ("man"). If Mark 10:7 did not originally have the words, καὶ προσκολληθήσεται πρὸς τὴν γυναῖκα αὐτοῦ ("and be joined to his wife"), then the use of ἄνθρωπος ("man/human being") would have made it possible to read the quotation as referring not only to a man but also to a woman.[5] It would also emphasise even more strongly the becoming one flesh, which without the "joining" would carry the full weight in describing the union, perhaps even more strongly emphasising the sexual aspect.

More significant is the question of LXX influence on the argument and on the assumptions of the anecdote. If one saw only the LXX as allowing Deut 24:1-4 to be read as 2 statements, as does Berger, with the first focused on the command to divorce by issuing a certificate of divorce, this could be seen as a sign of LXX influence, since 10:3 and 5 speak of a command to write a bill of divorce and to dismiss. But such a reading is also possible for the Hebrew text, as we have noted above.[6]

The use of οἱ δύο ("the two") may be indicative of LXX influence, as Berger suggests, and have influenced the conclusion, ὥστε οὐκέτι εἰσὶν δύο ἀλλὰ μία σάρξ ("so they are no longer two, but one flesh"), but it may well have been present in other versions and variants at the time.[7] It probably assumes a monogynous attitude towards marriage, but this can scarcely be seen as deriving

---

[3] Berger, *Gesetzesauslegung*, 575, see also 512-518. Against this T. Holtz, "'Ich aber sage euch': Bemerkingen zum Verhältnis Jesu zur Tora," in *Jesus und das jüdische Gesetz* ed. I. Broer (Stuttgart: Kohlhammer, 1992) 135-45, here 140.

[4] In agreement with the text as constructed in the LXX Göttingen edition Mark does not have the αὐτοῦ after μητέρα (although manuscript evidence is divided).

[5] So Berger, *Gesetzesauslegung*, 549, who argues for the shorter reading.

[6] See the discussion in Berger, *Gesetzesauslegung*, 513-14, who goes on to acknowledge that the Hebrew might also be understood in this way.

[7] Berger, *Gesetzesauslegung*, 528. Against this: D. R. Catchpole, "The Synoptic Divorce Material as a tradition historical problem," *BJRL* 57 (1974) 92-127, who argues that the point is still there without those words (116-17).

from LXX influence alone or at all, since the same tendency is evident in CD 4.20 - 5.2 and in 11QT 57.17-19. In the present context the issue of monogyny is present only incidentally if at all.

The presence of οἱ δύο ("the two") is but one aspect of the distinctive emphasis of the LXX and may not, in fact, be distinctive. More certain is the significance of ἄνθρωπος ("man"). As we have noted above, the LXX was unable to produce the pun אִשָּׁה אִישׁ (*ish-ishshah*; man-woman) with the result that the focus of the statement falls less on the commonality which binds man and woman and more on the creation (or recreation) of the single entity. The use of ἄνθρωπος ("man") in LXX instead of ἀνήρ ("male/man/husband") and the presence of οἱ δύο ("the two") will have made the link with Gen 1:27 easier and so enhanced the sense that the coming together in some way inaugurates a restored unity which corresponds to an original unity. It remains speculative whether there is some influence from the myth of the androgyny here.[8] There is in any case an argument that they belong together because they originate from one. As in the LXX the focus is unity of two rather than their commonality which Hebrew achieves through its pun. Certainly the focus lies on the coming together as fulfilling God's purpose in creation. The use in the LXX of σάρξ ("flesh") also throws the emphasis strongly on the aspect of sexual union, rather than on kinship of flesh.[9]

The passive form, προσκολληθήσεται ("join/be joined"), will have opened the possibility that the word be understood not as a deponent but as a true passive. People hearing it in this way would identify God as the agent who has brought about the joining, thus relating the text more closely to what was probably Jesus' original response: ὃ οὖν ὁ θεὸς συνέζευξεν ἄνθρωπος μὴ χωριζέτω ("Therefore what God has joined together, let no one [man] separate"). One might even speculate that the passive form invited the connection and so at least contributed to the expansion of the anecdote with the reference to Gen 2:24. The link between Gen 1:27 and 2:24 may have also contributed to this understanding, for it speaks of the action of God in creating male and female.[10] Then Gen 2:24 could be heard as indicating that the oneness restores what was God's intention in creation and therefore is not to be undone, that is, uncreated. As the LXX established stronger links between Gen 2:20-25 and Gen 1:26-28, so those using these texts associate the two closely. This reading of Gen 2:24 goes beyond the Hebrew of Gen 2:24 and probably what was intended by the LXX translator,

---

[8] For the view that the passage stands under the influence of the androgyny myth see K. Niederwimmer, *Askese und Mysterium: Über Ehe, Ehescheidung und Eheverzicht in den Anfängen des christlichen Glaubens* (FRLANT 113; Göttingen: Vandenhoeck und Ruprecht, 1975) 45-49; earlier Daube, *The New Testament and Rabbinic Judaism*, 81.

[9] So Berger, *Gesetzesauslegung*, 551.

[10] So Berger, *Gesetzesauslegung*, 548.

namely, a description of the way things are, that the man and the woman become one (doubtless in accord with God's will), to assert that the coming together is a yoking effected by God.[11] The role which the passive form προσκολληθήσεται ("be joined") appears to have played in the argument would support a textual decision that it was part of the original and later omitted.

One can in this sense speak of influence from the LXX on the anecdote, although, assuming the aphorism to be independent and to reflect a saying of Jesus, the notion of a divine initiative in the yoking will have already existed. A similar assumption of divine intention linked at least to Gen 1:27 may have been one line of interpretation of marriage in discussions of the day. It is reflected in CD 4, but also in the fact that the Pharisees even raise the question of divorce (and then respond in a way which is already conceding ground by saying "permit").

The passage is striking in its assumption that the coming together described in Gen 2:24 is something in which God is involved. Within the process of coming together προσκολληθήσεται ("be joined") is often taken as a reference to sexual intercourse. Here this will be included but the primary emphasis is on God's action, so that the whole process of coming together indicated by both προσκολληθήσεται ("be joined") and καὶ ἔσονται οἱ δύο εἰς σάρκα μίαν ("and the two shall become one flesh") is describing something which God does, to which Jesus refers in his statement: ὃ οὖν ὁ θεὸς συνέζευξεν ἄνθρωπος μὴ χωριζέτω ("Therefore what God has joined together, let no one [man] separate"). At the same time the fact that it is God's action does not remove the reality that this is union between two persons, including sexual union. That should not surprise us since the allusion is to God's creation and creativity. It does add a theological dimension to the widely held assumption in the world of the time that sexual intercourse really does create something which is much larger than the act itself or something of sheer physicality (which, as we shall see, Paul also assumes occurs even when it is contrary to divine will; 1 Cor 6:12-20). The use of the LXX helps reinforce this by the more directly sexual connotations of its language and indirectly by the passive προσκολληθήσεται ("be joined").

---

[11] J. A. Fitzmyer, "The Matthean Divorce Texts and some new Palestinian evidence," in *To Advance the Gospel: New Testament Studies* (2d ed., Grand Rapids: Eerdmans, 1988), mentions the parallel with Tob 6:18 LXX(BA) "she was destined for you from eternity" (85).

Matthew 19:3-9

3 Καὶ προσῆλθον αὐτῷ Φαρισαῖοι πειράζοντες αὐτὸν καὶ λέγοντες· εἰ ἔξεστιν ἀνθρώπῳ ἀπολῦσαι τὴν γυναῖκα αὐτοῦ κατὰ πᾶσαν αἰτίαν; 4 ὁ δὲ ἀποκριθεὶς εἶπεν· οὐκ ἀνέγνωτε ὅτι ὁ κτίσας ἀπ' ἀρχῆς *ἄρσεν καὶ θῆλυ ἐποίησεν αὐτούς; 5 καὶ εἶπεν· ἕνεκα τούτου καταλείψει ἄνθρωπος τὸν πατέρα καὶ τὴν μητέρα καὶ κολληθήσεται τῇ γυναικὶ αὐτοῦ, καὶ ἔσονται οἱ δύο εἰς σάρκα μίαν.* 6 ὥστε οὐκέτι εἰσὶν δύο ἀλλὰ σὰρξ μία. ὃ οὖν ὁ θεὸς συνέζευξεν ἄνθρωπος μὴ χωριζέτω. 7 λέγουσιν αὐτῷ· τί οὖν Μωϋσῆς ἐνετείλατο δοῦναι *βιβλίον ἀποστασίου* καὶ ἀπολῦσαι [αὐτήν]; 8 λέγει αὐτοῖς ὅτι Μωϋσῆς πρὸς τὴν σκληροκαρδίαν ὑμῶν ἐπέτρεψεν ὑμῖν ἀπολῦσαι τὰς γυναῖκας ὑμῶν, ἀπ' ἀρχῆς δὲ οὐ γέγονεν οὕτως. 9 λέγω δὲ ὑμῖν ὅτι ὃς ἂν ἀπολύσῃ τὴν γυναῖκα αὐτοῦ μὴ ἐπὶ πορνείᾳ καὶ γαμήσῃ ἄλλην μοιχᾶται.	3 Some Pharisees came to him, and to test him they asked, "Is it lawful for a man to divorce his wife for any cause?" 4 He answered, "Have you not read that the one who made them at the beginning 'made them male and female,' 5 and said, 'For this reason a man shall leave his father and mother and be joined to his wife, and the two shall become one flesh'? 6 So they are no longer two, but one flesh. Therefore what God has joined together, let no one separate." 7 They said to him, "Why then did Moses command us to give a certificate of dismissal and to divorce her?" 8 He said to them, "It was because you were so hard-hearted that Moses allowed you to divorce your wives, but from the beginning it was not so. 9 And I say to you, whoever divorces his wife, except for unchastity, and marries another commits adultery."

When we turn to Matthew, we find same Genesis texts, but now used as part of Jesus' initial response. Matthew has ἕνεκα ("for this reason") in place of ἕνεκεν ("for this reason"), has no possessive pronoun after πατέρα ("father") and the dative τῇ γυναικὶ ("to his wife") with κολληθήσεται ("be joined to") in place of πρὸς τὴν γυναῖκα ("to his wife") with προσκολληθήσεται ("be joined to"; some manuscripts have the latter by assimilation). It is only after a counter question referring to Deuteronomy 24 that Jesus brings the comment about hardness of heart. Yet Matthew had this passage in mind already in the opening question which the Pharisees bring. They ask not about the legitimacy of divorce but of its legitimacy κατὰ πᾶσαν αἰτίαν ("for any cause"). Jesus will go on to state that divorce is not permissible μὴ ἐπὶ πορνείᾳ ("except for unchastity"). Both κατὰ πᾶσαν αἰτίαν ("for any cause") and μὴ ἐπὶ πορνείᾳ ("except for unchastity") allude to the ground for divorce described in Deuteronomy 24 LXX as ἄσχημον πρᾶγμα ("something shameful"). The same issue of a ground for divorce lies behind the version of the divorce saying found earlier in Matt 5:31-32.

(31) Ἐρρέθη δέ· ὃς ἂν ἀπολύσῃ τὴν γυναῖκα αὐτοῦ, δότω αὐτῇ ἀποστάσιον. (32) ἐγὼ δὲ λέγω ὑμῖν ὅτι πᾶς ὁ ἀπολύων τὴν γυναῖκα αὐτοῦ παρεκτὸς λόγου πορνείας ποιεῖ αὐτὴν μοιχευθῆναι, καὶ ὃς ἐὰν ἀπολελυμένην γαμήσῃ, μοιχᾶται.

(31) It was also said, 'Whoever divorces his wife, let him give her a certificate of divorce.' (32) But I say to you that anyone who divorces his wife, except on the ground of unchastity, causes her to commit adultery; and whoever marries a divorced woman commits adultery.

What lies before us in both 5:32 and 19:9 are two differently formulated interpretations of the ground named in Deuteronomy. The meaning of πορνεία is much debated. For our study the following observations are pertinent. Matthew does not cite the words ἄσχημον πρᾶγμα ("something shameful"). The variant wording, especially λόγου πορνείας ("except on the ground of unchastity") appear to indicate a formulation in Greek independent of the LXX. This may also be the case in 5:31, where the summary of Deut 24:1-4 does not show the peculiarities of the LXX. ἀποστάσιον ("divorce") was a widely used technical term, as already noted above. Most probably Matthew is in touch with Hebrew or Aramaic discussions of the issue. Nothing indicates that his treatment of the exception clause stands under the influence of the LXX. These other traditions will have influenced his particular redaction of Mark's divorce anecdote.

In 5:31-32 Matthew is loosely citing Deut 24:1-4, assuming, as did others at the time, that the passage may be taken as implying that the provision to divorce and to give a bill of divorce was a commandment. As we have already noted, there is nothing peculiar to the LXX in such an interpretation.

The divorce anecdote is interesting in that it brings three key texts together. Deut 24:1-4 plays no further role in the New Testament beyond these texts. This is not the case for the Genesis texts. What was said above in relation to Mark also applies here. The passage assumes divine involvement in the joining to become one flesh represented in Gen 2:24 and is more easily able to do so on the basis of the LXX. Such divine involvement makes divorce problematic, as Mark's account makes clear, but the Matthean version contains a tension in this regard not present in Mark.

The two main ways in which exegetes have sought to explain the tension is by the assumption that (some Gentile) marriages were null and void because they were incestuous according to Leviticus and so could never be seen as divine joining.[12] The other is to contemplate that action can take place which subverts what God has done, namely sexual immorality, in particular: adultery.[13] The assumption on the basis of our passage and Matt 5:31-32 is that in the case of πορνεία, "illicit sexual relations", divorce is valid. If the reference were to incestuous marriage, then the marriage would be invalid in any case and should cease to be. The man should send the woman from his house, "divorce" her in that sense. Then no bill of divorce would be required because the marriage was never valid in the first place. Given the allusion to Deut 24:1-4 here and in 5:31, this is unlikely to be the focus.

The possibility that what God has created can be destroyed is already contemplated in Jesus' saying: ὃ οὖν ὁ Θεὸς συνέζευξεν ἄνθρωπος μὴ χωριζέτω ("Therefore what God has joined together, let no one [man] separate"), an exhortation which would not otherwise make sense. Its assumption is that

---

[12] H. Baltensweiler, *Die Ehe im Neuen Testament* (ATANT 52; Zurich: Zwingli, 1967) 87-107; J. P. Meier, *Law and History in Matthew's Gospel: A Redactional Study of Mt 5:17-48* (AnBib 71; Rome: PBIPr., 1976) 147-50; F. J. Moloney, "Matthew 19:3-12 and Celibacy," in *"A Hard Saying": The Gospel and Culture* (Collegeville: Liturgical, 2001) 35-52; in an earlier form: *JSNT* 2 (1979) 42-60, esp. 44-45; Fitzmyer, "Matthean Divorce Texts," 88-89; B. Witherington, "Matthew 5.32 and 19.9 – Exception or Exceptional Situation," *NTS* 31 (1985), 571–76; *Women in the Ministry of Jesus* (Cambridge: CUP, 1984) 145 n. 111.

[13] P. Sigal, *The Halakah of Jesus of Nazareth according to the Gospel of Matthew*, (Lanham: Univ. of America Pr., 1986) 96-97; U. Luz, *Das Evangelium nach Matthäus (Mt 1–7)* (EKKNT I/1; Zurich: Benziger Verlag; Neukirchen–Vluyn: Neukirchener Verlag, 1985) 274; R. B. Hays, *The Moral Vision of the New Testament: A contemporary introduction to New Testament Ethics* (Edinburgh: T&T Clark, 1996) 354-55; W. D. Davies and D. C. Allison, *A Critical and Exegetical Commentary on the Gospel according to Saint Matthew*: Vol III, XIX-XXVIII (ICC; Edinburgh: T&T Clark, 1997) 16; C. L. Blomberg, "Marriage, Divorce, Remarriage, and Celibacy: An Exegesis of Matthew 19:3–12," *TrinJourn* 11 (1990) 161-96, here 177-78. See also the proposal that it might refer to premarital relations: So A. Isaksson, *Marriage and Ministry in the New Temple: A Study with Special References to Mt 19:13-22 and 1 Cor 11:3-16* (ASNU XXIV; Lund 1965) 116-52, argues that it means pre-marital sex and is relating what applied in Lev 21:7 to priests to Christians. Similarly L. W. Countryman, *Dirt, greed, and sex: Sexual ethics in the New Testament and their implications for today* (Philadelphia: Fortress Press, 1988) 175. But, as Blomberg, "Marriage, Divorce, Remarriage, and Celibacy," 176, observes, it is not evident that Leviticus 21 is applied to Christians; it is mostly ceremonial and the effect would be to be more concerned with pre-marital sex than adultery. Similarly W. D. Davies and D. C. Allison, *A Critical and Exegetical Commentary on the Gospel according to Saint Matthew*: Vol I.: I–VII (ICC; Edinburgh: T&T Clark, 1988) 529, who claim that such an interpretation "would make sex before marriage worse than adultery (because only the former would be grounds for divorce)". For further critical discussion see also Luz, *Matthäus (Mt 1–7)*, 274.

something can occur which is of sufficient impact to undo what was created in the coming together of man and wife. As sexual intercourse was an essential element in creating a psychosomatic union, so sexual intercourse can destroy that unity. Just as there is an assumption that a union is created in this way, so there is an assumption that such a unity is broken in this way - not on grounds of hurt or anger as doubtless would be present and would be prominent in modern discussions, but because it was widely believed that something was created and uncreated by sexual intercourse which had an ontic quality. Adultery does not just create a potential crisis; it creates something new and destroys the old. There can be no turning back, no return to the original marriage.

2.   Paul

1 Corinthians 6:12-20

12 Πάντα μοι ἔξεστιν ἀλλ᾽ οὐ πάντα συμφέρει· πάντα μοι ἔξεστιν ἀλλ᾽ οὐκ ἐγὼ ἐξουσιασθήσομαι ὑπό τινος. 13 τὰ βρώματα τῇ κοιλίᾳ καὶ ἡ κοιλία τοῖς βρώμασιν, ὁ δὲ θεὸς καὶ ταύτην καὶ ταῦτα καταργήσει. τὸ δὲ σῶμα οὐ τῇ πορνείᾳ ἀλλὰ τῷ κυρίῳ, καὶ ὁ κύριος τῷ σώματι· 14 ὁ δὲ θεὸς καὶ τὸν κύριον ἤγειρεν καὶ ἡμᾶς ἐξεγερεῖ διὰ τῆς δυνάμεως αὐτοῦ. 15 οὐκ οἴδατε ὅτι τὰ σώματα ὑμῶν μέλη Χριστοῦ ἐστιν; ἄρας οὖν τὰ μέλη τοῦ Χριστοῦ ποιήσω πόρνης μέλη; μὴ γένοιτο. 16 [ἢ] οὐκ οἴδατε ὅτι ὁ *κολλώμενος* τῇ *πόρνῃ ἓν σῶμά ἐστιν; ἔσονται γάρ, φησίν, οἱ δύο εἰς σάρκα μίαν. 17 ὁ δὲ κολλώμενος τῷ κυρίῳ ἓν πνεῦμά ἐστιν.* 18 Φεύγετε τὴν πορνείαν. πᾶν ἁμάρτημα ὃ ἐὰν ποιήσῃ ἄνθρωπος ἐκτὸς τοῦ σώματός ἐστιν· ὁ δὲ πορνεύων εἰς τὸ ἴδιον σῶμα ἁμαρτάνει. 19 ἢ οὐκ οἴδατε ὅτι τὸ σῶμα ὑμῶν ναὸς τοῦ ἐν ὑμῖν ἁγίου πνεύματός ἐστιν οὗ ἔχετε ἀπὸ θεοῦ, καὶ οὐκ ἐστὲ ἑαυτῶν; 20 ἠγοράσθητε γὰρ τιμῆς· δοξάσατε δὴ τὸν θεὸν ἐν τῷ σώματι ὑμῶν.	12 "All things are lawful for me," but not all things are beneficial. "All things are lawful for me," but I will not be dominated by anything. 13 "Food is meant for the stomach and the stomach for food," and God will destroy both one and the other. The body is meant not for fornication but for the Lord, and the Lord for the body. 14 And God raised the Lord and will also raise us by his power. 15 Do you not know that your bodies are members of Christ? Should I therefore take the members of Christ and make them members of a prostitute? Never! 16 Do you not know that whoever *joins himself to* a prostitute becomes one body with her? For it is said, *"The two shall be one flesh."* 17 But anyone *joining himself* to the Lord becomes one spirit with him. 18 Shun fornication! Every sin that a person commits is outside the body; but the fornicator sins against the body itself. 19 Or do you not know that your body is a temple of the Holy Spirit within you, which you have from God, and that you are not your own? 20 For you were bought with a price; therefore glorify God in your body.

The statement, ἔσονται γάρ, φησίν, οἱ δύο εἰς σάρκα μίαν ("For it is said, *"The two shall be one flesh"*), includes a quotation from Gen 2:24 cited exactly according to the LXX, including the possibly distinctive οἱ δύο ("the two").The use of κολλώμενος (*"joins himself to"*) also alludes to Gen 2:24, but differs from the LXX: προσκολληθήσεται πρὸς ("will join himself to, be joined to") in the use of the simple verb and the dative construction (as in Matthew's citation in 19:5). It also clearly understands the participle as a deponent, certainly not a divine passive! Given the uncertainty about οἱ δύο it is difficult to identify a distinctively LXX influence in its use here, but is probably to be seen in the emphasis on sexual union. While this is implied in both the Hebrew and LXX of Gen 2:24, the use of σάρξ ("flesh") in the LXX, as we have seen, emphasises sexual union more strongly, whereas the focus of the Hebrew is more on kinship.

Paul's concern with sexual themes begins already in 1 Cor 5:1, where he cites a case of immorality. It continues in 5:9 where Paul urges the congregation to distance itself from people who practise immorality, which includes as its first item: sexual immorality. While the issue of taking fellow believers to the public courts (6:1-8) does not indicate the nature of the cases, it could well be that, given the context, they relate to sexual matters.[14] The reference to saints judging angels (6:3), may well have in mind the sexual immorality of the fallen angels. If we, the saints, can judge sexual cases among angels then we should be able to deal with them here and now. This increases in likelihood when we find that the verses which follow declare who may or may not enter the kingdom and begin with sexual immorality. It is then striking that in contrast to the defilement of sin represented in people who perpetrate such sins, 6:11 speaks of the believers in terms of being washed, sanctified and justified in the name of the Lord Jesus Christ and in the Spirit of God. This statement both reflects baptismal imagery and brings together two key motifs central to early understandings of baptism: baptism in the name of Christ and the receiving the Holy Spirit. Thus Paul draws attention to the moment of entry into this relationship. This is important because 6:12-20 also focuses on the moment of entry and the abiding nature of this and other potential relationships. 6:11will find its echo in 6:19 which speaks of the Spirit of God, but already in 6:12-13 where the relationship of the believer and the Lord is a key presupposition.

---

[14] This does not have to be as specific as entailing the case addressed in 5:1-3, as J. H. Bernhard, "The Connexion between the Fifth and Sixth Chapters of 1 Cor," *ExpT* 7 (1907) 433-43; W. Deming, "The Unity of 1 Corinthians 5-6," *JBL* 115 (1992) 289-312, Michael D. Goulder, "Libertines? (1 Cor. 5-6)," *NovT* 41 (1999) 334-48 argue or the matter dealt with in 6:12-19, as suggested by P. Richardson, "Judgement in Sexual Matters in 1 Cor 6:1-11," *NovT* 25 (1983) 37-58. See also Raymond F. Collins, *First Corinthians* (SacPag 7; Collegeville: Liturgical, 1999) 225-26 and the discussion in Brian S. Rosner, "Temple prostitution in 1 Corinthians 6:12-20," *NovT* 40 (1998) 336-51.

In 6:12 part of Paul's response is to speak of the danger of coming under the power/authority of something or someone (else!).[15] 6:11 has signalled that we are now under the power of the Lord. Paul is already addressing what he believes happens when someone has intercourse with a prostitute, as becomes apparent in the following verses. Already Gen 2:24 is in the background. He will cite it explicitly to show precisely how one comes under such power. Sexual intercourse leads to people becoming "one flesh" which has as its focus not the moment of joined flesh, but its outcome, here hinted at as being in a relation of power.[16]

6:13 appears to be a digression in making reference to food and the stomach. On the contrary it reflects a widespread linkage between sexual appetite and appetite for food, which can be the basis of quite diverse arguments in support of sexual licence or against it.[17] Paul's response is to declare that God will destroy both.[18] This follows the pattern of the slogans in 6:12 where Paul cites and then counter-asserts immediately. Alternatively one might read the statement about God destroying as part of the Corinthian slogan, to which Paul would then be responding with a statement of similar structure in τὸ δὲ σῶμα οὐ τῇ πορνείᾳ ἀλλὰ τῷ κυρίῳ, καὶ ὁ κύριος τῷ σώματι ("The body is meant not for

---

[15] On the so-called slogans in 1 Cor 6:12-20 see Kirchhoff, *Sünde gegen den eigenen Leib*, 70-103, who argues against the dominant view of exegetes that these are not the slogans of the Corinthians themselves reflecting their own gnostic anthropology or libertine philosophy, but are Paul's formulation of slogans present in the wider community, used by Paul to help the Corinthians come to terms with their own behaviour where some, especially from the lower classes were still engaging in prostitution and using prostitutes as a matter of course as an normal pattern of society of the day. This is difficult, given the range of issues Paul addresses in Corinth which reflect much more than a naive lack of appreciation of values.

[16] While not identifying influence on the text from Gen 2:24, W. Schrage, *Der erste Brief an die Korinther (1 Kor 6,12 - 11,16)* (EKKNT VII/2; Zürich: Benziger Verlag; Neukirchen-Vluyn: Neukirchener Verlag, 1995) 19, notes the link to the theme of sexuality and points appropriately to the issue of "authority" in the context of male-female relations in 1 Corinthians 7. See also G. Dautzenberg, "'Φεύγετε τὴν πορνείαν' (1 Kor 6,18): Eine Fallstudie zur paulinischen Sexualethik in ihrem Verhältnis zur Sexualethik des Frühjudentums," in *Neues Testament und Ethik: Für Rudolf Schnackenburg* ed. H. Merklein (Freiburg: Herder, 1989) 271-98, esp. 282-84.

[17] Similar slogans are applied to issues of food specifically in 10:23 (cf. also 8:1). See also Mark 7:15-19 which disparages concern about food. See also Thiselton, *1 Corinthians*, 463.

[18] See the discussion in Schrage, *1 Korintherbrief (1 Kor 6,12 - 11,16)*, 10-11 n. 237, who notes that καταργήσει "shall destroy") is Pauline eschatological vocabulary (1:28; 2:6; 13:8,10-11; 15:24,26). The verb indicates that God's eschatological action is in view in contrast to what the Corinthians might have seen as a natural process. See also his comments on pp. 20-21.

fornication but for the Lord, and the Lord for the body") and by 6:14 when he asserts the resurrection of the body.[19]

If the words, ὁ δὲ θεὸς καὶ ταύτην καὶ ταῦτα καταργήσει ("and God will destroy both one and the other") are part of Paul's counter-assertion, they are more than just a euphemism for the fact that everyone will die, but reflect Paul's eschatology according to which in the world to come food and the stomach will no longer play a role. By association Paul is probably also implying that in the world to come sexual appetite will play no role, a view reflected in Mark 11:25, that in the age to come people neither marry nor are given in marriage but are like the angels. That, in itself, is already an argument why sexuality should be kept in its place (and for some, given up altogether).

When Paul states that the body is not for πορνεία ("sexual immorality") but for the Lord and the Lord for the body, he could simply be saying that it is to be used for the Lord and not for sexual immorality. The language of power, already introduced in 6:12 and implicit in the reference to the Lord into whose name the believers have been baptised, suggests that something more is intended. Using the body for πορνεία ("sexual immorality") is parallel to being under something or someone else's authority. The implication is: sexual immorality is more than a generic category for sexual sins; it is a power which is able to be exercised because of a relationship once entered. The mutuality, the body for the Lord and the Lord for the body, echoes the structure of mutuality assumed to be created in Gen 2:24 between a man and a woman and may stand under its influence indirectly.

The focus on power continues in 6:14 where Paul links Christ's resurrection to the believers. διὰ τῆς δυνάμεως αὐτοῦ ("by his power") is emphatically placed in the final position. This is not simply a flourish on Paul's part to underline the might of this power, but a statement about resurrected bodies. The issues is about bodies and the powers which govern them. 6:15 presses home the point by identifying the bodies of believers as members of Christ. Different from in 1 Cor 11 the focus is not on diversity and equality among the limbs belonging to the one body, the body of Christ, but on Christians as bodies who are members of Christ.

The question ἄρας οὖν τὰ μέλη τοῦ Χριστοῦ ποιήσω πόρνης μέλη; ("Should I therefore take the members of Christ and make them members of a prostitute?") is enlightening with regard to how Paul understands the relation of bodies. Again we have to draw on Gen 2:24. I make myself a member of a prostitute[20] by having sexual intercourse with her. As sexual intercourse was

---

[19] So, for instance, Thiselton, *I Corinthians*, 462-63; Collins, *1 Corinthians*, 243.

[20] On the meaning of πορνεία and πόρνη see Kirchhoff, *Sünde gegen den eigenen Leib*, 18-37, who reviews the use of both in pagan and Jewish (and Jewish Christian) texts, concluding that whereas the words refer to prostitution in pagan literature and are used

widely understood to constitute a marriage, a permanent state of affairs, so sexual intercourse with a prostitute brings me into a relationship with a prostitute in which my body becomes a member of hers and hers a member of mine.[21] The mutuality alluded to in 6:13 finds its counterpart here, although Paul does not appear to imply that, as the Lord is our master, so the prostitute exercises such mastery. In 6:13 the mastery is attributed to πορνεία ("sexual immorality") itself rather than the πόρνη ("prostitute"). In 6:12 τινος ("by anything") is probably best taken as a neuter.

Finally in 6:16 Paul makes explicit the implicit assumption of the preceding statements and its basis, Gen 2:24. Paul cites and alludes to only that part of the text which is relevant. κολλώμενος (" joining himself") in 6:16 and 17 alludes to the statement προσκολληθήσεται πρὸς τὴν γυναῖκα αὐτοῦ ("shall join himself/be joined to his wife") but omits πρὸς τὴν γυναῖκα αὐτοῦ ("to his wife") because the focus is not on the prescribed order to be achieved, but on the effects of the action. That action - here certainly not read as a passive indicating divine action! - is understood here as sexual intercourse, not surprising given the stronger focus on the sexual element in the LXX.[22] That act brings into being a

---

infrequently, they have a broader compass in Jewish and Jewish Christian sources. The translation, sexual immorality, for πορνεία is appropriate and for πόρνη one could include any woman who engages in sexual intercourse beyond what is permitted, including prostitutes, but not limited to prostitutes. Of our passage she writes: "Paulus verbiete also in 6,12-20 nicht speziell den Verkehr mit Frauen, die sich gewerbsmässig prostituieren, sondern den Verkehr mit einer Frau, für die der betreffende Christ nicht der einzige (noch lebende) Sexualpartner ist" (36) (Tr. So Paul is not forbidding specifically relations with women, who work as prostitutes professionally, but relations with a woman, for whom the respective Christian is not the sole (living) partner) .

[21] Kirchhoff, *Sünde gegen den eigenen Leib*, 163-164, draws attention to the understanding of Gen 2:24 behind *Gen.Rab.* 18 where it is argued that when two men engage in sexual intercourse with a prostitute, only the second commits adultery because the first through sexual intercourse creates a marriage. This understanding of the effects of sexual union and thus its key role in establishing marriage reflects a widespread assumption in the texts and informs Paul's argument here. The focus certainly includes sexual intercourse, but the primary concern is not the act but what it produces. See also Dautzenberg, "'Φεύγετε τὴν πορνείαν'," 271-98, who speaks of a power relation which is established, similar to that exercised by cultic impurity: "Die πορνεία ist vielmehr als den Körper oder Leib in besondererer Weise betreffende negative Macht aufzufassen, vergleichbar der kultischen Unreinheit" (283-84). (Tr. πορνεία is rather to be understood as a negative power, which affects the body in a special way, comparable to cultic impurity). He goes on to note the appropriateness of the shift to the metaphor of the temple in v. 19.

[22] For the understanding of Gen 2:24 consistently as a statement about marriage see the discussion in Kirchhoff, *Sünde gegen den eigenen Leib*, 160-64, where she examines its use

new reality. Here Paul cites the LXX εἰς σάρκα μίαν ("one flesh"). While the Hebrew focuses particularly on the creation of kinship, Paul, following the LXX, focuses more on the effects of the act of sexual intercourse in creating "one body". "Body" here means more than flesh and blood. It is a unity like marriage in which two are joined in such a way that they embody together what Paul will explain later, when speaking of marriage, as mutual belonging and ownership (7:4). That, then, is the situation created which Paul could describe earlier as being under an authority, being for the other, becoming a member of the other. Paul would give no credence to the notion of casual sex. His understanding of a person's sexuality is inseparable from his considering the person as a whole. σῶμα "body" refers to the integrated whole with a focus on the bodily aspect, but not to body as in any way separable from soul or spirit.[23]

Its counterpoint, already highlighted in the baptismal statement in 6:11, in the use of "Lord" and in the reference to becoming members of Christ, is according to 6:17 to become one spirit by joining the Lord: ὁ δὲ κολλώμενος τῷ κυρίῳ ἓν πνεῦμά ἐστιν ("But anyone *joining himself* to the Lord becomes one spirit with him"). One might have expected σῶμα ("body"). Perhaps εἰς σάρκα ("one flesh") prompted Paul to switch to ἓν πνεῦμα ("one spirit"). Perhaps it was to echo the baptismal theology of 6:11 and to prepare for the argument in 6:19. It was clearly not on the basis of a dualism which would have seen the body as material and the spirit only as belonging to God. Already the use of σῶμα ("body") in relation to Christ in 6:13 shows this was not Paul's perspective. πνεῦμα ("spirit") like σῶμα ("body") refers to the whole person, but with focus on the aspect of the spirit.

---

in *Jub.* 3:7; *Jos. Asen.* 20:4; 1 Esdr 4:17b-22; Philo *Q.G.* 1.29 and *Gen. Rab.* 18, noting that the joining is interpreted as a sexual reference, as here in Paul (165). Kirchhoff does not differentiate between the emphasis of the Hebrew and the Greek of Gen 2:24.

[23] On σῶμα ("body") see the discussion in R. H. Gundry, *Sōma in Biblical Theology: with emphasis on Pauline anthropology* (Cambridge: CUP, 1976) 51-80, who argues against the view that sōma means the whole person; rather "where used of whole people, soma directs attention to their bodies, not to the wholeness of their being" (80). "Ancient writers do not usually treat sōma in isolation. Rather, apart from its use for a corpse, sōma refers to the physical body in its proper and intended union with the soul/spirit" (79-80). Gundry's work is a corrective to an overemphasis on σῶμα in the work of R. Bultmann, *Theology of the New Testament*, Vol 1 (London: SCM; New York: Scribner, 1951) and subsequent writers as referring to the whole person, but his assessment that Paul's objection here is to the casualness and superficiality of the liaison with the prostitute fails to take into account the argument of the context where clearly issues of competing power spheres of influence are at stake.

Gen 2:24 continues its influence in 6:18 which in exhorting the hearers to flee sexual immorality argues that, unlike other sins, sexual immorality sins against one's own body.[24] This is not a reference to Christ's body, but to the Christian's body and is based on the assumption that sexual intercourse actually changes people by creating a new reality: oneness with another person, as Gen 2:24 is understood.[25] Recognising the influence of Gen 2:24 in the way Paul understands it makes sense of the otherwise strange sounding statement that the person engaging in sexual immorality is sinning against their own body.[26] Paul really does believe that something happens which actually changes a person's being/body in a way that no act of self inflicted abuse can.[27] Paul's language of power is not so much focused on the prostitute nor on πορνεία ("sexual immorality") as a power, but on the power embodied in the new oneness which he sees indicated by Gen 2:24.[28]

It would be interesting to know how Paul would have understood this effect. Was it irreversible? We assume it must have been. Otherwise those exhorted to flee immorality could never escape it. How would he have envisaged what was happening with a believer who was both one with a prostitute and one with Christ? Did one relationship automatically have the effect of terminating the other? Or would such a relationship allow power or contamination to flow from one to the other? Might not Christ's power then flow to the prostitute to benefit her, perhaps after the model of Paul's notion that because of the union which coming together had created the believing wife sanctifies the unbelieving husband and children (7:14)? Paul does not countenance such a benefit for the prostitute. Is the body of

---

[24] For discussion of the various attempts to define the difference see Thiselton, *1 Corinthians*, 471-73.

[25] "There may be many sins of *thought* (διαλογισμοὶ πονηροὶ) Matt. 15:19), but the only sin which a man can *do* (ποιήσῃ) from within the body is πορνεία; for, as Gen. 2:24 makes clear, the sexual sinner unites himself for eternity in one flesh with the whore." So Goulder, "Libertines?," 347.

[26] Musonius Rufus speaks of dishonouring oneself by such action (Fr. 12), but Paul's assumptions are driven rather by Gen 2:24. See also Kirchhoff, *Sünde gegen den eigenen Leib*, 94-98; Dautzenberg, "'Φεύγετε τὴν πορνείαν'," 272-73, 288.

[27] Dautzenberg, "'Φεύγετε τὴν πορνείαν'," 275 correctly observes: "Man wird der Aussage von V 18bc nur gerecht, wenn man sie nicht als situationsbezogene paulinische Übertreibung abschwächt, sondern sie als Ausdruck paulinischer Überzeugung und paulininscher σῶμα -Anthropologie liest." (Tr. One can only do justice to the saying in v 18bc if one does not weaken it down to a Pauline exaggeration dictated by the context, but reads as an expression of Pauline conviction and Pauline σῶμα -anthropology).

[28] Kirchhoff, *Sünde gegen den eigenen Leib*, 151, make this point well against Dautzenberg, "'Φεύγετε τὴν πορνείαν'," 291-92, although without seeing the specific connection with Gen 2:24, whereas this features more strongly in Dautzenberg's account beside his discussion of πορνεία as a sphere of power (277-84).

Christ or Christ, himself, contaminated or influenced by this other unity? Apparently not. The point seems to be rather one of irreconcilable conflict between two entities: the new reality in Christ and the new reality entered with the prostitute. Paul's use of ἄρας ("take" 6:15) to describe taking away a limb from Christ indicates the irreconcilability of belonging to both. It suggests mutilation.[29]

There are two aspects to these competing unities: the inaugural act and the resultant body of unity. Gen 2:24 clearly informs the understanding of the man-woman relationship. Is it also informing Paul's understanding of the relation between the believer and Christ? Had it already had such influence in the tradition before Paul wrote or is this a fruit of his argument? One cannot miss the allusion to Gen 2:24 in the κολλώμενος ("joining himself to") of 6:17. It could be a Pauline innovation inspired by the context of his argument and nothing more and have informed his discussion from 6:12 onwards. Alternatively Paul assumes use of the metaphor of sexual intimacy to describe the believer's relation to Christ, imagery which has its roots in the prophetic literature, but which has been developed christologically.[30]

One of the most interesting developments in this respect is how Paul continues in 6:19. He is referring to the bodies of believers when he describes their bodies as temples of the Holy Spirit. This is an argument using the imagery of contamination. Their bodies/temples (not they as together the body of Christ) will be defiled if believers use prostitutes. 6:19 contains a second argument which continues in 6:20. They are owned by someone else, not by themselves. In this we see a return to the notion of authority, indicated already in 6:12.

One possible consequence of this line of thought in 1 Corinthians 6 is that any such psychosomatic union with another person competes with our relationship with Christ, so that what applies to prostitutes also applies to sexual union in marriage.[31] The following chapter shows that this is not a conclusion which Paul

---

[29] Collins, *1 Corinthians*, 247.

[30] Kirchhoff, *Sünde gegen den eigenen Leib*, disputes that it is typological here as in Eph 5:31-32, understanding typology as indicating type and antitype with one superior to the other (166). Here it is a matter of direct conflict (167). On the nuptial metaphor see, however, Brian S. Rosner, *Paul, Scripture and Ethics: A Study of 1 Corinthians 5-7* (AGAJU 22; Leiden: Brill, 1994) 131-34.

[31] So G. Delling *Paulus' Stellung zu Frau und Ehe* (BWANT 4/5; Stuttgart: Kohlhammer, 1931) 62-69,86, who argued that Paul saw sexual intercourse as an act incompatible with possession of the Spirit, but was inconsistent on the matter. A. C. Wire *The Corinthian Women Prophets: A Reconstruction through Paul's Rhetoric* (Minneapolis: Fortress, 1990) 90, observes: "The only explanation developed theologically for the danger of immorality argues that a body destined for resurrection with the Lord is no longer neutral ground subject to human authority, but becomes the spirit's temple, which may not be violated. This would seem to require sexual abstinence of all believers. Instead Paul locates immorality in 'your (plural) body,' meaning the community as a whole, and calls for

drew,[32] though some at Corinth may have drawn it. The point of mediation, one might speculate, is that sexual union with another who is also in relation to Christ remains within the one body of Christ and is therefore not in conflict.[33]

The imagery of temple and being bought for a price appears to move away from the imagery of sexual intercourse with a prostitute. Or does it? With cult prostitution in mind one might hear Paul's words as developing a vary daring metaphor. As one pays for a prostitute, so Christ has purchased us for service. As one participates in the temple through cult prostitution in a way that the prostitute is understood as part and parcel of the temple, so Christ sends the Spirit into us and we become a holy place, a temple. The analogy does not fit precisely because the initiator in the case of cult prostitution is not on the side of the temple, whereas in relation to Christ and the believer, it is not the believer's initiative but Christ's. Probably by implication, instead of entering the body of a temple prostitute, which might be claimed as part of the temple and holy place, we should see ourselves as bought to be a holy place and temple where God is glorified. Paul merges an understanding of sexual union based on Gen 2:24 with an understanding of temple prostitution to turn it upside down and plead for a new kind of intercourse. If Paul is, indeed, developing Gen 2:24 in this direction, it gives greater coherence to his argument than the usual interpretations which assume that Paul leaves behind the imagery of prostitution and turns instead to the slave market and to temples. [34] Prostitution, slavery, and temples are doubtless more closely linked and Paul can therefore engage in the daring extension of his metaphor without losing coherence.[35]

---

marriage to prevent immorality in this body, conceding parenthetically the ideal of abstinence (7:1-2)."

[32] Schrage, *1 Korintherbrief (1 Kor 6,12 - 11,16)*, 28-29, denies that Paul would have sensed a tension here or simply not have noticed the potential for one. Rather, he argues, Paul would have been aware of using "body" in different ways.

[33] I find Gundry's explanation at this point unconvincing where he writes: "Coitus with a prostitute is casual, occasional, momentary, and non-indicative of any larger union. On the other hand, union with Christ is fundamental, constant, and all-embracing - as is also marriage. Therein lies the reason that sexual union within marriage does not take away virtue and consequently does not contradict union with Christ" (*Sōma in Biblical Theology*, 53). Paul's point is surely that the so-called casual encounter does in fact create something more substantial. In this R. Jewett, *Paul's Anthropological Terms* (Leiden: Brill, 1971) 269-70, is right. It does mean entering an evil sphere.

[34] Similarly J. Héring, *La Première Épitre de Saint Paul aux Corinthiens* (Neuchatel/Paris: Delachaux et Niestlé, 1949) 48; J. Ruef, *Paul's First Letter to Corinth*; (Pelican NT Comm; Harmondsworth: Penguin, 1971) 51.

[35] Rosner, "Temple Prostitution," points to the condemnation of all forms of prostitution in the Jewish scriptures and to the linking of apostasy and idolatry with sexual

Might Paul have been playing with such images assuming his hearers would have sufficient familiarity with such practices to understand the allusions? Possibly. At least at the level of purchasing slaves as (non cultic) prostitutes, this is probable. The difficulty with assuming more than this is that we do not have evidence of sacral prostitution at Corinth in the Roman period,[36] so that we would have to assume that Paul would be attacking use of ordinary non sacral prostitutes while playing with the image of sacral prostitution to develop the positive side of argument about becoming one with Christ. It may not depend on actual practices in Corinth so much as what might have been in the world of the imagination of the hearers. It takes us in any case beyond the immediate influence of Gen 2:24, but the sexual metaphor for describing the believer's relation with Christ opened such rich possibilities.

Galatians 3:28

Gal 3:26 Πάντες γὰρ υἱοὶ θεοῦ ἐστε διὰ τῆς πίστεως ἐν Χριστῷ ᾽Ιησοῦ· 27 ὅσοι γὰρ εἰς Χριστὸν ἐβαπτίσθητε, Χριστὸν ἐνεδύσασθε. 28 οὐκ ἔνι ᾽Ιουδαῖος οὐδὲ ῞Ελλην, οὐκ ἔνι δοῦλος οὐδὲ ἐλεύθερος, οὐκ ἔνι *ἄρσεν καὶ θῆλυ*· πάντες γὰρ ὑμεῖς εἷς ἐστε ἐν Χριστῷ ᾽Ιησοῦ. 29 εἰ δὲ ὑμεῖς Χριστοῦ, ἄρα τοῦ ᾽Αβραὰμ σπέρμα ἐστέ, κατ᾽ ἐπαγγελίαν κληρονόμοι.	Gal 3:26 For in Christ Jesus you are all children of God through faith. 27 As many of you as were baptized into Christ have clothed yourselves with Christ. 28 There is no longer Jew or Greek, there is no longer slave or free, there is no longer male and female; for all of you are one in Christ Jesus. 29 And if you belong to Christ, then you are Abraham's offspring, heirs according to the promise

---

immorality (342-45). He points in particular to 1 Cor 10:7 which he argues assumes presence of prostitutes at temple meals and where the same kind of slogans of freedom occur, to 6:9-11 which also links sexual immorality and idolatry, but especially to the imagery of 6:19 (345-47).

[36] On this see Kirchhoff, *Sünde gegen den eigenen Leib*, 42-47; Schrage, *1 Korintherbrief (1 Kor 6,12 - 11,16)*, 13; Rosner, "Temple prostitution," 347-48. Rosner goes on to point out however that prostitutes were commonly present at special feasts in temples and that 1 Cor 10:7 appears to reflect this situation (348-51). "Thus a solution to the puzzle of the historical context of 1 Cor. 6:12-20 presents itself when we recognise the link between feasting and πορνεία, and note that both the Corinthians Christians who were eating in pagan temples and those who were using prostitutes were defending their behaviours with the same slogan: 'all things are lawful for me,' It is this: some Corinthians were attending temple feasts and using prostitutes who offered their services on such festive occasions" (350).

The words ἄρσεν καὶ θῆλυ ("male and female") appear to be drawn from Gen 1:27 ἄρσεν καὶ θῆλυ ἐποίησεν αὐτούς ("male and female he created them") or Gen 5:2 which is identical. This accounts for the καὶ construction which appears here. The other contrasts use the οὐκ ἔνι ... οὐδὲ ("there is neither ... nor") form. In Ephesians the focus is oneness in marriage and oneness with Christ as the bridegroom. Here the focus is also oneness, but it is alluding horizontally to the oneness not of marriage but of different groups in Christ.

Isolated, the words, οὐκ ἔνι ἄρσεν καὶ θῆλυ· πάντες γὰρ ὑμεῖς εἷς ἐστε ("there is no male and female; for you are all one"), might recall Gen 2:24. Male and female have become one. Speculation might run rife about how such oneness is consummated in Christ, including through sexual union. The context shows that Paul is, indeed, speaking about becoming one with Christ, who, he argues is the seed of Abraham, and so in him qualifying to receive the promises. But the image of male and female is not being used of Christ and the church, respectively, as in Ephesians 5 (or 1 Corinthians 6), but of the oneness of male and female in Christ.

The focus is not males ceasing to be male nor females ceasing to be female but on their oneness in the single seed who is Christ. Seed is being used in the sense of descendant and heir, not reproductive seed. The result of being baptised into Christ and putting on Christ is that all are children of God. Paul is also focusing on differences. Those between Jew and Gentile are the primary concern of the context. His argument is not that such differences should be eliminated, but that being Jew or Greek, slave or free, male and female, creates no barrier to this reality. All have equal access. None is privileged. None is excluded.[37]

While the focus of the context is on the inclusion of Gentiles on an equal basis, Paul goes beyond the concerns of the context to name also "slave or free, and male and female", most likely because he is using an established formula probably associated with the celebration of baptism. It would be speculative to wonder how a tradition about oneness in relation to these additional pairs, slave and free, male and female, might have been understood and, for our study, in

---

[37] For a review of recent exegesis of Gal 3:28 see J. M. Gundry-Volf, "Christ and Gender: A Study of Difference and Equality in Gal 3,28" in *Jesus Christus als Mitte der Schrift: Studien zur Hermeneutik des Evangeliums: FS für O. Hofius* ed. C. Landmesser, H. J. Eckstein and H. Lichtenberger (Berlin: de Gruyter, 1997) 439-79. She writes: "Gal 3,28 does not declare sex difference in any sense abolished in a new creation of a unified, sexually undifferentiated humanity. Rather, it refers to the adiaphorization of sex difference in a new creation where being male or female is no advantage or disadvantage in relation to God and others and where man and woman are reconciled and united as equals" (439). See also J. M. Gundry-Volf, "Male and Female in Creation and New Creation: Interpretations of Galatians 3:28c and 1 Corinthians 7" in *To Tell the Mystery: Essays on New Testament Eschatology in Honor of Robert H. Gundry*, ed. T. E. Schmidt and M. Silva (JSNTSup 100; Sheffield: JSOTPr., 1994) 95-121.

particular, what people might have understood by the allusion to Gen 1:27 and whether distinctive emphases of the LXX played a role. The pair, slave and free, could have been read as a radical statement which in effect obliterated the distinction or it could have been read as implying no social change, but a sense of unity nevertheless. The latter appears to be Paul's position. The Colossian and Ephesian household codes emphatically reinforce the distinctions. It has the potential, nevertheless, to subvert the social distinctions.

The three pairs of categories are different in kind. Jews and Gentiles is racial and cultural; slaves and free is social; male and female is gender and sexual. Clearly the first pair implies equality in Christ between different groups which remain different. In the case of the second pairing one might argue that the distinctions should be obliterated, if equality is to count. This raises the possibility that the third might be understood either as like the first or like the second pair. If it is like the second then one might expect that what makes the difference, gender and sexuality, is to be overcome or set aside. If it is like the first then one might expect equality between the sexes which retain their distinctiveness and their worth as such. It is very likely that both options were espoused.

The tradition behind Galatians 3:28 in 1 Corinthians 12:13; Colossians 3:11 and 1 Corinthians 7

The tradition reflected in Gal 3:28 reappears, it seems, in 1 Cor 12:13 and in Col 3:11.

1 Cor 12:13 καὶ γὰρ ἐν ἑνὶ πνεύματι ἡμεῖς πάντες εἰς ἓν σῶμα ἐβαπτίσθημεν, εἴτε Ἰουδαῖοι εἴτε Ἕλληνες εἴτε δοῦλοι εἴτε ἐλεύθεροι, καὶ πάντες ἓν πνεῦμα ἐποτίσθημεν.	13 For in the one Spirit we were all baptized into one body-Jews or Greeks, slaves or free-and we were all made to drink of one Spirit.
Col 3:11 ὅπου οὐκ ἔνι Ἕλλην καὶ Ἰουδαῖος, περιτομὴ καὶ ἀκροβυστία, βάρβαρος, Σκύθης, δοῦλος, ἐλεύθερος, ἀλλὰ [τὰ] πάντα καὶ ἐν πᾶσιν Χριστός.	11 where is no longer Greek and Jew, circumcised and uncircumcised, barbarian, Scythian, slave and free; but Christ is all and in all!

Like Gal 3:26-28 the context is baptism and unity in Christ, but strikingly absent from both is any reference to male and female. Had it become a non issue for Paul in writing to the Corinthians and for the writer of Colossians? The contrary appears to be the case. The author of Colossians is confronting asceticism, as 2:23 indicates.[38] The "male-female" pair may have been used in support of that asceticism. In 3:9-11 the author alludes to Gen 1:26-27 in affirming, at least, the cultural diversity which living out the restored "image of God" affirms. This is then the prelude to the household code which affirms male and female relations.

Similarly there are indications in 1 Corinthians that male-female relations in the church had become a major issue. While Paul was comfortable with, in fact, insistent on the equality of Jew and Gentile in Christ and must have come close to this in his view of slaves and masters, there are indications that the status of men and women was something different, particularly at Corinth. 1 Corinthians 7 includes all three pairs: circumcision: uncircumcision (7:18-20); slave: free (7:21-24); and male: female as a major focus of the chapter. In the first two pairs the implication is that each is of equal worth before God. For the second pair Paul is espousing the strategy of slaves remaining slaves and seeking freedom only when the opportunity arises, not otherwise. In his treatment of male and female in 1 Corinthians 7 it is clear that Paul rejects the setting aside of maleness and femaleness as an implied requirement, although he appears to assume that, as with slavery, the distinctions will one day cease to be. Some will even choose to live this way in the present, like Paul, himself, but he refuses to impose this on all, as some were doing. Until then, however, the current order of male and female remains, including its ordering through marriage.

The tradition of Gal 3:28, at least in the form of the three contrasting pairs, does, then, appear in 1 Corinthians 7, but in each case with the exhortation not to seek to abandon the status. Paul urges such constraint in face of the prospect of troubles in the last days, but he is also influenced throughout by an underlying preference for disengagement from sexual relations which probably reflects his eschatological vision. In other words, just as he resists notions of resurrection already, so he resists the claim that we should live now sexually as we will in the resurrection on the grounds that this is too difficult for many.

Without seeking to unravel the complexities of the Corinthian situation,[39] which would take us far beyond the scope of this discussion, it is appropriate for

---

[38] On this see Margaret Y. MacDonald, "Citizens of heaven and earth: Asceticism and social integration in Colossians and Ephesians, in *Asceticism and the New Testament*, ed. Leif E. Vaage and Vincent L. Wimbusch (New York: Routledge, 1999) 269-98, esp. 280-83.

[39] For recent discussion see Gundry-Volf, "Christ and Gender" and "Male and Female" and J. Dorcas Gordon, *Sister or Wife? 1 Corinthians 7 and Cultural Anthropology* (JSNTSup 149; Sheffield: JSOTPr., 1997); W. Deming, *Paul on marriage and celibacy* (SNTMS 83; Cambridge: CUP, 1995); Wire, *Corinthian women prophets*; D. R. MacDonald, *There is no male and female: the fate of a dominical saying in Paul and Gnosticism* (Philadelphia: Fortress, 1987). Gundry-Volf, "Male and female," writes: "Early

us to ask in relation to it what role the particular emphases of the LXX might have played. There is little in 1 Corinthians 7 that could be shown to be the result of a distinctive influence from the LXX, although in broad terms the affirmation of sexual union in marriage reflected in Gen 2:24 underlies Paul's comments throughout and holds him from espousing denial of sexual relations or limiting sexual relations to procreation. He has directly applied Gen 2:24 LXX to argue negatively against sexual union with prostitutes in 6:12-20. Sexual union becomes in that context a metaphor for our relation to Christ, as we have seen. By implication sexual union is to be affirmed - in the right relationship and the right context. This is to be upheld, despite the alternative choices made by some including himself.

Paul does appear to be aware of the Gal 3:28 tradition in 1 Corinthians and continues to affirm it, but within certain parameters. The absence of the pair, male: female, in 1 Cor 12:13 may well be in response to the danger which it posed when uncommented. His commentary comes in 1 Corinthians 7 where significantly the other two pairs also occur. Beyond 1 Corinthians 7 Paul also reveals important assumptions about how he understood male and female in 1 Cor 11:2-16, where, again, we find his thought standing under the influence of Genesis 1-2 LXX.

1 Corinthians 11:2-16

The hierarchy of being which the LXX of Genesis 1-2 brings to the fore lies behind Paul's statements about the status of women in 1 Corinthians 11.[40] Paul is countering a practice which had developed at Corinth in which women at worship abandoned their distinctively female attire of their head or face being covered or veiled. In 11:2 he praises their observance of received traditions. In 11:16 he returns to reinforce that such traditions are to be upheld and to point out that the practice at Corinth was out of line with established practice in Paul's churches and in "the churches of God".

Christians familiar with the biblical creation account or with early Christian or Jewish interpretation of it could have thus understood the words of the baptismal tradition, 'there is no male and female', to alter or abolish the implications of the created sexual distinctions, 'male' and 'female' for marriage, sexual union and procreation. In the hands of sexual ascetes such as those in Corinth, the eschatological formula could be taken to justify sexual asceticism" (107).

[40] Paul shows in 1 Corinthians 15 that he was also aware of the kind of Platonic interpretation of Genesis 1-2 which the LXX made possible and which is reflected in a different form in Philo. Giving it his own twist he identifies Christ as the heavenly man, matching the image of God of Genesis 1.

Paul seeks to bolster the case for the accepted practice with a range of arguments, some interrelated. He begins with the matter at hand: the "head", using it first metaphorically to assert a hierarchy of being: God-Christ-man-woman (11:3).[41] In isolation from its intertextual relation and in the light of normal Greek usage of κεφαλή ("head/source"), one might argue that the focus is source and origin not any sense of superiority. In the LXX not κεφαλή ("head/source") but ἀρχων ("ruler") or ἀρχηγός ("leader") translate שׁיר ("head") when it means authority. It is however possible that κεφαλή has acquired such connotations already in the LXX. It is present in Philo's usage and in the deuteropaulines (eg. Eph 1:22; Col 2:10). Even if one decides that "source" or "prominence" is in mind here, Paul will have been working within the framework of Genesis 1-2 LXX, which does indicate a sense of hierarchy and appears to see some analogy between the man in the likeness of God and the woman in the likeness of man and so is probably to be assumed here and reflects the context. The statements are not reversible (eg. Christ is not the κεφαλή of God). Paul is assuming that to be the origin and source is to have a priority in more than just time.

His primary concern comes first: the relation of the male to Christ and the woman to the man. In 11:4-6 Paul describes the effect of inappropriate practice. First he states that a male praying or prophesying with his head covered[42] shames his head. The transition from 11:3 to 11:4-6 is awkward because in 11:3 the head of one person is the next superior person. Here in 11:4-6 the head refers literally to the person's physical head. This suggests that when a man shames "his head", it still refers to his own head and not to Christ who according to 11:3 is head in a different sense. The reference to shaming oneself receives support from 11:6 which speaks of shame a woman brings on herself and in 11:14 which refers to dishonour being brought upon oneself. The matter is, however, more complex.

When Paul speaks of a woman praying and prophesying with her head uncovered,[43] he repeats the same claim: she shames her head. He then adds an

---

[41] See Michael Lattke, "κεφαλή," *EWNT*, 2.701-708, who sees Paul combining the meaning, "Spitze, Führer, Oberhaupt" (Tr. prominence, leader, chief) found in Hellenistic Judaism in the LXX, Philo and T. 12 Patr., with the notion of origin in a way that enables him to bring together the sociologically given patriarchy of his world with the theological notions of origin and rule. On the range of possible meanings for κεφαλή here see also the discussion in Thiselton, *1 Corinthians*, 812-22; Collins, *1 Corinthians*, 405-406, who speaks of a "three-part chain" expressing origin; Schrage, *1 Korintherbrief (1 Kor 6,12 - 11,16)*, 501-503.

[42] The precise reference of κατὰ κεφαλῆς ἔχων is unclear. It may refer to a covering or it may refer to a hairstyle (long hair). See the discussion in Collins, *1 Corinthians*, 406-407; Thiselton, *1 Corinthians*, 823-26.

[43] On the various interpretations of ἀκατακαλύπτῳ τῇ κεφαλῇ see Collins, *1 Corinthians*, 407-409.

explanation which provides a clue for understanding the relation between 11:3 and 11:4-6. He equates the uncovered head with a shaven head. Having a shaven head or having one's hair cut off was a mark of shame for a woman. It was a sign she had disgraced herself. Given the hierarchy of belonging which was embedded in social relations, any disgrace of herself was also a disgrace of her master, her husband. This means that 11:4 and 5-6 refer simultaneously to the head of (on!) the person and to the head over the person, as set out in Paul's understanding of the levels of authority in 11:3.[44]

Paul's arguments are informed not only by what he assumes to be social norms (to which he appeals explicitly in 11:13-14),[45] but also from his understanding of Genesis 1-2,[46] whereby he is clearly influenced by the stronger emphasis in the LXX on the chain of being. This is evident not only in the hierarchy of being assumed in 11:3, where he introduces Christ between the man and God, but also in the description in 11:7 of the man as the image and glory of God and the woman as the glory of man.[47] Ἀνὴρ μὲν γὰρ οὐκ ὀφείλει κατακαλύπτεσθαι τὴν κεφαλὴν εἰκὼν καὶ δόξα θεοῦ ὑπάρχων· ἡ γυνὴ δὲ δόξα ἀνδρός ἐστιν ("For a man ought not to have his head veiled, since he is the image and reflection {Or [glory] } of God; but woman is the reflection {Or [glory] } of man"). Genesis 2 clearly informs the argument in 11:8 where Paul argues for the order of being on the basis of woman being made from the man and in 11:9 where the woman is created for the sake of the man.

In 11:10 Paul draws his argumentation to its interim conclusion: διὰ τοῦτο ὀφείλει ἡ γυνὴ ἐξουσίαν ἔχειν ἐπὶ τῆς κεφαλῆς διὰ τοὺς ἀγγέλους ("Therefore the woman ought to have authority on her head because of the angels."). This should not be seen as a parenthesis, following the specific argument of 11:9, but as the major concern Paul is seeking to address. It would have doubtless been seen by him as representing the conclusion of his arguments.

---

[44] So also Thiselton, *1 Corinthians*, 827. See also his excurse on head covering and shame (828-833).

[45] See Collins, *1 Corinthians*, 397-399, who quotes extensively from contemporary philosophical discussion of hairstyling. Roman and Jewish custom was that men should pray with covered heads; the Greek custom was the opposite: for men to pray with heads uncovered (401).

[46] Cf. Watson, *Agape, Eros, Gender*, 42, who argues that Paul's statement of praise in 11:2 indicates that the practice at Corinth was not contrary to the traditions which Paul handed on. Alternatively it is a Pauline rhetorical ploy. See also Watson, "Strategies of recovery," 92-93, 96. On the passage as a whole see also J. D. Beduhn, "'Because of the angels': unveiling Paul's anthropology in 1 Corinthians 11," *JBL* 118 (1999) 295-320 and the extensive discussion in Thiselton, *1 Corinthians*, 800-848.

[47] Watson *Agape, Eros, Gender*, explains the use of glory in the expression, "glory of man", as evident of a "semantic slippage" (56): it refers to what the man delights in and therefore is wont to gaze at, whereas "glory" of God refers to something derived from God.

The fact that it is formulated differently from what precedes, especially when it speaks of "authority on her head" ἐξουσίαν .. ἐπὶ τῆς κεφαλῆς and of "angels", may indicate that Paul is indeed citing a traditional formulation. This would explain also why there is a surplus of argument beyond what has been indicated thus far and which is picked up by "therefore", διὰ τοῦτο, namely, the concern about angels.

If we interpret the statement in the language which Paul has used thus far, we can understand having authority on one's head as making a statement about having a covered or veiled head. As we have seen, the treatment of one's head also has implications for whether shame or honour is brought on the person who is one's "head". It is a sign of that person's authority. It is by implication also a sign of one's own authority.[48] Provided the signs of proper authority are present, women are to pray and prophesy. The latter is not even in question for Paul; it is assumed; it does not have to be argued.

"Because of the angels" probably belonged to the tradition which Paul, I think, is citing, whether directly or indirectly. Paul is happy to include it and would doubtless have understood it within his frame of reference. The reference to angels could reflect an interpretation of the plural ποιήσωμεν ("let us make" Gen 2:18) as implying, as does Philo, that women are part of the faulty creation in which angels were at work,[49] but more likely it reflects the concern about nakedness and shame: nakedness is inappropriate in the presence of the holy angels.[50] That understanding may also have gone so far as seeing potential danger to women (and to angels) if women's naked beauty (at least in relation to the head and face) is exposed in the presence of angels, given the story of the fall of angels in Gen 6:2 and the traditions it spawned.

The context does not suggest that the concern is with other men being enticed to sin (or from true worship) by women's beauty,[51] which might subvert her authority.[52] The authority would be seen as relating to a particular male, namely

---

[48] So M. Hooker, "Authority on her head: An examination of 1 Cor 11:10," *NTS* 10 (1964) 410-16. See the discussion of research in Thiselton, *1 Corinthians*, 838-39.

[49] So Beduhn, "'Because of the angels'," 308-309, 317. Cf. the similar assumption in relation to the Law in Gal 3:19-20.

[50] This interpretation coheres to my mind better with the emphasis on shame and nakedness which Watson, *Agape, Eros, Gender*, appeals to in relation to the gaze of men, than his suggestion that the gaze of men symbolically representing the old order now holds no fears (70). It is also possible that the shame and nakedness connects to fears about the gaze of angels linked to the myth of Genesis 6. On the presence of the holy angels in worship see 1QM 7.4-6; 1QS 2.3-11.

[51] Cf. Watson, *Agape, Eros, Gender*, 45-50.

[52] So Watson, *Agape, Eros, Gender*, 40: "The veil is the symbol not of woman's enforced silence but of her authority to speak." See his argument about the erotic gaze in

the woman's husband. The woman is to continue to wear the symbols which express this relationship. This symbol did make a statement to other males, but the traditional focus was less on other men than on angels. Within this framework the woman is free to exercise authority.

In 11:11-12 we see Paul countering potential misunderstanding which might diminish the place of women in the community. This is the strength of his "but" πλήν with which he begins. In 11:11 he asserts that both women and men belong together "in the Lord". This may already reflect Gen 2:18 according to which it is not good for man to be alone, but it finds its expression christologically: "in the Lord" ἐν κυρίῳ. But then in 11:12 Paul playfully asserts on the basis of Gen 2 and human reproduction that while the woman came out of man, so man comes into being through woman and all are from God. These balancing comments had the potential to undermine all of the previous argument, but Paul does not indicate this.[53] At most one may suspect that the shift to a "common sense" observation in 11:13-15 could reflect a sense of vulnerability in the argument thus far.

In 11:13-15 Paul appeals to what he sees as a common assumption of his culture: long hair for men is shameful (for Paul: according to "nature"!); long hair for women is glorious and appropriate. The point of the argument, however, is that long hair covers; covering is "natural"; therefore covering in worship is appropriate. Paul is "getting desperate"! Finally he returns to the argument of conformity with accepted tradition.

In the process of urging a return to what he accepts as proper practice, expressed as the need for women to wear the signs of their status in worship in the presence of the angels, Paul employs arguments from custom (and "nature") and the creation narrative of Genesis 1-2. In the latter he reflects the stronger emphasis in the LXX on the chain of being where as man is the image of God, so woman is the image of man and subordinate. His concern is not to diminish the status of women. He assumes that their actions of praying and prophesying in the community are fully appropriate.[54] If anything he senses the need to counter any

---

44-55. "The shame is the shame of nakedness. Hair is given to a woman 'for a covering' (v. 15), as a garment provided by nature herself. It is just one small step, although a necessary one, from the covering of woman's head by her hair to the covering of her face with a veil" (54-55). He also comments: "Paul's attempt to interpose the veil was questionable not only culturally and politically but also theologically - as himself later tacitly acknowledges" (41), pointing to 2 Cor 3:12-18.

[53] Cf. Collins, *1 Corinthians*, 403: "Paul's explanatory aside proclaims that from the standpoint of a Christian understanding of creation there is radical equality between men and women."

[54] See also Francis Watson, "The authority of the voice: a theological reading of 1 Cor 11.2-16," *NTS* 46 (2000) 520-36, who argues that Paul is concerned to argue for

tendencies towards diminishing women's status, especially in 11:12-13. His concern is with practice.

We can only imagine why. Clearly some had abandoned the accepted practice. Why? Such a countercultural initiative probably reflects an assertion of freedom and equality. It would be consistent with an approach that read "no longer male and female" as warranting abandonment of the signs of authority of one over the other. Why does that matter to Paul? Paul believes in an order of creation which includes a hierarchy of being. His view is informed by his reading of Genesis 1-2 LXX. This provides assumptions which he then brings to his Christian understanding. The result is, on the one hand, his assertion that male and female belong together in Christ, but that in coming together and acknowledging each other's value, on the other, they are not to abandon their status in the hierarchy of being and so should not abandon the symbols of that status.

It is likely that the women who abandoned their veils were doing so on the basis of a radical interpretation of the kind of tradition we find in Gal 3:28. This might explain why Paul no longer includes the male-female pair when he repeats the tradition elsewhere.[55] We may at least assume that they saw their behaviour as consonant with their being in Christ. If they understood their position in the light of Genesis 1-2, it would probably have been in a manner that saw what Christ had achieved as restoring a oneness in which sexual differentiation was no longer relevant. It is also possible that 1 Corinthians 7 provides further evidence of the development of such an approach. For there it appears that some had taken this even further and reckoned that abandonment of sexual differentiation also implied abandonment of sexual relations and of marriage. One can hardly make the LXX responsible for this, but its linking of Genesis 2:20-25 more closely with Genesis 1:26-28 than in the Hebrew may have contributed.

---

interdependence, but in the process uses a hierarchical understanding of male female relations which he argues is in tension with his real objective.

[55] So for instance H. D. Betz, *Galatians* (Hermeneia; Philadelphia: Fortress, 1979) 200, who also notes the reluctance which Paul shares with Philo to embrace the androgyny myth.

2 Corinthians 11:2-3

2 ζηλῶ γὰρ ὑμᾶς θεοῦ ζήλῳ, ἡρμοσάμην γὰρ ὑμᾶς ἑνὶ ἀνδρὶ παρθένον ἁγνὴν παραστῆσαι τῷ Χριστῷ· 3 φοβοῦμαι δὲ μή πως, ὡς ὁ ὄφις ἐξηπάτησεν Εὕαν ἐν τῇ πανουργίᾳ αὐτοῦ, φθαρῇ τὰ νοήματα ὑμῶν ἀπὸ τῆς ἁπλότητος [καὶ τῆς ἁγνότητος] τῆς εἰς τὸν Χριστόν.	2 I feel a divine jealousy for you, for I promised you in marriage to one husband, to present you as a chaste virgin to Christ. 3 But I am afraid that as the serpent deceived Eve by its cunning, your thoughts will be led astray from a sincere and pure devotion to Christ.

The other allusion to Genesis 1-3 comes in Paul's words of warning to the Corinthians in 2 Cor 11:2-3. Here he uses Eve's seduction by the serpent as a basis for warning the Corinthians as virgins wedded to Christ not be seduced by false teachers (see also the reference in 11:14 to seduction by Satan's transforming himself into an angel of light, an allusion to *Life of Adam and Eve* 9). Adam's sin in Rom 5:12-21 is not sexualised, but Eve's appears to be in 2 Cor 11:2-3. This reflects the use of ἡπάτησεν ("deceived/seduced") in Gen 3:13 LXX, which opened the possibility that the woman's deception might be read as sexual seduction on the part of the serpent.

Given Paul's interpretation of the deception of Eve as seduction here, we might also assume a similar nuance in the use of ἐξηπάτησεν ("deceived/ seduced") in Romans 7:11 which would reinforce a sexual interpretation of ἐπιθυμίαν ("desire/lust") and οὐκ ἐπιθυμήσεις ("you shall not desire/lust after") in 7:7. Can one say that the LXX has contributed to this understanding? This is almost certainly the case. In the sense that LXX allows for confusion between the creation of sexuality in Gen 2:24 and the curse in Gen 3:16, Gen 3:13 would have led to speculation that this "uncontrollable" aspect of the woman already played a role in her downfall.

Conclusion

Genesis 2:24 LXX formed the basis for Paul's argument against use of prostitutes in 1 Cor 6:12-20. Through the use of the word, σάρξ ("flesh"), the inability of the LXX to reproduce the אִשָּׁה אִישׁ (*ish-ishshah*; man-woman) pun, and the resultant focus not on commonality but unity of two into one (reflected also in the presence of δύο in the text), the LXX of Gen 2:24 lends itself to a focus on sexual intercourse. Paul's concern is both the act and what it achieves in bringing about a unity which persists far beyond the act itself. In a daring use of the image Paul challenges the Corinthians to see themselves as entering such a unity with Christ who has purchased them and made them into a sacral entity.

Genesis 2:24 LXX continues to inform the discussion which follows where, contrary to many influences of the time, Paul asserts the validity of sexual intercourse in itself - and not just for the sake of procreation - and of marriage, even though it is not his choice. 1 Corinthians 7 also reflects the tradition identified in Gal 3:28 which speaks of "no male and female" in Christ, alluding to Gen 1:27, beside the pairs, Jew-Gentile and slave-free. Both 1 Corinthians 7 and 1 Corinthians 11 indicate that there have been problems in understanding male and female and their respective roles in Corinth. Indirectly both Gen 2:24 and Gen 1:27 are influencing the discussion in 1 Corinthians 7. The LXX of at least the former plays a significant role.

In 1 Corinthians 11, where Paul again addresses an issue which has arisen from differing understandings of the role of male and female in Christ and in Christian community, Paul employs Genesis 1-2 to make his point about the need to preserve the common church practice which retained the differentiation between men and women's head attire in the context of worship. Here the LXX emphasis which more strongly reflects a hierarchical chain of being of God-(Christ)-male-female is apparent. As in 1 Corinthians 7 Paul advocates retaining what he sees as the created order and recognising authority (including women's authority to pray and prophesy) within that frame of reference. As he resists abandonment of marriage and sexual union there, so here he resists abandonment of differentiation and orders of being in the created order. He holds in tension his belief, rooted in the creation story, in orders of being and his belief that in Christ male and female are one. Others appear to have argued that the oneness in Christ belongs to a new creation and new order which applies already. Paul probably agreed with their vision, but insisted that its realisation was still to come and that in the interim the created order applied. He could do so, even though his own choice had been already to disengage from sexual relations.

Paul's attitudes to sexuality reflect diverse influences. Behind them is doubtless some reflection on Genesis 1-3. Beyond the potential which is already there in the Hebrew, a reading of the LXX will have played a role. This is certainly the case in the interpretation of Gen 3:13 as referring to the woman's seduction by the serpent, as reflected in 2 Cor 11:2-3. It is probably so also at a broader level, particularly in the distinction that was able to be made between the man of Genesis 1 and the Adam of Genesis 2, in a manner that the ultimate hope is to return to be as the being in Genesis 1 where male and female aspects are present, but - despite 1:28 - are not acted upon.

Other Pauline excurses related to Genesis 1-3, 1 Cor 15:20-57 and Rom 5:12-21, might suggest that he saw Christ as the heavenly or original Adam or at least as the one in whom male and female come together as one, as heavenly man and second Adam. The oneness is now no longer sexual union, but going back behind that to a stage where the separation has not yet taken place and sexual union is irrelevant. This need not be a full blown androgyny, but it assumes that in this state the male and female aspects cease to be relevant. His focus is, however, not protology but eschatology and while using the language of Genesis which applies well to Philo's first Adam, Paul retains the contrast between the earthly and the heavenly, but uses it in relation to the coming Christ (1 Corinthians 15) or the Christ who has come (Romans 5). He makes no connection in either place between the new Adam and issues of male and female, even though we may assume on the basis of 1 Corinthians 7 that he would have affirmed what we hear in Mark's anecdote about the resurrection of the dead, that "they neither marry nor are given in marriage" (12:25).

3.   Deuteropauline Literature

Ephesians 5

25 Οἱ ἄνδρες, ἀγαπᾶτε τὰς γυναῖκας, καθὼς καὶ ὁ Χριστὸς ἠγάπησεν τὴν ἐκκλησίαν καὶ ἑαυτὸν παρέδωκεν ὑπὲρ αὐτῆς, 26 ἵνα αὐτὴν ἁγιάσῃ καθαρίσας τῷ λουτρῷ τοῦ ὕδατος ἐν ῥήματι, 27 ἵνα παραστήσῃ αὐτὸς ἑαυτῷ ἔνδοξον τὴν ἐκκλησίαν, μὴ ἔχουσαν σπίλον ἢ ῥυτίδα ἤ τι τῶν τοιούτων, ἀλλ᾽ ἵνα ᾖ ἁγία καὶ ἄμωμος. 28 οὕτως ὀφείλουσιν [καὶ] οἱ ἄνδρες ἀγαπᾶν τὰς ἑαυτῶν γυναῖκας ὡς τὰ ἑαυτῶν σώματα. ὁ ἀγαπῶν τὴν ἑαυτοῦ γυναῖκα ἑαυτὸν ἀγαπᾷ· 29 Οὐδεὶς γάρ ποτε τὴν ἑαυτοῦ σάρκα ἐμίσησεν ἀλλὰ ἐκτρέφει καὶ θάλπει αὐτήν, καθὼς καὶ ὁ Χριστὸς τὴν ἐκκλησίαν, 30 ὅτι μέλη ἐσμὲν τοῦ σώματος αὐτοῦ. 31 *ἀντὶ τούτου καταλείψει ἄνθρωπος [τὸν] πατέρα καὶ [τὴν] μητέρα καὶ προσκολληθήσεται πρὸς τὴν γυναῖκα αὐτοῦ, καὶ ἔσονται οἱ δύο εἰς σάρκα μίαν.* 32 τὸ μυστήριον τοῦτο μέγα ἐστίν· ἐγὼ δὲ λέγω εἰς Χριστὸν καὶ εἰς τὴν ἐκκλησίαν. 33 πλὴν καὶ ὑμεῖς οἱ καθ᾽ ἕνα, ἕκαστος τὴν ἑαυτοῦ γυναῖκα οὕτως ἀγαπάτω ὡς ἑαυτόν, ἡ δὲ γυνὴ ἵνα φοβῆται τὸν ἄνδρα.	22 Wives, be subject to your husbands as you are to the Lord. 23 For the husband is the head of the wife just as Christ is the head of the church, the body of which he is the Savior. 24 Just as the church is subject to Christ, so also wives ought to be, in everything, to their husbands. 25 Husbands, love your wives, just as Christ loved the church and gave himself up for her, 26 in order to make her holy by cleansing her with the washing of water by the word, 27 so as to present the church to himself in splendor, without a spot or wrinkle or anything of the kind-yes, so that she may be holy and without blemish. 28 In the same way, husbands should love their wives as they do their own bodies. He who loves his wife loves himself. 29 For no one ever hates his own body, but he nourishes and tenderly cares for it, just as Christ does for the church, 30 because we are members of his body. 31 "For this reason a man will leave his father and mother and be joined to his wife, and the two will become one flesh." 32 This is a great mystery, and I am applying it to Christ and the church. 33 Each of you, however, should love his wife

	as himself, and a wife should respect her husband.

Instead of ἕνεκεν τούτου ("therefore") of the LXX Ephesians 2:31 has ἀντὶ τούτου (also meaning: "therefore"). There is no possessive after πατέρα ("father") and μητέρα ("mother") although manuscripts are divided about inclusion of the articles before them. The writer may be using a variant Greek translation or citing the LXX loosely.[56] Distinctive features of the LXX are present: ἄνθρωπος ("man/human being") and προσκολληθήσεται πρὸς ("join himself to, be joined to").

The preceding context in Ephesians alludes also to the context of Gen 2:24. The writer will already have Gen 2:24 in mind in the formulation of 5:25b-27. It belongs to the tradition which sees Christ's relation to the church in marital terms.[57] Earlier still the statement in 5:23, "the husband is the head of the wife" ἀνήρ ἐστιν κεφαλὴ τῆς γυναικός, will doubtless reflect the LXX emphasis in Gen 2:18-25, which implies subordination, as it does in 1 Corinthians 11. κεφαλή, "head", has already featured in Ephesians as a term indicating authority and superiority (1:22-23; 4:15-16). The woman is assumed not to be his equal in the LXX, but to be his βοηθός ("helper"), which, as we have shown, is understood in the context as reflecting inferiority in the chain of being. That makes the analogy with the unequal partnership of Christ and the church possible. The value system which subordinates women derives also from other sources here, not least, from the traditional household order.

The shift from τὰ ἑαυτῶν σώματα ("their own bodies") in 5:28 to τὴν ἑαυτοῦ σάρκα ("his own flesh") in 5:29 reflects the influence of Gen 2:24 in its use of σάρκα ("flesh"). The argument in 5:28 that to love one's wife is to love one's own body makes sense in the light of the Genesis account, where the sexual union (understood here as marital union) creates a single body and also restores the single body represented in the man, Adam.[58] In the LXX, the man in 2:24, as

---

[56] On the longer text, which picks up the references to flesh and bone in Gen 2:23, as a secondary expansion see the discussion in Thorsten Moritz, *A Profound Mystery: The Use of the Old Testament in Ephesians* ((SuppNovTest 85; Leiden: Brill, 1999) 117, n. 1 and Metzger, *Textual Commentary*, 541.

[57] For washing as part of the wedding ritual see Ezek 16:9. Ezek 16:8-14 stands behind the passage. See Andrew T. Lincoln, *Ephesians* (WBC 42; Dallas: Word, 1990) 375-76.

[58] J. P. Sampley, *"And the two shall become one flesh": A study of traditions in Ephesians 5:21-33* (SNTSMS 16; Cambridge: CUP, 1971) 57-58, points to the relationship between 5:33a, πλὴν καὶ ὑμεῖς οἱ καθ᾽ ἕνα, ἕκαστος τὴν ἑαυτοῦ γυναῖκα οὕτως ἀγαπάτω ὡς ἑαυτόν ("Each of you, however, should love his wife as himself") and Lev 19:18 LXX, ἀγαπήσεις τὸν πλησίον σου ὡς σεαυτόν ("you shall love your neighbor as yourself"), noting the use of πλησίον ("neighbor") for the beloved bride in the Song of

the ἄνθρωπος ("man") of 1:27 and as the ἄνθρωπος ("man") of 2:18, is restoring unity.

1 Cor 6:15-20 is useful background for understanding ὅτι μέλη ἐσμὲν τοῦ σώματος αὐτοῦ ("for we are members of his body") in 5:30. The focus of the latter is not on the diversity of parts of the body as in 1 Corinthians 12 but on us as bodies, persons, belonging to Christ, the objects of his love, as 5:25b-27 has explained, using marital imagery. A number of manuscripts contain the words, "of his flesh and bones" an allusion to Gen 2:23, but the balance favours seeing this as an addition.[59] Using Gen 2:24 the writer explains that this has been achieved through the equivalent of sexual union with Christ, a daring metaphor, but one already developed by Paul in 1 Cor 6:15-20. We are members of his body (μέλη ἐσμὲν τοῦ σώματος αὐτοῦ 5:30) by becoming "one flesh" with him (εἰς σάρκα μίαν 5:31).

The use of the word, "mystery", τὸ μυστήριον, may suggest that the author is conscious of the striking nature of the metaphor and of its existence in tradition and teaching as a way of explaining the relationship with Christ, but its primary context is the use elsewhere in Ephesians (1:9; 3:3; 4:9; 6:19) to describe the unfolding or revelation of God's purpose in Christ.[60] The emphasis on sexual union in Gen 2:24 conveyed by the loss of the pun, אִשָּׁה אִישׁ (ish-ishshah; man-woman), the translation of לְבָשָׂר אֶחָד by εἰς σάρκα μίαν ("one flesh"), and the focus on oneness from two-ness, may well lie behind the τὸ μυστήριον ("the mystery") here. The metaphorical use of sexual union to describe the divine human relationship occurs in many cultures and continues to do so. It is assumed in Jewish prophetic and wisdom literature. Later streams of Christian thought would elaborate the marital image so that conversion became a moment of sexual consummation in the spiritual bridal chamber (so Gos. Phil. 64; 70; 82; Gos.

Songs LXX (1:9,15; 2:2,10,13; 4:1,7; 5:2; 6:4) and points to a similar use of neighbor in later rabbinic discussions of marriage (30-31). Sampley argues that Lev 19:18 is also influencing 5:28-29a (32). The influence of Gen 2:24 is evident in 5:29a: Οὐδεὶς γάρ ποτε τὴν ἑαυτοῦ σάρκα ἐμίσησεν ("No one hates his own flesh"). He also points to the linking of Gen 2:24 and Lev 19:18 in Sir 13:15-16 (57-58). On this cf. Moritz, *Profound Mystery*, 121 n. 13. Even more extraordinary is *T. Naph.* 8:8-9 which creates an analogy between the two great commandments and the need sometimes to pray and sometimes to engage in sexual intercourse with one's wife. The implicit association of the latter with love of neighbor is remarkable.

[59] See the discussion in Lincoln, *Ephesians*, 351.

[60] So Lincoln, *Ephesians*, 380-83.

Thom. 22).[61] Paul uses Gen 2:24 LXX to explicate the relationship in 1
Corinthians 6.

To speak of LXX influence is to describe particular influences from these
LXX texts on the form that this speculation took within early Christianity. This
appears to be the case in Ephesians where it occurs in an expansion of the
household code found in Colossians. The expansion appears to reflect a tradition
of thought, which may well have been influenced by the LXX. The following
passages, which reflect Gen 1:27, may provide further evidence for such influence.

1 Timothy 2:11-15

11 Γυνὴ ἐν ἡσυχίᾳ μανθανέτω ἐν πάσῃ ὑποταγῇ· 12 διδάσκειν δὲ γυναικὶ οὐκ ἐπιτρέπω οὐδὲ αὐθεντεῖν ἀνδρός, ἀλλ᾽ εἶναι ἐν ἡσυχίᾳ. 13 Ἀδὰμ γὰρ πρῶτος ἐπλάσθη, εἶτα Εὕα. 14 καὶ Ἀδὰμ οὐκ ἠπατήθη, ἡ δὲ γυνὴ ἐξαπατηθεῖσα ἐν παραβάσει γέγονεν· 15 σωθήσεται δὲ διὰ τῆς τεκνογονίας, ἐὰν μείνωσιν ἐν πίστει καὶ ἀγάπῃ καὶ ἁγιασμῷ μετὰ σωφροσύνης·	11 Let a woman learn in silence with full submission. 12 I permit no woman to teach or to have authority over a man; she is to keep silent. 13 For Adam was formed first, then Eve; 14 and Adam was not deceived, but the woman was deceived and became a transgressor. 15 Yet she will be saved through childbearing, provided they continue in faith and love and holiness, with modesty.

This deuteropauline passage assumes a difference stance from the one we find in 1
Corinthians 11. It is concerned to silence women and restrict their authority,[62] but
it also uses Genesis 1-3. The assertion that Adam was first "formed" (ἐπλάσθη)
reflects the language of the LXX of Genesis 2. It goes beyond both the Hebrew
and the LXX in its interpretation of Genesis 3 when it contrasts Adam and Eve; in
doing so it reflects exegetical tradition (already Sir 25:24; see also Life of Adam
and Eve 18:1; Apoc Adam and Eve 14:2) which assumes Eve was sexually
seduced (ἐξαπατηθεῖσα "deceived/seduced"; similarly 2 Cor 11:2-3; cf. Gen 3:6 ,
esp. 3:13 LXX: ὁ ὄφις ἠπάτησέν με "the snake deceived/seduced me"). 2:15
interprets the curse of the woman in Genesis 3:16 in accordance with the LXX as
meaning that she will keep returning to her husband (but similarly in the Hebrew
which speaks of sexual desire for her husband) and becoming pregnant and so
giving birth.

---

[61] On these and related traditions see Lincoln, *Ephesians*, 382-383; Elaine H. Pagels,
"Adam and Eve, Christ and the Church," in *The New Testament and Gnosis*; ed. A. H. B.
Logan and A. J. M. Wedderburn (Edinburgh: T&T Clark, 1983) 146-75.

[62] See Watson, *Agape, Eros, Gender*, 73.

The words, σωθήσεται δὲ διὰ τῆς τεκνογονίας ("she shall be saved through childbearing") have evoked a range of explanations from being saved in some physical way in the process of childbearing to being saved as a result of Eve's descendent giving birth to the Messiah.[63] 2:15 is most naturally understood as an allusion to Gen 3:16. The context in 1 Timothy suggests that two elements of 3:16 have relevance: childbirth (διὰ τῆς τεκνογονίας "through childbearing"; cf. πληθύνων πληθυνῶ τὰς λύπας σου καὶ τὸν στεναγμόν σου ἐν λύπαις τέξῃ τέκνα καὶ πρὸς τὸν ἄνδρα σου ἡ ἀποστροφή σου "I will greatly increase your pangs in childbearing; in pain you shall bring forth children, yet your desire shall be for your husband" Gen 3:16) and security through submission to the husband as master (σωθήσεται; "she shall be saved" cf. καὶ αὐτός σου κυριεύσει "and he shall rule over you" Gen 3:16). Being saved probably refers neither to spiritual salvation in the abstract nor to some relief from pain during childbirth, but to being rescued from danger by being with a husband who cares for her and to whom she submits (the point of the context). The pain of childbirth, part of the curse, appears here as something through which she then finds security with a husband provided she then remains ἐν πίστει καὶ ἀγάπῃ καὶ ἁγιασμῷ μετὰ σωφροσύνης ("in faith and love and holiness, with modesty").

4. The Gospel of Thomas

While the Gospel of Thomas takes us beyond the New Testament writings, it is appropriate briefly to examine its sayings, both because, in the minds of some, they embody early traditions, and because they contain traditions which appear also to stand under the influence of Genesis 1-2 and may be related to traditions we find in Paul.

---

[63] See the discussion in George W. Knight III, *Commentary on the Pastoral Epistles* (NIGTC; Grand Rapids: Eerdmans, Carlisle: Paternoster, 1992) 144-48; Jürgen Roloff, *Der erste Brief an Timotheus* (EKKNT XV; Zurich: Benziger Verlag; Neukirchen-Vluyn: Neukirchener Verlag, 1988), 140-42, who aptly notes: "Die meisten vorliegenden Deutungsversuche verfolgen das Ziel, das Ärgernis dieser Aussage aus der Welt zu schaffen" (140-41). (Tr. Most of the available attempts at interpretation have as their aim to get rid of the offensiveness of the saying). He favours the view that σωθήσεται refers to spiritual salvation which is open to the woman despite her having to bear the curse of childbirth. Similarly T. Holtz, *Die Pastoralbriefe* (ThHK 13; Berlin: Evangelische Verlagsanstalt, 1980) 71.

One such saying is *Gos. Thom.* 22 which like Gal 3:28 incorporates an allusion to Gen 1:27, and appears to be attested independently in the Gospel of the Egyptians and in 2 Clement 12:2-6.[64]

> Jesus saw infants being suckled. He said to his disciples, "These infants being suckled are like those who enter the kingdom." They said to him, "If we then become children, shall we enter the kingdom?" Jesus said to them, "When you make the two one, and when you make the inside as the outside, and the outside as the inside, and the upper as the lower, and when you make the male and the female into a single one, so that the male is not male and the female not female, and you make eyes in place of an eye, and hand in place of a hand, and a foot in place of a foot, and an image (IKⲰN) in place of an image (IKⲰN), then you will enter [the kingdom]."[65] *Gos. Thom.* 22:1-4

> When Salome asked when what she had inquired about would be known, the Lord said, "When you have trampled on the garment of shame and when the two become one and the male with the female (is) neither male nor female." *Gospel of the Egyptians* (Clement *Strom.* 3.92).

> When the Lord himself was asked by someone when his kingdom would come, he said, "When the two shall be one, and the outside as the inside, and the male with the female neither male nor female." Now "the two are one" when we speak with one another in truth, and there is but one soul in two bodies without dissimulation. And by "the outside as the inside" he means this, that the inside is the soul, and the outside is the body. Therefore, just as your body is visible, so let your soul be apparent in your good works. And by "the male and the female neither male nor female" he means this, that when a brother sees a sister he should have no thought of her as female, nor she of him as male. When you do this, he says, the kingdom of my Father will come.[66] *2 Clem* 12:2-6.

---

[64] On this see, for instance, MacDonald, *There is no male and female*. See also A. Lindemann, *Die Clemensbriefe* (HNT 17; Die Apostolischen Väter 1; J. C. B. Mohr [Paul Siebeck]: Tübingen, 1992) 234-36; M. Fieger, *Das Thomasevangelium: Einleitung, Kommentar und Systematik* (NTAbh NF 22; Münster: Aschendorff, 1991) 98-101.

[65] The *Gos. Thom.* logia and the following citation from *Gos. Eg.* are cited according to the translation in *New Testament Apocrypha, Volume One: Gospels and Related Writings*, ed. W. Schneemelcher (2d ed., Cambridge: James Clarke; Louisville: Westminster/John Knox, 1991).

[66] Cited in the translation by Kirsopp Lake, *Apostolic Fathers I* (LCL 24; Cambridge, Mass.: Harvard Univ. Press, 1970).

The constant feature in these texts is the reference to male and female, probably under the influence of Gen 1:27, directly or indirectly, and the two becoming one, probably under the influence of Gen 2:24. They also assume a reading of Genesis 1-2 according to which the goal must be to return to a state of being where male and female as such no longer play a role. *Gos. Thom.* 22 points to suckling infants, on the assumption that they are asexual.[67] In *Gos. Thom.* 22 "and an image (IKⲱN) in place of an image (IKⲱN)," doubtless reflect the influence of Gen 1:27. See also *Gos. Thom.* 11: "On the day when you were one, you became two". It also recalls the language of Gen 1:26-27 in speaking of a restored image.[68] The *Gos. Eg.*, which *2 Clem* appears to be citing, speaks of the garment of shame, doubtless an allusion to the sense of shame in Genesis 3, and understood in relation to sexuality. The term appears also in *Gos. Thom.* 37:

> His disciples said; "On what day will you be revealed to us and on what day will we see you? Jesus said: When you unclothe yourselves and are not ashamed, and take your garments (and) lay them beneath your feet like the

---

[67] "Die Rückkehr zu einer ontologischen Einheit und die Ablehnung der Ehe und der Sexualität sind die Kerngedanken des zweiten Teils (Log 22b)" (Tr. The return to an ontological oneness and the rejection of marriage and sexuality are the central thoughts of the second part [Log 22b]) - so Fieger, *Thomasevangelium*, 101.

[68] Elaine H. Pagels, "Exegesis of Genesis 1 in the Gospels of Thomas and John," *JBL* 118 (1999) 477-96, demonstrates that Thomas can be read as beginning with sayings which reflect on Genesis 1 and portray a two-step understanding of Gen 1:27 according to which first the man was created and then the male and female, a view also present in Philo, Poimandres and later rabbinic exegetes (482). On the first 11 sayings she writes: "The central theme that connects the cluster of sayings here discussed is the disciple's hope of being restored from his present, divided existence back into the image of the original 'single one' - the unity with the primordial *anthropos* enjoyed in the 'place of light'" (482-483). The exchange with Salome whose address to Jesus is overtly sexual illustrates that this primordial existence is asexual. Jesus "rejects the divisive categories of sexual identity (cf. Gen 1:27b) and declares instead that 'I am he who is from the undivided' (ⲡⲉⲧϢⲎⲱ), that is, from the singular one of Gen 1:27a." (483). The pun made possible by the LXX translation of Gen 1:3 and its use of φῶς (φῶς or φῶς) made it possible to identify the primordial being as light (484) and to see it within (see Logia 77 and 50). "Thus the cluster of logia that interpret Genesis 1 directs those who seek access to God towards the divine image given in creation" (487). This is not a gnosticism seeking divine origin. "Instead, the disciple is to recover the form of the original creation κατ᾽ εἰκόνα θεοῦ" (488). "Such exegesis connects *eikon* of Gen 1:26-27 with the primordial light (or: light/*anthropos* of Gen 1:3), to show that the divine image implanted at creation enables humankind to find - by means of baptism - the way back to its origins in the mystery of the primordial creation." (488). Saying 37 is taken as referring to baptismal rite.

little children (and) trample on them, then [you will see] the Son of the living One, and you will not be afraid". [69]

Gos. Thom. 114 also reflects the oneness theme, but stands in some tension with the rest of the gospel and may be a secondary expansion: [70]

Simon Peter said to them: Let Mariham go out from among us, for women are not worthy of the life. Jesus said: Look, I will lead her, that I may make her male, in order that she too may become a living spirit resembling you males. For every woman who makes herself male will enter into the kingdom of heaven.

Logically, this should mean a return to what we have in Genesis 2: embodied human beings, "living spirits" (an allusion to Gen 2:7?), among whom sexual union of male and female is natural, and in which there is no sense of shame. Contrary to Genesis 3, however, it appears to assume that embodied nakedness will not bring shame because sexual passion will no longer exist. Similarly the references to the replacement of eye, hand and foot in *Gos. Thom.* 22, are probably to their sexual roles. The tradition will be related to the sayings in Mark 9:43-48 and Matthew 5:29-30, the latter related explicitly to sexuality, the former probably presupposing it. [71] It probably means either that they are replaced by asexual organs or are now constituted in a way that sexual functions cease.

---

[69] So Fieger, *Thomasevangelium*: "Sowohl Sexualität also auch Leiblichkeit sollen geniert werden" (131). (Tr. Both sexuality and physicality are to be negated).

[70] On the relationship between Thomas 22 and 114 see most recently Annti Marjanen, "Women disciples in the *Gospel of Thomas*," in *Thomas at the Crossroads: Essays on the Gospel of Thomas* ed. Risto Uro (*Studies of the New Testament and its World*; Edinburgh: T&T Clark, 1998) 89-106, esp. 94-104, where having reviewed the possible meanings of making a female male (physical, androgyny, attitudinal) she argues that 114 is in contradiction with 22, reflects different rhetorical technique from the rest of the collection, appears as an addition beyond 113 which forms an inclusio, and reflects late second century values, concluding that it is probably an addition made at that time. S. L. Davies, *The Gospel of Thomas and Christian Wisdom* (New York: Seabury, 1983) 152-53, 155, had also suggested 114 may be secondary.

[71] See also the discussion in Risto Uro, "Is *Thomas* an encratite gospel?" in *Thomas at the Crossroads: Essays on the Gospel of Thomas* ed. Risto Uro (Studies of the New Testament and its World; Edinburgh: T&T Clark, 1998) 140-62, here 149-56 who reviews interpretations of the theme of "becoming one" in Thomas (esp. 22, 23, 40). He notes the presence of the androgyny myth in Philo and later rabbinic literature, the eschatological focus of statements of "becoming one" in *Gos. Thom.* and Valentinian texts, the quasi-ethical interpretations of the saying about "becoming one" in *2 Clem* and Clement of Alexandria, citing *Gos. Eg.*, the possible influence of baptismal tradition. He concludes:

Is it any easier to read this into the LXX than into the Hebrew? Perhaps only in the sense that there is a greater suggestion of duality in the LXX by its use of Platonic categories and that Gen 2:24 LXX has put greater emphasis on oneness and on the link with Gen 1:27 and so made such speculation more possible. Such protology which looked to an asexual restoration will have developed diversely and under diverse influences, among which the LXX played a minor role, but its interpretation, probably a major one. Such other influences will have included ideals about sexuality as serving only procreation, cultic notions of the heavenly where sexual activity is out of place, as well as negative assessments of physicality.

"But even if the saying in *Gos. Thom.* 22.4-7 preserves a baptismal reunification formula, as is often suggested, it is still unclear whether one should suggest strictly encratite requirements for baptism, such as was the case in the teaching of Marcion (see e.g. Tertullian, *Adv. Marc.* 1.29), or whether the ethical consequences of the rite were understood more loosely as an encouragement to diminish the power of sexual desire (cf. 2 Clement)" (155). Probably the focus, as also in Philo's allusion to the myth, is on asexuality rather than bisexuality or androgyny (cf. 150 n. 36).

Conclusion

The studies in this book have attempted to identify possible influences in the area of sexuality which the LXX text might have had in the writings of Philo and, in particular, in the writings of the New Testament. Their aim has not been to imagine the intention of the translator(s), but to examine what they produced. Even to speak of a Septuagint text evokes problems. It was at least possible to approach three key passages or sets of passages which would have been influential in themselves, both in Hebrew and in Greek, because of their substance and to deal with the complex issues in relation to each.

The two passages which give an account of the decalogue, the "ten commandments", Exod 20:1-17 and Deut 5:6-21, may be assumed to have been widely known and used and so to have been influential. In comparison with the most commonly accepted Hebrew text they contain some distinctive features in relation to the broad area of sexuality which open the possibility of identifying distinctive influence where these are reflected in writings which have used the Septuagint. Those features include a difference in order. The prohibition of adultery is the first of the second half of the commandments, compared with the Hebrew text where the first is the prohibition of murder. This may be an innovation of the Septuagint perhaps reflecting greater concern with adultery and related matters. It could however have already been present in the Hebrew text used by the translators. This possibility must be considered because of the existence of a second century BCE liturgical text, the Nash Papyrus, which includes the decalogue in Hebrew with the same order of commandments as we find in the LXX version of Deuteronomy: adultery-murder-theft. The matter is further complicated by the fact that the Codex Alexandrinus manuscript of the LXX has the order of the majority Hebrew text: murder-adultery-theft. The latter, however, probably reflects an adaptation of the Septuagint to the Hebrew, a characteristic of later manuscripts.

In any event a Septuagint version did exist in the first century CE which put adultery first. We saw that Philo made a special point of the order as indicating that sexual sins, which he lumped together with adultery, were the first to be mentioned in the second table of the Law because they were most serious. Some other features of the Septuagint versions of the decalogues would have also contributed to this emphasis. Already the Hebrew version of Deuteronomy lists not coveting one's neighbor's wife as a separate prohibition before going on to prohibit coveting one's neighbor's house and chattels. Exodus lists "wife" among the chattels of the household. Both the Exodus and the Deuteronomy version now follow the order in the Hebrew of Deuteronomy. Coveting one's neighbor's wife gets a separate listing. The Greek makes it even more directly a statement on its own. In addition it uses the word ἐπιθυμέω ("to desire") to translate the word to covet in Exodus and the two words used in Deuteronomy. While the translation adequately captures the meaning of the Hebrew, there are some subtle differences. The context in the Hebrew texts, especially in Exodus, is greed, the desire to possess as property. With the prohibition now standing on its own, it would have been easier to read the word in terms not just of greed to possess, but of sexual lust. The Hebrew text of Deuteronomy may already be tending in this direction, since one can read this prohibition in close association with the prohibition of adultery and the prohibition of coveting in close association with theft. In hearing the Greek version, however, the listener might easily have brought to the word ἐπιθυμέω ("to desire") the associations which it has with passions and sexual desire, so that it would be heard as directly addressing sexual passion. Negative depictions of sexual passion had become a commonplace in some circles where popular philosophies of life, influenced above all by Stoic thought, warned against the grave dangers of human passion and enjoined strict self control, even to the extent of advising that sexual intercourse was to serve procreation only and anything beyond that, whether outside or inside marriage, was depraved. We found such thought in Philo. The Septuagint of the decalogue served his expositions well.

No New Testament writer makes a special point of the prominence given adultery in the order of the commandments. The listing of the commandments in the anecdote of Jesus' meeting with a rich man in Mark reflects the Hebrew order of Deuteronomy (at least according to the strongest manuscript evidence, while the text in Codex Alexandrinus at this point reflects the Greek order), as does Matthew's version. This may mean they were using a Greek text with that order or it may mean they are preserving a tradition which reflects influence from the Hebrew order. Luke, on the other hand, appears influenced by the Septuagint order in Deuteronomy. This order is more evident in lists, such as we find in Mark 7:21-22 (Exodus LXX order), Romans 13:9-14 and behind James (both following the

Deuteronomy LXX order). The order is probably more than simply a matter of sequence, but reflects an emphasis (already embodied in the Septuagint text) on the gravity of sexual sins, a matter consistently to the fore among issues which Jews faced at the interface with the Hellenistic culture of the period. Romans 1 illustrates the way sexual sin becomes paradigmatic of all sin for Paul and Jews whom he is rhetorically courting in confronting the pagan world.

Neither Philo nor any New Testament writer draws attention to the prohibition of desiring one's neighbor's wife as a separate entity. Perhaps this simply reflects their lack of interest in the subtle changes of translation and transposition which interest us. We do, however, find allusions to the Septuagint language used for "covet" and its range of meaning, especially in relation to sexual lust. Sexual connotations are present in both contexts where Paul cites the prohibition (Rom 7:7; 13:9). An allusion is likely in Matthew's saying about the lusting eye and adultery in 5:28. Desire is frequently interpreted in sexual terms (like the English word, "lust") in Paul (Rom 7:7-8; 13:14; Gal 5:16-17,24; 1 Thess 4:3-6; and beyond Paul: Col 3:5; Eph 2:3; 4:22; Tit 2:12; 3:3; 2 Tim 2:22; 3:6; Jas 1:14-15; 4:1-4; 1 John 2:15-17 and possible 1 Pet 1:14; 2:11; 4:2-3).

Overall, given the prominence of adultery, the separate emphasis on desiring another's wife and the sexual connotations of the word used to translate that desire, we can assume that people hearing the Greek version of the decalogue might have received the impression that sexual sin and sexual desire were very dangerous. This is not to suggest that such seriousness would not have been evoked by the Hebrew text. Writers in Hebrew during the Hellenistic period also see fit to emphasise its menace. Rather the form and substance of the Septuagint version of the decalogues opened the possibility that these would be used as a particular vehicle for addressing sexual immorality and would influence such discourse. While it is reasonable to speculate this might have been so - which is not inappropriate given the paucity of what has survived - we are able to go further and point to some evidence. Superficially it is most solid in the case of Philo's exploitation of the prominence of adultery as first of the second table of the Law. At a broader and more significant level it is to be found where moral concerns reflect a particular reading of the prohibition of desiring another's wife. Here one cannot necessarily speak of direct influence, but at least of influence along with other factors which include sexual connotations of the word for "desire" and perceptions of the dangers of sexual immorality latent in non Jewish culture, an anxiety which may have already played a role in the reordering of the text, itself.

The creation stories are also key texts. Here, too, I sought to identify distinctive elements and the way they might influence understandings of sexuality in relation to the text. There were many minor differences, some of which had a cumulative effect. One key feature is the difficulty the translators had in dealing with puns and wordplays in the Hebrew text. This is so with Adam, which in the

Hebrew text (אָדָם *adam*) means a human being (or humankind generally; "earthling") and thence becomes also a proper name and is derived according to the Hebrew account from אֲדָמָה *adamah*, the ground or "earth". The Septuagint translator is aware that Adam is a name given to the human species (so: 5:2) and uses the generic Greek word, ἄνθρωπος ("man/human"), to translate Adam, but does not attempt to reproduce the link with *adamah*. The sense of the "Adam" as "earthling" is thus lost and without it, it is much easier for the hearer, familiar with the flow of the story to hear ἄνθρωπος ("man/human") as a reference to the male, Adam.

It is almost to be expected that the translator would treat Genesis 1-2 as a whole. We see minor indications of this in the smoothing of the transition between the two accounts of creation. Genesis 2 is now an account of how God formed the creation which he "began" to create in Genesis 1. By adding "began" to 2:4 the translator effects a neat bracket with "in the beginning" of Gen 1:1, but also makes the move into the so-called second account easier. Little words like ἔτι ("yet"; 2:9,19) allow us to imagine that the created plants had not yet appeared and the same we must assume for the animals. All of this lent itself to being interpreted according to Platonic models of thought so that Genesis 1 depicts either the creation of ideas or the creation of each genus, after which the second account describes the concretisation.

The closer integration between the two is also apparent in the creation of woman from the man in 2:18-25. The language more closely echoes 1:26-27 with the result that the hearer can relate the account of the creation of man in the image and likeness of God to the formation of woman in the likeness of man. The linkage is evident in the Septuagint's repetition of ποιήσωμεν ("let us make") from 1:26 (Hebrew: נַעֲשֶׂה) in 2:18 instead of the singular, אֶעֱשֶׂה ("I shall make"); in the words, ὅμοιος αὐτῷ ("like, or in the likeness of, him") in 2:20 instead of using the same words as in 2:18, as does the Hebrew, meaning something similar (κατ' αὐτόν; כְּנֶגְדּוֹ "according to him") but without the verbal allusion to "likeness" in 1:26 (καθ' ὁμοίωσιν). Even the use of ἄνθρωπος ("man/human") in 2:24 where one might have expected "male, man" (the usual translation of the Hebrew, אִישׁ) appears to reflect the influence of 1:26-27. The overall effect of this linkage is to see the two events as in some way analogous and connected. As man is the image and likeness of God, so woman is in the likeness of man. By implication as man seeks oneness with God, so woman seeks oneness with man. A hierarchy appears to be assumed; or at least, it can be heard in this way. Even the word, "helper", which in the Hebrew (עֵזֶר) is not a term for subservience and in the Septuagint (βοηθός) is also mainly used of God as helper, could be heard as indicating an inferior stance, as we find, for instance, in Philo.

The passage is also important for its word plays. In 2:23 the naming of woman, אִשָּׁה (*ishshah*), plays on the word for man, אִישׁ (*ish*). English can approximate the word play by using "woman" and "man", but the Septuagint does not and cannot. Where in Hebrew the focus falls on common substance, emphasised in the word play, and the appropriateness of the oneness of coming together and so creating new kin, the Greek inevitably places the focus on two coming together as one. The context still includes the background of their commonality, but the focus shifts from commonality and kinship to two-ness and the coming together of the two as one flesh. The Septuagint has, in addition to the .standard Hebrew text, the words, "the two", although it may have used a Hebrew text which included them. This invites reflection perhaps more directly on the coming together as restoring an original unity. Further, the use of the word, σάρξ, for "flesh", opens possibilities for the hearer of seeing this act primarily in terms of sexual union, and less as formation of new "flesh" as kind, ie. flesh and blood. The use of the Greek word προσκολλάω ("join to") in the passive deponent form also opened the possibility that people would hear the text as indicating a joining that God initiates. This is certainly the case in the divorce anecdote in the gospels but certainly not the case in Paul's use of the same text in 1 Corinthians 6. In both instances the Genesis text is being heard as having strongly sexual overtones, probably because of the use of the word σάρξ, whereas, though sexual union is certainly implied in the Hebrew, the focus is more on creation of new flesh and blood, kin.

The account of the snake's encounter with Eve includes language which opened the possibility that the scene took on sexual overtones. When Eve reports that the snake deceived her, she used the word, ἠπάτησεν, which could also mean seduce, in contrast to the Hebrew, הִשִּׁיאַנִי, which means "tricked me". Paul picks up the sense of the Greek word in a sexual sense in 2 Cor 11:3 and may be thinking similarly in Romans 7. The Septuagint's apparent alteration of the appeal of the tree and its fruit from being something which would bring wisdom (as the Hebrew puts it) to something which was attractive to the eyes, beautiful (Gen 3:6), may reflect what was a common concern about seduction through the eyes, often with sexual overtones.

The account of the curses is particularly interesting. The woman is have increased pain in childbearing (3:16). In this both the Hebrew and the Septuagint agree. The Hebrew then speaks of her having desire (וְאֶל־אִישֵׁךְ תְּשׁוּקָתֵךְ) for her husband and his ruling over her. This is doubtless sexual. By contrast, the Septuagint speaks of her *returning* (ἡ ἀποστροφή σου) to her husband and his ruling over her. Though not explicitly sexual, the context suggests that this is meant. She will keep going back to her husband and getting pregnant. The word used for returning is the same as used for the man, who will *return* (ἀποστρέψαι) to the earth from which he was taken. This produces in the Septuagint a closer analogy between what happens to the woman and what happens to the man. He returns to his origin, the earth, and will work for it amid great pains; she will return to the man and will toil for him with great pains (in childbearing). It is a neater symmetry. The Septuagint enhances it by the bracket created between "the earth" in 2:7 (γῆ) and 3:19 (γῆ; where Hebrew has עָפָר "dust").

Thus in the Septuagint account we find two patterns: man is formed from the earth; woman is formed from the man. Cursed, woman keeps returning sexually and in subservience to the man and man keeps returning in toil and ultimately death to the earth. At the same time, man has also been created in the likeness of God and woman has been created in the likeness of man. I suspect that many would draw from the text the implication: so man should seek oneness in obedience to God and woman should seek oneness in obedience to man. That is not, however, said. 2:24 even speaks of the man leaving his father and mother and joining himself to his wife. One might want to read from this a contradiction of the normal pattern according to which the woman leaves her parents' house and joins the man in his. But such does not appear to have been the common understanding. The focus is the changed loyalties of the man from his parents to the woman, not his change of location. Nevertheless, even in the Septuagint text, with its implied chain of being: God-man-woman, the assumption is clearly that the relationship so established does not deny all rights to the woman.

The hearer of 2:18-25 who knows the stories to follow would not have put it aside as now superseded by 3:16. Rather the two will have been "thought together". The subservience implied in 3:16 would have informed the understanding of the relationship in 2:18-25. The intervening events if seen as seduction might then underline the need for the rule of which 3:16 speaks. This would at least have cohered well with the widespread assumption that women were a danger and needed to be controlled, especially because they were not able to control their sexuality. Though not at all the focus in either the Hebrew or the Greek text, a connexion between sexual danger and nakedness could then be read into the garden scene. From the inappropriateness of nakedness in the presence of deity (such as in the temple), one could move to the inappropriateness of sexuality in the presence of God to the inappropriateness of sexuality absolutely.

Part of our discussion of Philo focused on how he appears to have understood the relation between the two creation accounts, reaching the conclusion that, in effect, he sees three aspects: the creation of the ideas, the creation of the genera and the creation of the species. He understands the mind of the man as being the image of God, but the body, formed from the ground as being of a lower order. The man after the image of God seeks union with God. We also noted that while he appears to have been familiar with the myth of androgyny, it is not how he interprets Gen 1:27, which he takes as a description of the species. Philo clearly reads 2:18-25 as indicating subordination and allegorises woman as the representation of passions, dangers to the mind, although he can also describe them as "helpers" (clearly read as subordinate), if they are held in check. Women appear to be flawed, the result of God's imperfect co-workers to whom the text alludes when it has God say: "Let us make" in relation to the woman. Philo does not appear to differentiate 2:18-25 from 3:16. It was not the intervening events which ruined women, but their flawed nature from the beginning.

Our consideration of the potential influence of Genesis 1-3 on the New Testament writers was postponed until after we looked at Deuteronomy, because the Genesis and Deuteronomy texts appear together in the divorce pericope, Mark 10:2-9 and Matt 19:3-9, and are therefore best considered together. Deut 24:1-4 in the Septuagint, as in the Hebrew, is one long sentence, setting out a hypothetical situation in which then to declare remarriage of one's former wife an abomination. In both the Hebrew and the Septuagint it would have been possible to isolate elements of the description and treat them as declarations in their own right. This happened in particular in relation to the statement that the first husband wrote a bill of divorce and gave it to his wife, the only reference to divorce in the laws of the Pentateuch, and to the statement about the grounds for the divorce. The Septuagint translation of the grounds assumed to justify the divorce in the hypothetical case remains close to the Hebrew and retains a similar ambiguity. It is difficult to identify particular nuances distinctive to the Septuagint text. The latter uses the same word for describing the defilement of the woman and the defilement of the land, whereas the Hebrew speaks of sinning against the land. If anything, the focus of the Septuagint may be more on ritual defilement than on the moral outrage at greed which may have originally informed the Hebrew.

Philo's exposition assumes the offence is adultery on the part of the woman, and that she thereby contravened and treated with disrespect traditional laws. He suppresses the second divorce, instead speaking of her as widowed and, while forbidding remarriage to the first husband, saying nothing about ritual defilement. Rather the prohibition is justified according to Philo because remarriage would show the man guilty of adultery and acting as a panderer. Here Philo reads Deuteronomy 24 in the light of the Lex Julia which also forbids such remarriage. Perhaps the open ended expression, ἄσχημον πρᾶγμα ("something shameful"), helped the move away from the focus on ritual defilement, but the same could have been true of the Hebrew text, which seems less focussed on ritual defilement.

In Mark 10:2-9 we find an allusion to Deut 24:1-4 and a citation together of Gen 1:27 and 2:24. The latter reflects tell-tale features of the Septuagint form: the use of ἄνθρωπος ("man/human being") and the inclusion of the words, "the two", not present in the Hebrew. In addition we find the deponent passive, προσκολληθήσεται ("be joined to"). The latter enables a link to Jesus' aphorism, "What God has yoked, let no one separate". It may also have at least contributed to the link between Gen 2:24 and Gen 1:27, which speaks of God's action in creation.

Here, too, in 2:24 we are to hear God's action. For in contrast to Paul in 1 Cor 6:16, Mark and probably Mark's tradition understands the passive as indicative that the joining is effected by God. The Septuagint makes this possible. But both Mark and Paul in 1 Cor 6:16 understand becoming one flesh as including a strong sexual reference, in accordance with the use of σάρξ, rather than as emphasising kinship.

The Septuagint may well therefore have influenced the text as we have it, although there is a note of caution. The notion of God's action in joining the man and the woman is already present in Jesus' aphorism, so is scarcely derived from the LXX use of προσκολληθήσεται ("be joined to"). In addition the application of Gen 1:27 to marriage already occurs in CD 4, which assumes that marriage as the joining of the male and female is to be seen as in some way an act of God, not to be subverted. The claim that the Markan anecdote depends on the Septuagint because of its use of the reference in Deut 24:2 as an instruction cannot really be maintained, because the Hebrew of Deut 24:2 could be read in isolation in a similar way. At most one could say that presence of words like προσκολληθήσεται ("be joined to") and σάρξ ("flesh") gave focus to the coming together as something God effected, including the coming together in sexual union, which is represented as something positive.

Matthew's version of the story takes over the same biblical texts in slightly variant form. Both here in 19:9 and in 5:31, where Matthew refers to again to Deut 24:1-4, Matthew mentions an exceptional ground for divorce, but in neither text is it a citation of the Septuagint, ἀσχημον πρᾶγμα ("something shameful"). There is nothing which might suggest particular influence from the Septuagint in his interpretation of Deuteronomy 24.

While Deut 24:1-4 does not appear elsewhere in the New Testament, relevant passages from Genesis 1-3 do. We have already noted Paul's use of Gen 2:24 in 1 Cor 6:16-17. The (possibly) distinctive use of "the two" is present; like Matthew, Paul has, perhaps, a text which contains the simple verb, κολληθήσεται ("shall be joined to") followed by the dative (thus his κολλώμενος, "the one joining/joining himself to") rather than the compound form προσκολληθήσεται ("shall be joined to"); and he cites the concluding words: ἔσονται γάρ, φησίν, οἱ δύο εἰς σάρκα μίαν ("For it is said, *The two shall be one flesh*"). Paul understands this as a sexual reference, an emphasis strongly present in the LXX text. Paul's reading implies, however, much more than a single physical act. He is speaking in the context of rival allegiances and systems of power, so that while, unlike in Mark's anecdote, he does not see the act as a mode of God's creation of something permanent, he does nevertheless consider it in similar terms, as creating a oneness capable of competing with a believer's oneness with Christ. This extrapolation from the Septuagint text will have been informed by values beyond the text, but the text lent itself to reflection on oneness which reached far beyond the sexual realm.

Gal 3:28 alludes directly to Gen 1:27 (or 5:2) when it lists "male and female" (οὐκ ἔνι ἄρσεν καὶ θῆλυ) beside other pairs: "neither Jew nor Greek; slave nor free" (οὐκ ἔνι Ἰουδαῖος οὐδὲ Ἕλλην, οὐκ ἔνι δοῦλος οὐδὲ ἐλεύθερος) and preserves the different form of construction of using "and". The reference to their being "one" (πάντες γὰρ ὑμεῖς εἷς; "for you are all one") may allude to Gen 2:24. Beyond that it is difficult to say anything about a distinctive influence from the LXX on this important text. The tradition of Gal 3:28 reappears in 1 Cor 12:13 and Col 3:11 without the male-female reference, but it probably informs the discussion in 1 Corinthians 7. It is speculative to wonder if a particular emphasis of the LXX is also reflected from these texts in 1 Corinthians 7. One might at most point to the presence of Gen 2:24 in the previous chapter and its focus on sexual intercourse in its LXX form as background to Paul's positive affirmation of sexual intercourse in marriage in 1 Corinthians 7, even if not his preferred option and not the ultimate state for the believer.

Remaining with Paul, but moving to other texts in Genesis 1-3 LXX, we noted the influence of the Septuagint's assumption of a hierarchy of being in Paul's discussion in 1 Corinthians 11. While there has been much argument about the meaning of κεφαλή ("head"; "source"?), the context does assume a relationship which is not reciprocal, as though the one might be the head of the other, and which, much like Gen 2:18-25 understands woman's relation to God on the analogy of man's relation to God (or Christ). Within that framework Paul is not seeking to diminish women's roles, but to affirm them. In doing so, however, his understanding is informed by Genesis 1-2 LXX, where the formation of woman is set more closely in analogy to the creation of man. On the one hand, that explains the conceptuality of hierarchy; on the other hand, Paul can also use the argument from origin at two levels, so that while according to Genesis 2 woman comes from man, in natural birth man comes from woman (11:12).

In 2 Cor 11:2-3 Paul takes up the account of Eve's temptation by the snake. The LXX of Gen 3:13 uses ἠπάτησεν, which, unlike the Hebrew it translates, הִשִּׁיאַנִי, can mean "seduced" as well as "deceived". Paul clearly understand it in the former sense. This is probably how he understands the allusion to the same verse in Rom 7. We are left to imagine the degree to which Paul would have seen a sexual component to the temptation story.

Beyond Paul we find Gen 2:24 reappearing in Ephesians 5. The passage clearly alludes to the LXX version as the tell-tale features ἄνθρωπος ("man/human") and προσκολληθήσεται ("be joined to") indicate. The subordination of women implicit in Genesis 2:18-25 LXX finds expression in the passage and coheres well with the household values which underlie the passage. Gen 2:24's use of σάρξ ("flesh") already informs 5:29 which identifies woman as the man's own flesh. The metaphor of sexual union with Christ is daring, although already countenanced by Paul in 1 Cor 6:15-20. It warrants the description, mystery, for that alone although the term has its broader context in depicting the plan and purpose of God.

In contrast to 1 Cor 11 where Paul is concerned for appropriate order in which women have their place including the performance of roles such as praying and prophesying, 1 Tim 2:11-15 seeks to silence them and restrict their authority. It, too, draws on the subordination implicit in the LXX, but goes beyond both the Hebrew and Greek accounts by asserting the tradition that it was not Adam who was deceived, but Eve. Like 2 Cor 11:2-3 it assumes that Eve was sexually seduced. It also draws on the LXX version of Gen 3:16 which portrays the woman as constantly returning to her husband, becoming pregnant, and giving birth as her cursed lot. She is condemned to being dependent on her husband.

A further allusion to Gen 1:27 and possibly Gen 2:24 may be present in the logion found in Gos. Eg., 2 Clem. 12:2-6 and Gos. Thom. 22:1-4 (which also alludes to "image", Gen 1:27). It assumes asexuality as the ideal and appears to link this to restoration of a primal state in which male and female are merged into one. It is possible that the development of such speculation was fostered more through the LXX which links 2:18-25 and 1:27 more closely together, but many other factors will have been at work.

This study has examined three important sets of texts, which are likely to have been well known and influential. This is particularly so of the decalogue and the creation stories. In each instance we sought to identify distinctive features of the Septuagint in relation to matters pertaining broadly to sexuality. The Septuagint accounts will have been influential even when they were not distinctive or different in substance from the Hebrew. They will certainly have informed Paul's understanding of human beings as male and female, of marriage, and of appropriate sexual behaviours. We began with the question whether despite this there were distinctive aspects of the Septuagint text in the area of sexuality to which we might attribute influence. This was not the same as saying what the LXX translators intended, nor was it the same as trying to determine a single meaning or interpretation which belonged to the text.

In one sense our discussion of those texts opened up a range of possibilities. This was especially the case with the creation stories. This range of possible interpretations created by the Septuagint was far more extensive than what we were able to trace in the extant writings of Philo and of the New Testament. We have limited the discussion in this study to only this sample of writings. Even then it has been possible to make a case that some distinctive elements of the Septuagint did contribute to what Paul and some New Testament writers wrote. In relation to the decalogue there is sufficient evidence to say that the greater prominence given to adultery (and sins of sexual lust) had an impact. In the case of the Genesis stories the passages do appear to have generated an understanding of the way male and female relate to each other and to God and to have done so in a way that portrayed women as subordinate and in some sense problematic because of their sexuality. This was not novel, but reflected widespread assumptions of the time which the text then had the effect of reinforcing.

The fact that such influence is evident even in the relatively few relevant texts we have at our disposal allows the speculation that such influence was relatively widespread where the LXX was read and heard. Beyond speculation our findings invite further study in two directions: traces of influence in other writings of the period in Hellenistic Judaism, but also in literature of the early centuries of Christianity where the LXX assumed great authority. This study sees itself as contributing one piece to that broader picture of the impact of the LXX and at the same time casting light on aspects of the understanding of sexuality.

In very broad terms the encounter between the stream of the Jewish tradition and the diverse streams of Hellenistic cultures will have been very important for the development of attitudes towards sexuality. Some attitudes are deeply engrained in cultural assumptions which are very often ancient and unquestioned. Others are simply so central to life, relationships and society, that they are the focus of ancient stories and myths and of laws. The encounter between Judaism and Hellenism frequently saw a linkage between attacks on pagan idolatry and attacks on pagan sexual practices. At the same time self-critical voices within the non Jewish world attracted Jewish moral teachers. The much older interchange of "international" wisdom found expression in the Hellenistic period in "baptizing" the "wisdom of Greece" in many areas. Some of this influence is probably to be seen already in the Septuagint, not least in the creation narratives, as we have seen. It becomes influential later in attitudes to sexual intercourse which want to limit it to procreation and frown on its passion (such as we find in Philo, Josephus and the Testaments of the Twelve Patriarchs).

Christianity emerged from this conflux of traditions. Where sexuality did not form an element of conflict, attitudes and assumptions would continue unchanged and unchallenged. But occasionally one sees the turbulence where the streams meet and values collide. The Septuagint and the way it was able to be read certainly belonged to that flow beside much else which had already mingled with popular Hellenistic assumptions. There were streams which located sexuality within a hierarchical order. There were others which saw it is an interim phenomenon to be succeeded by an age in which they neither marry nor are given in marriage. Control of passions, even denial of passions, met affirmations of creation; cultic and ritual assumptions of impurity met trends towards making purity of moral attitude and behaviour paramount. Notions of flawed creation met assertions of creation's goodness. The dangers of women and their allegedly uncontrollable sexuality met invitations to mutual respect and responsibility. The

Septuagint was but one factor in the stream, but it flowed strongly. The samples we have taken indicate something of that. They have also shown the potential influence at an important time when people were affirming and shaping attitudes and values which have continued their influence into modern times.

Appendices

Appendix A1: The Decalogue

Exod 20:1-17 (LXX)	Exod 20:1-17 (BHS)	Deut 5:6-21 (BHS)	Deut 5:6-21 (LXX)
1 καὶ ἐλάλησεν κύριος πάντας τοὺς λόγους τούτους λέγων	1 וַיְדַבֵּר אֱלֹהִים אֵת כָּל־הַדְּבָרִים הָאֵלֶּה לֵאמֹר׃ ס		
2 ἐγώ εἰμι κύριος ὁ θεός σου, ὅστις ἐξήγαγόν σε ἐκ γῆς Αἰγύπτου, ἐξ οἴκου δουλείας.	2 אָנֹכִי יְהוָה אֱלֹהֶיךָ אֲשֶׁר הוֹצֵאתִיךָ מֵאֶרֶץ מִצְרַיִם מִבֵּית עֲבָדִים	10	6 ἐγώ κύριος ὁ θεός σου ὁ ἐξαγαγών σε ἐκ γῆς Αἰγύπτου, ἐξ οἴκου δουλείας.
3 οὐκ ἔσονταί σοι θεοὶ ἕτεροι πλὴν ἐμοῦ.	3 לֹא יִהְיֶה־לְךָ אֱלֹהִים אֲחֵרִים עַל־פָּנָיַ	אָנֹכִי יְהוָה אֱלֹהֶיךָ אֲשֶׁר הוֹצֵאתִיךָ מֵאֶרֶץ מִצְרַיִם מִבֵּית עֲבָדִים	7 οὐκ ἔσονταί σοι θεοὶ ἕτεροι πρὸ προσώπου μου.
4 οὐ ποιήσεις σεαυτῷ εἴδωλον οὐδὲ παντὸς ὁμοίωμα, ὅσα ἐν τῷ οὐρανῷ ἄνω καὶ ὅσα ἐν τῇ γῇ κάτω καὶ ὅσα ἐν τοῖς ὕδασιν ὑποκάτω τῆς γῆς.	4 לֹא יִהְיֶה־לְךָ אֱלֹהִים אֲחֵרִים עַל־פָּנָיַ	6 לֹא יִהְיֶה־לְךָ אֱלֹהִים אֲחֵרִים עַל־פָּנָיַ	8 οὐ ποιήσεις σεαυτῷ γλυπτὸν οὐδὲ παντὸς ὁμοίωμα, ὅσα ἐν τῷ οὐρανῷ ἄνω καὶ ὅσα ἐν τῇ γῇ κάτω καὶ ὅσα ἐν τοῖς ὕδασιν ὑποκάτω τῆς γῆς.
5 οὐ προσκυνήσεις αὐτοῖς οὐδὲ μὴ λατρεύσῃς αὐτοῖς· ἐγὼ γάρ εἰμι κύριος ὁ θεός σου, θεὸς ζηλωτὴς ἀποδιδοὺς ἁμαρτίας πατέρων ἐπὶ τέκνα ἕως τρίτης καὶ τετάρτης γενεᾶς τοῖς μισοῦσίν με,	5	7	9 οὐ προσκυνήσεις αὐτοῖς οὐδὲ μὴ λατρεύσῃς αὐτοῖς, ὅτι ἐγώ εἰμι κύριος ὁ θεός σου, θεὸς ζηλωτὴς ἀποδιδοὺς ἁμαρτίας πατέρων ἐπὶ τέκνα ἐπὶ τρίτην καὶ τετάρτην γενεᾶν τοῖς μισοῦσίν με,
6 καὶ ποιῶν ἔλεος εἰς χιλιάδας τοῖς ἀγαπῶσίν με καὶ τοῖς φυλάσσουσιν τὰ προστάγματά μοι.	6	8	10 καὶ ποιῶν ἔλεος εἰς χιλιάδας τοῖς ἀγαπῶσίν με καὶ τοῖς φυλάσσουσιν τὰ προστάγματά μου..
	9	9	

(Deuteronomy 5:11–15)

Greek (LXX)

11 οὐ λήμψη τὸ ὄνομα κυρίου τοῦ θεοῦ σου ἐπὶ ματαίῳ· οὐ γὰρ μὴ καθαρίσῃ κύριος τὸν λαμβάνοντα τὸ ὄνομα αὐτοῦ ἐπὶ ματαίῳ.

12 φύλαξαι τὴν ἡμέραν τῶν σαββάτων ἁγιάζειν αὐτήν, ὃν τρόπον ἐνετείλατό σοι κύριος ὁ θεός σου.

13 ἓξ ἡμέρας ἐργᾷ καὶ ποιήσεις πάντα τὰ ἔργα σου·

14 τῇ δὲ ἡμέρᾳ τῇ ἑβδόμῃ σάββατα κυρίῳ τῷ θεῷ σου· οὐ ποιήσεις ἐν αὐτῇ πᾶν ἔργον, σὺ καὶ οἱ υἱοί σου καὶ ἡ θυγάτηρ σου, ὁ παῖς σου καὶ ἡ παιδίσκη σου, ὁ βοῦς σου καὶ τὸ ὑποζύγιόν σου καὶ πᾶν κτῆνός σου καὶ ὁ προσήλυτος ὁ ἐντὸς τῶν πυλῶν σου, ἵνα ἀναπαύσηται ὁ παῖς σου καὶ ἡ παιδίσκη σου ὥσπερ καὶ σύ·

15 καὶ μνησθήσῃ ὅτι οἰκέτης ἦσθα ἐν γῇ Αἰγύπτῳ καὶ

Hebrew

11 לֹא תִשָּׂא אֶת־שֵׁם־יְהוָה אֱלֹהֶיךָ לַשָּׁוְא כִּי לֹא יְנַקֶּה יְהוָה אֵת אֲשֶׁר־יִשָּׂא אֶת־שְׁמוֹ לַשָּׁוְא׃

12 שָׁמוֹר אֶת־יוֹם הַשַּׁבָּת לְקַדְּשׁוֹ כַּאֲשֶׁר צִוְּךָ יְהוָה אֱלֹהֶיךָ׃

13 שֵׁשֶׁת יָמִים תַּעֲבֹד וְעָשִׂיתָ כָּל־מְלַאכְתֶּךָ׃

14 וְיוֹם הַשְּׁבִיעִי שַׁבָּת לַיהוָה אֱלֹהֶיךָ

(Exodus 20:7–11)

Greek (LXX)

7 οὐ λήμψη τὸ ὄνομα κυρίου τοῦ θεοῦ σου ἐπὶ ματαίῳ· οὐ γὰρ μὴ καθαρίσῃ κύριος τὸν λαμβάνοντα τὸ ὄνομα αὐτοῦ ἐπὶ ματαίῳ.

8 μνήσθητι τὴν ἡμέραν τῶν σαββάτων ἁγιάζειν αὐτήν.

9 ἓξ ἡμέρας ἐργᾷ καὶ ποιήσεις πάντα τὰ ἔργα σου·

10 τῇ δὲ ἡμέρᾳ τῇ ἑβδόμῃ σάββατα κυρίῳ τῷ θεῷ σου· οὐ ποιήσεις ἐν αὐτῇ πᾶν ἔργον, σὺ καὶ ὁ υἱός σου καὶ ἡ θυγάτηρ σου, ὁ παῖς σου καὶ ἡ παιδίσκη σου, ὁ βοῦς σου καὶ τὸ ὑποζύγιόν σου καὶ πᾶν κτῆνός σου καὶ ὁ προσήλυτος ὁ παροικῶν ἐν σοί.

11 ἐν γὰρ ἓξ ἡμέραις ἐποίησεν κύριος τὸν οὐρανὸν καὶ τὴν γῆν καὶ τὴν θάλασσαν καὶ πάντα τὰ ἐν αὐτοῖς, καὶ

Hebrew

7 לֹא תִשָּׂא אֶת־שֵׁם־יְהוָה אֱלֹהֶיךָ לַשָּׁוְא כִּי לֹא יְנַקֶּה יְהוָה אֵת אֲשֶׁר־יִשָּׂא אֶת־שְׁמוֹ לַשָּׁוְא׃

8 זָכוֹר אֶת־יוֹם הַשַּׁבָּת לְקַדְּשׁוֹ׃

9 שֵׁשֶׁת יָמִים תַּעֲבֹד וְעָשִׂיתָ כָּל־מְלַאכְתֶּךָ׃

10 וְיוֹם הַשְּׁבִיעִי שַׁבָּת לַיהוָה אֱלֹהֶיךָ

11 כִּי שֵׁשֶׁת־יָמִים עָשָׂה יְהוָה אֶת־הַשָּׁמַיִם וְאֶת־הָאָרֶץ

(Hebrew – Exodus)	Greek (Exodus)	(Hebrew – Deuteronomy)	Greek (Deuteronomy)
שבת... ויקדשהו׃	κατέπαυσεν τῇ ἡμέρᾳ τῇ ἑβδόμῃ· διὰ τοῦτο εὐλόγησεν κύριος τὴν ἡμέραν τὴν ἑβδόμην καὶ ἡγίασεν αὐτήν.	שמור את־יום השבת לקדשו כאשר צוך יהוה אלהיך׃ ס	ἐξήγαγέν σε κύριος ὁ θεός σου ἐκεῖθεν ἐν χειρὶ κραταιᾷ καὶ ἐν βραχίονι ὑψηλῷ, διὰ τοῦτο συνέταξέν σοι κύριος ὁ θεός σου ὥστε φυλάσσεσθαι τὴν ἡμέραν τῶν σαββάτων καὶ ἁγιάζειν αὐτήν.
12 כבד את־אביך ואת־אמך למען יארכון ימיך על האדמה אשר־יהוה אלהיך נתן לך׃ ס	12 τίμα τὸν πατέρα σου καὶ τὴν μητέρα, ἵνα εὖ σοι γένηται καὶ ἵνα μακροχρόνιος γένῃ ἐπὶ τῆς γῆς τῆς ἀγαθῆς, ἧς κύριος ὁ θεός σου δίδωσίν σοι.	16 כבד את־אביך ואת־אמך כאשר צוך יהוה אלהיך למען יאריכן ימיך ולמען ייטב לך על האדמה אשר־יהוה אלהיך נתן לך׃ ס	16 τίμα τὸν πατέρα σου καὶ τὴν μητέρα σου, ὃν τρόπον ἐνετείλατό σοι κύριος ὁ θεός σου, ἵνα εὖ σοι γένηται, καὶ ἵνα μακροχρόνιος γένῃ ἐπὶ τῆς γῆς, ἧς κύριος ὁ θεός σου δίδωσίν σοι.
13 לא תרצח ס	13 οὐ μοιχεύσεις.	17 לא תרצח ס	17 οὐ μοιχεύσεις.
14 לא תנאף ס	14 οὐ κλέψεις.	18 ולא תנאף ס	18 οὐ φονεύσεις.
15 לא תגנב ס	15 οὐ φονεύσεις.	19 ולא תגנב ס	19 οὐ κλέψεις.
16 לא־תענה ברעך עד שקר ס	16 οὐ ψευδομαρτυρήσεις κατὰ τοῦ πλησίον σου μαρτυρίαν ψευδῆ.	20 ולא־תענה ברעך עד שוא ס	20 οὐ ψευδομαρτυρήσεις κατὰ τοῦ πλησίον σου μαρτυρίαν ψευδῆ.
17 לא תחמד בית רעך ס לא־תחמד אשת רעך ועבדו ואמתו ושורו וחמרו וכל אשר לרעך׃	17 οὐκ ἐπιθυμήσεις τὴν γυναῖκα τοῦ πλησίον σου. οὐκ ἐπιθυμήσεις τὴν οἰκίαν τοῦ πλησίον σου οὔτε τὸν ἀγρὸν αὐτοῦ οὔτε τὸν παῖδα αὐτοῦ οὔτε τὴν παιδίσκην αὐτοῦ	21 ולא תחמד אשת רעך ס ולא תתאוה בית רעך שדהו ועבדו ואמתו שורו וחמרו וכל אשר לרעך׃ ס	21 οὐκ ἐπιθυμήσεις τὴν γυναῖκα τοῦ πλησίον σου. οὐκ ἐπιθυμήσεις τὴν οἰκίαν τοῦ πλησίον σου οὔτε τὸν ἀγρὸν αὐτοῦ οὔτε τὸν παῖδα αὐτοῦ οὔτε τὴν παιδίσκην αὐτοῦ

οὔτε τοῦ βοὸς αὐτοῦ οὔτε τοῦ ὑποζυγίου αὐτοῦ οὔτε παντὸς κτήνους αὐτοῦ οὔτε ὅσα τῷ πλησίον σού ἐστιν.

οὔτε τοῦ βοὸς αὐτοῦ οὔτε τοῦ ὑποζυγίου αὐτοῦ οὔτε παντὸς κτήνους αὐτοῦ οὔτε ὅσα τῷ πλησίον σού ἐστιν.

Appendix A2: The Decalogue in English Translation

Exod 20:1-17 (LXX ET)	Exod 20:1-17 (BHS ET)	Deut 5:6-21 (LXX ET)	Deut 5:6-21 (BHS ET)
Then the Lord spoke all these words: 2 I am the LORD your God, who brought you out of the land of Egypt, out of the house of slavery; 3 you shall have no other gods besides me. 4 You shall not make for yourself an idol, whether in the form of anything that is in heaven above, or that is on the earth beneath, or that is in the water under the earth. 5 You shall not bow down to them and do not worship them; for I am the LORD your God, a jealous God, paying back children for the sins of parents, to the third and the fourth generation of those who	Then God spoke all these words: 2 I am the LORD your God, who brought you out of the land of Egypt, out of the house of slavery; 3 you shall have no other gods before/beside me. 4 You shall not make for yourself a graven image, whether in the form of anything that is in heaven above, or that is on the earth beneath, or that is in the water under the earth. 5 You shall not bow down to them or worship them; for I the LORD your God am a jealous God, punishing children for the iniquity of parents, to the third and the fourth generation of those	6 I am the LORD your God, who brought you out of the land of Egypt, out of the house of slavery; 7 you shall have no other gods before me. 8 You shall not make for yourself a graven image, whether in the form of anything that is in heaven above, or that is on the earth beneath, or that is in the water under the earth. 9 You shall not bow down to them and do not worship them; for I am the LORD your God, a jealous God, paying back children for the sins of parents, to the third and fourth generation of those who	6 I am the LORD your God, who brought you out of the land of Egypt, out of the house of slavery; 7 you shall have no other gods before/beside me. 8 You shall not make for yourself a graven image, whether in the form of anything that is in heaven above, or that is on the earth beneath, or that is in the water under the earth. 9 You shall not bow down to them or worship them; for I the LORD your God am a jealous God, punishing children for the iniquity of parents, to the third and fourth generation of those who

reject me, 6 but showing mercy to the thousandth generation of those who love me and keep my statutes. 7 You shall not make wrongful use of the name of the LORD your God, for the LORD will not pronounce anyone pure who misuses his name. 8 Remember the sabbath day, and keep it holy. 9 Six days you shall labor and do all your work. 10 But the seventh day is a sabbath to the LORD your God; you shall not do any work on it, you, your son or your daughter, your male or female slave, your ox or your donkey, your livestock, or the alien resident living with you. 11 For in six days the LORD made heaven and earth, the sea, and all that is in them, but rested the seventh day; therefore the	who reject me, 6 but showing steadfast love to the thousandth generation of those who love me and keep my commandments. 7 You shall not make wrongful use of the name of the LORD your God, for the LORD will not acquit anyone who misuses his name. 8 Remember the sabbath day, and keep it holy. 9 Six days you shall labor and do all your work. 10 But the seventh day is a sabbath to the LORD your God; you shall not do any work - you, your son or your daughter, your male or female slave, your livestock, or the alien resident within your gates.	reject me, 10 but showing mercy to the thousandth generation of those who love me and keep my statutes. 7 You shall not make wrongful use of the name of the LORD your God, for the LORD will not pronounce anyone pure who misuses his name. 12 Observe the sabbath day and keep it holy, as the LORD your God commanded you. 13 Six days you shall labor and do all your work. 14 But the seventh day is a sabbath to the LORD your God; you shall not do any work on it, you, or your sons or your daughter, your male or female slave, your ox or your donkey, or any of your livestock, or the resident alien within your gates, so that your male and female slave may rest as well as you. 15 Remember that you were a slave in the land of Egypt, and the LORD your God brought you out from there with a mighty hand	reject me, 10 but showing steadfast love to the thousandth generation of those who love me and keep my commandments. 11 You shall not make wrongful use of the name of the LORD your God, for the LORD will not acquit anyone who misuses his name. 12 Observe the sabbath day and keep it holy, as the LORD your God commanded you. 13 Six days you shall labor and do all your work. 14 But the seventh day is a sabbath to the LORD your God; you shall not do any work - you, oryour son or your daughter, or your male or female slave, or your ox or your donkey, or any of your livestock, or the resident alien within your gates, so that your male and female slave may rest as well as you. 15 Remember that you were a slave in the land of Egypt, and the LORD your God brought you out from there with a mighty hand

LORD blessed the seventh day and consecrated it. 12 Honor your father and your mother, so that that it may go well with you and your days may be long in the good land that the LORD your God is giving you. 13 You shall not commit adultery. 14 You shall not steal. 15 You shall not murder. 16 You shall not bear false witness against your neighbor. 17 You shall not covet your neighbor's wife; you shall not covet your neighbor's house, or field or male or female slave, or ox, or donkey, or any livestock or what belongs to your neighbor.	LORD blessed the sabbath day and consecrated it. 12 Honor your father and your mother, so that your days may be long in the land that the LORD your God is giving you. 13 You shall not murder. 14 You shall not commit adultery. 15 You shall not steal. 16 You shall not bear false witness against your neighbor. 17 You shall not covet your neighbor's house; you shall not covet your neighbor's wife, or male or female slave, or ox, or donkey, or anything that belongs to your neighbor.	and an outstretched arm; therefore the LORD your God commanded you to keep the sabbath day and to consecrate it. 16 Honor your father and your mother, as the LORD your God commanded you, so that it may go well with you and that your days may be long in the land that the LORD your God is giving you. 17 You shall not commit adultery. 18 You shall not murder. 19 You shall not steal. 20 You shall not bear witness against your neighbor falsely. 21 You shall not desire your neighbor's wife; you shall not desire your neighbor's house, or field or male or female slave, or ox, or donkey, or any livestock or what belongs to your neighbor.	and an outstretched arm; therefore the LORD your God commanded you to keep the sabbath day. 16 Honor your father and your mother, as the LORD your God commanded you, so that your days may be long and that it may go well with you in the land that the LORD your God is giving you. 17 You shall not murder. 18 Neither shall you commit adultery. 19 Neither shall you steal. 20 Neither shall you bear false witness against your neighbor. 21 Neither shall you covet your neighbor's wife. Neither shall you desire your neighbor's house, or field, or male or female slave, or ox, or donkey, or anything that belongs to your neighbor.

Appendix B1: Selected Texts from the Creation Stories: Hebrew and Greek

Genesis 1:26-28 (LXX)	Genesis 1:26-28 (BHS)
26	26
καὶ εἶπεν ὁ θεός	וַיֹּאמֶר אֱלֹהִים
Ποιήσωμεν ἄνθρωπον κατ᾽ εἰκόνα ἡμετέραν καὶ καθ᾽ ὁμοίωσιν,	נַעֲשֶׂה אָדָם בְּצַלְמֵנוּ כִּדְמוּתֵנוּ
καὶ ἀρχέτωσαν τῶν ἰχθύων τῆς θαλάσσης	וְיִרְדּוּ בִדְגַת הַיָּם
καὶ τῶν πετεινῶν τοῦ οὐρανοῦ καὶ τῶν κτηνῶν	וּבְעוֹף הַשָּׁמַיִם וּבַבְּהֵמָה
καὶ πάσης τῆς γῆς καὶ πάντων τῶν ἑρπετῶν τῶν ἑρπόντων ἐπὶ τῆς γῆς.	וּבְכָל־הָאָרֶץ וּבְכָל־הָרֶמֶשׂ הָרֹמֵשׂ עַל־הָאָרֶץ׃
27	27
καὶ ἐποίησεν ὁ θεὸς τὸν ἄνθρωπον,	וַיִּבְרָא אֱלֹהִים אֶת־הָאָדָם בְּצַלְמוֹ
κατ᾽ εἰκόνα θεοῦ ἐποίησεν αὐτόν,	בְּצֶלֶם אֱלֹהִים בָּרָא אֹתוֹ
ἄρσεν καὶ θῆλυ ἐποίησεν αὐτούς.	זָכָר וּנְקֵבָה בָּרָא אֹתָם׃
28	28
καὶ ηὐλόγησεν αὐτοὺς ὁ θεὸς λέγων	וַיְבָרֶךְ אֹתָם אֱלֹהִים
Αὐξάνεσθε καὶ πληθύνεσθε καὶ πληρώσατε τὴν γῆν καὶ	וַיֹּאמֶר לָהֶם אֱלֹהִים פְּרוּ וּרְבוּ וּמִלְאוּ אֶת־הָאָרֶץ וְכִבְשֻׁהָ
κατακυριεύσατε αὐτῆς καὶ ἄρχετε τῶν ἰχθύων τῆς θαλάσσης	וּרְדוּ בִּדְגַת הַיָּם
καὶ τῶν πετεινῶν τοῦ οὐρανοῦ καὶ πάντων τῶν κτηνῶν καὶ	וּבְעוֹף הַשָּׁמַיִם וּבְכָל־חַיָּה הָרֹמֶשֶׂת עַל־הָאָרֶץ׃
πάσης τῆς γῆς καὶ πάντων τῶν ἑρπετῶν τῶν ἑρπόντων ἐπὶ τῆς γῆς.	
Genesis 2:18-24; 3:1 (LXX)	**Genesis 2:18-25 (BHS)**
18	18
καὶ εἶπεν κύριος ὁ θεός Οὐ καλὸν εἶναι τὸν ἄνθρωπον μόνον·	וַיֹּאמֶר יְהוָה אֱלֹהִים לֹא־טוֹב הֱיוֹת הָאָדָם לְבַדּוֹ
ποιήσωμεν αὐτῷ βοηθὸν κατ᾽ αὐτόν.	אֶעֱשֶׂה־לּוֹ עֵזֶר כְּנֶגְדּוֹ׃
19	19
καὶ ἔπλασεν ὁ θεὸς ἔτι ἐκ τῆς γῆς	וַיִּצֶר יְהוָה אֱלֹהִים מִן־הָאֲדָמָה כָּל־חַיַּת הַשָּׂדֶה וְאֵת כָּל־עוֹף הַשָּׁמַיִם
πάντα τὰ θηρία τοῦ ἀγροῦ καὶ πάντα τὰ πετεινὰ τοῦ οὐρανοῦ,	וַיָּבֵא אֶל־הָאָדָם לִרְאוֹת מַה־יִּקְרָא־לוֹ
καὶ ἤγαγεν αὐτὰ πρὸς τὸν Αδαμ ἰδεῖν, τί καλέσει αὐτά,	

Genesis 3:16-19 (BHS)

16

אֶל־הָאִשָּׁה אָמַר הַרְבָּה אַרְבֶּה עִצְּבוֹנֵךְ וְהֵרֹנֵךְ בְּעֶצֶב תֵּלְדִי בָנִים

20
וַיִּקְרָא הָאָדָם שֵׁמוֹת לְכָל־הַבְּהֵמָה וּלְעוֹף הַשָּׁמַיִם וּלְכֹל חַיַּת הַשָּׂדֶה וּלְאָדָם לֹא־מָצָא עֵזֶר כְּנֶגְדּוֹ׃

21
וַיַּפֵּל יְהוָה אֱלֹהִים תַּרְדֵּמָה עַל־הָאָדָם וַיִּישָׁן וַיִּקַּח אַחַת מִצַּלְעֹתָיו וַיִּסְגֹּר בָּשָׂר תַּחְתֶּנָּה׃

22
וַיִּבֶן יְהוָה אֱלֹהִים אֶת־הַצֵּלָע אֲשֶׁר־לָקַח מִן־הָאָדָם לְאִשָּׁה וַיְבִאֶהָ אֶל־הָאָדָם׃

23
וַיֹּאמֶר הָאָדָם זֹאת הַפַּעַם עֶצֶם מֵעֲצָמַי וּבָשָׂר מִבְּשָׂרִי לְזֹאת יִקָּרֵא אִשָּׁה כִּי מֵאִישׁ לֻקֳחָה־זֹּאת׃

24
עַל־כֵּן יַעֲזָב־אִישׁ אֶת־אָבִיו וְאֶת־אִמּוֹ וְדָבַק בְּאִשְׁתּוֹ וְהָיוּ לְבָשָׂר אֶחָד׃

Genesis 3:16-19 LXX

16
καὶ τῇ γυναικὶ εἶπεν Πληθύνων πληθυνῶ
τὰς λύπας σου καὶ τὸν στεναγμόν σου, ἐν λύπαις τέξῃ τέκνα·

20
καὶ πᾶν, ὃ ἐὰν ἐκάλεσεν αὐτὸ Αδαμ ψυχὴν ζῶσαν,
τοῦτο ὄνομα αὐτῷ.
καὶ ἐκάλεσεν Αδαμ ὀνόματα πᾶσιν τοῖς κτήνεσιν
καὶ πᾶσιν τοῖς πετεινοῖς τοῦ οὐρανοῦ καὶ πᾶσιν τοῖς θηρίοις
τοῦ ἀγροῦ,
τῷ δὲ Αδαμ οὐχ εὑρέθη βοηθὸς ὅμοιος αὐτῷ.

21
καὶ ἐπέβαλεν ὁ θεὸς ἔκστασιν ἐπὶ τὸν Αδαμ, καὶ ὕπνωσεν· καὶ
ἔλαβεν μίαν τῶν πλευρῶν αὐτοῦ
καὶ ἀνεπλήρωσεν σάρκα ἀντ' αὐτῆς.

22
καὶ ᾠκοδόμησεν κύριος ὁ θεὸς τὴν πλευράν,
ἣν ἔλαβεν ἀπὸ τοῦ Αδαμ, εἰς γυναῖκα, καὶ ἤγαγεν αὐτὴν πρὸς
τὸν Αδαμ

23 καὶ εἶπεν Αδαμ Τοῦτο νῦν ὀστοῦν ἐκ τῶν ὀστέων μου καὶ
σὰρξ ἐκ τῆς σαρκός μου· αὕτη κληθήσεται γυνή, ὅτι
ἐκ τοῦ ἀνδρὸς αὐτῆς ἐλήμφθη.

24
ἕνεκεν τούτου καταλείψει ἄνθρωπος τὸν πατέρα αὐτοῦ
καὶ τὴν μητέρα καὶ προσκολληθήσεται πρὸς τὴν γυναῖκα
αὐτοῦ, καὶ ἔσονται οἱ δύο εἰς σάρκα μίαν

3:1
25
Καὶ ἦσαν οἱ δύο γυμνοί, ὅ τε Αδαμ καὶ ἡ γυνὴ αὐτοῦ, καὶ οὐκ
ᾐσχύνοντο.

	Genesis 5:1-3 (BHS)
<div dir="rtl">וְאֶל־אִישֵׁךְ תְּשׁוּקָתֵךְ וְהוּא יִמְשָׁל־בָּךְ׃ ס 17 וּלְאָדָם אָמַר כִּי־שָׁמַעְתָּ לְקוֹל אִשְׁתֶּךָ וַתֹּאכַל מִן־הָעֵץ אֲשֶׁר צִוִּיתִיךָ לֵאמֹר לֹא תֹאכַל מִמֶּנּוּ אֲרוּרָה הָאֲדָמָה בַּעֲבוּרֶךָ בְּעִצָּבוֹן תֹּאכֲלֶנָּה כֹּל יְמֵי חַיֶּיךָ׃ 18 וְקוֹץ וְדַרְדַּר תַּצְמִיחַ לָךְ וְאָכַלְתָּ אֶת־עֵשֶׂב הַשָּׂדֶה׃ 19 בְּזֵעַת אַפֶּיךָ תֹּאכַל לֶחֶם עַד שׁוּבְךָ אֶל־הָאֲדָמָה כִּי מִמֶּנָּה לֻקָּחְתָּ כִּי־עָפָר אַתָּה וְאֶל־עָפָר תָּשׁוּב׃</div>	<div dir="rtl">1 זֶה סֵפֶר תּוֹלְדֹת אָדָם בְּיוֹם בְּרֹא אֱלֹהִים אָדָם בִּדְמוּת אֱלֹהִים עָשָׂה אֹתוֹ׃ 2 זָכָר וּנְקֵבָה בְּרָאָם וַיְבָרֶךְ אֹתָם וַיִּקְרָא אֶת־שְׁמָם אָדָם בְּיוֹם הִבָּרְאָם׃ ס 3 וַיְחִי אָדָם שְׁלֹשִׁים וּמְאַת שָׁנָה וַיּוֹלֶד בִּדְמוּתוֹ כְּצַלְמוֹ וַיִּקְרָא אֶת־שְׁמוֹ שֵׁת׃</div>
καὶ πρὸς τὸν ἄνδρα σου ἡ ἀποστροφή σου, καὶ αὐτός σου κυριεύσει. 17 τῷ δὲ Αδαμ εἶπεν Ὅτι ἤκουσας τῆς φωνῆς τῆς γυναικός σου καὶ ἔφαγες ἀπὸ τοῦ ξύλου, οὗ ἐνετειλάμην σοι τούτου μόνου μὴ φαγεῖν ἀπ' αὐτοῦ, ἐπικατάρατος ἡ γῆ ἐν τοῖς ἔργοις σου· ἐν λύπαις φάγῃ αὐτὴν πάσας τὰς ἡμέρας τῆς ζωῆς σου. 18 ἀκάνθας καὶ τριβόλους ἀνατελεῖ σοι, καὶ φάγῃ τὸν χόρτον τοῦ ἀγροῦ. 19 ἐν ἱδρῶτι τοῦ προσώπου σου φάγῃ τὸν ἄρτον σου ἕως τοῦ ἀποστρέψαι σε εἰς τὴν γῆν, ἐξ ἧς ἐλήμφθης ὅτι γῆ εἶ καὶ εἰς γῆν ἀπελεύσῃ.	Genesis 5:1-3 LXX 1 Αὕτη ἡ βίβλος γενέσεως ἀνθρώπων· ᾗ ἡμέρᾳ ἐποίησεν ὁ θεὸς τὸν Αδαμ, κατ' εἰκόνα θεοῦ ἐποίησεν αὐτόν· 2 ἄρσεν καὶ θῆλυ ἐποίησεν αὐτούς. καὶ εὐλόγησεν αὐτούς. καὶ ἐπωνόμασεν τὸ ὄνομα αὐτῶν Αδαμ, ᾗ ἡμέρᾳ ἐποίησεν αὐτούς. 3 Ἔζησεν δὲ Αδαμ ἔτη διακόσια τριάκοντα καὶ ἐγέννησεν κατὰ τὴν ἰδέαν αὐτοῦ καὶ κατὰ τὴν εἰκόνα αὐτοῦ καὶ ἐπωνόμασεν τὸ ὄνομα αὐτοῦ Σηθ.

Appendix B2: Selected Texts from the Creation Stories in English translation

Genesis 1:26-28 (LXX)	Genesis 1:26-28 (BHS)
Then God said, "Let us make *anthropon* in our image and according to our likeness; and let them have dominion over the fish of the sea, and over the birds of the air, and over the cattle, and over all the earth and over every creeping thing that creeps upon the earth." 27 So God created (the) *anthropon*, in the image of God he created him; male and female he created them. 28 God blessed them, saying, "Be fruitful and multiply, and fill the earth and rule over it; and have dominion over the fish of the sea and over the birds of the air and over all animals and over all the earth and over every living thing that moves upon the earth."	Then God said, "Let us make *adam* in our image, according to our likeness; and let them have dominion over the fish of the sea, and over the birds of the air, and over the cattle, and over all the earth and over every creeping thing that creeps upon the earth." 27 So God created (the) *adam* in his image, in the image of God he created him; male and female he created them. 28 God blessed them, and God said to them, "Be fruitful and multiply, and fill the earth and subdue it; and have dominion over the fish of the sea and over the birds of the air and over every living thing that moves upon the earth."
Genesis 2:18-24; 3:1 (LXX)	Genesis 2:18-25 (BHS)
18 Then the LORD God said, "It is not good that the *anthropos* should be alone; let us make him a helper like him." 19 So out of the ground the LORD God formed still every animal of the field and every bird of the air, and brought them to Adam to see what he would call them; and whatever Adam called every living creature, that was its name. 20 Adam gave names to all cattle, and to all the birds of the air, and to every animal of the field; but for Adam there was not found a helper similar to him. 21 So the LORD God cast a spell upon Adam, and he slept; then he took one of his ribs and filled up flesh in its place.	18 Then the LORD God said, "It is not good that the *adam* should be alone; I will make him a helper as his partner." 19 So out of the ground the LORD God formed every animal of the field and every bird of the air, and brought them to the man to see what he would call them; and whatever the man called every living creature, that was its name. 20 The man gave names to all cattle, and to the birds of the air, and to every animal of the field; but for the *adam* there was not found a helper as his partner. 21 So the LORD God caused a deep sleep to fall upon the man, and he slept; then he took one of his ribs and closed up its place with flesh.

22 And the rib that the LORD God had taken from Adam he built it into a woman and brought her to Adam. 23 Then Adam said, "This is now bone of my bones and flesh of my flesh; she shall be called Woman, for she was taken out of her husband." 24 Therefore a man (*anthropos*) leaves his father and his mother and is joined to his wife, and the two become one flesh. 3:1 And the two, Adam and his wife, were naked, and were not ashamed. Genesis 3:16-19 LXX 16 And to the woman he said, "I will greatly increase your pains and groaning; in pain you shall bring forth children, yet your return shall be for your husband, and he shall rule over you." 17 And to Adam he said, "Because you have listened to the voice of your wife, and have eaten of the tree about which I commanded you only of this one not to eat from it, cursed is the ground in your toils; in pain you shall eat of it all the days of your life; 18 thorns and thistles it shall bring forth for you; and you shall eat the grass of the field. 19 By the sweat of your face you shall eat your bread until you return to the ground, from which you were taken; because you are earth and to earth you shall return."	22 And the rib that the LORD God had taken from the man he made into a woman and brought her to the man. 23 Then the man said, "This at last is bone of my bones and flesh of my flesh; this one shall be called Woman, {Heb [ishshah] } for out of Man {Heb [ish] } this one was taken." 24 Therefore a man leaves his father and his mother and clings to his wife, and they become one flesh. 25 And the man and his wife were both naked, and were not ashamed Genesis 3:16-19 (BHS) 16 To the woman he said, "I will greatly increase your pangs in childbearing; in pain you shall bring forth children, yet your desire shall be for your husband, and he shall rule over you." 17 And to the *adam* he said, "Because you have listened to the voice of your wife, and have eaten of the tree about which I commanded you, 'You shall not eat of it,' cursed is the ground because of you; in toil you shall eat of it all the days of your life; 18 thorns and thistles it shall bring forth for you; and you shall eat the plants of the field. 19 By the sweat of your face you shall eat bread until you return to the ground, for out of it you were taken; you are dust, and to dust you shall return."

Genesis 5:1-3 LXX	Genesis 5:1-3 (BHS)
This is the book of the origin of human beings (*anthropon*);	This is the list of the descendants of Adam.
when God created Adam,	When God created *adam*,
he created him according to the image of God.	he made him in the likeness of God.
2 Male and female he created them, and he blessed them and named them Adam,	2 Male and female he created them, and he blessed them and named them *adam*,
when he created them.	when they were created.
3 When Adam had lived two hundred and thirty years, he became the father of a son according to his appearance and according to his image, and named him Seth.	3 When Adam had lived one hundred and thirty years, he became the father of a son in his likeness, according to his image, and named him Seth.

Appendix C1: Deuteronomy 24:1-4, Greek and Hebrew

Deut 24:1 (LXX)	Deut 24:1 (BHS)
ἐὰν δέ τις λάβη γυναῖκα	כִּי־יִקַּח אִישׁ אִשָּׁה וּבְעָלָהּ
καὶ συνοικήσῃ αὐτῇ,	וְהָיָה
καὶ ἔσται	אִם־לֹא תִמְצָא־חֵן בְּעֵינָיו
ἐὰν μὴ εὕρῃ χάριν ἐναντίον αὐτοῦ,	כִּי־מָצָא בָהּ עֶרְוַת דָּבָר
ὅτι εὗρεν ἐν αὐτῇ ἄσχημον πρᾶγμα,	וְכָתַב לָהּ סֵפֶר כְּרִיתֻת
καὶ γράψει αὐτῇ βιβλίον ἀποστασίου	וְנָתַן בְּיָדָהּ
καὶ δώσει εἰς τὰς χεῖρας αὐτῆς	וְשִׁלְּחָהּ מִבֵּיתוֹ
καὶ ἐξαποστελεῖ αὐτὴν ἐκ τῆς οἰκίας αὐτοῦ,	
2	2
καὶ ἀπελθοῦσα	וְיָצְאָה מִבֵּיתוֹ
γένηται ἀνδρὶ ἑτέρῳ,	וְהָלְכָה
3	וְהָיְתָה לְאִישׁ־אַחֵר׃
καὶ μισήσῃ αὐτὴν ὁ ἀνὴρ ὁ ἔσχατος	3
καὶ γράψει αὐτῇ βιβλίον ἀποστασίου	וּשְׂנֵאָהּ הָאִישׁ הָאַחֲרוֹן
καὶ δώσει εἰς τὰς χεῖρας αὐτῆς	וְכָתַב לָהּ סֵפֶר כְּרִיתֻת
καὶ ἐξαποστελεῖ αὐτὴν ἐκ τῆς οἰκίας αὐτοῦ,	וְנָתַן בְּיָדָהּ
ἢ ἀποθάνῃ ὁ ἀνὴρ ὁ ἔσχατος,	וְשִׁלְּחָהּ מִבֵּיתוֹ
ὃς ἔλαβεν αὐτὴν ἑαυτῷ γυναῖκα,	אוֹ כִי יָמוּת הָאִישׁ הָאַחֲרוֹן
4 οὐ δυνήσεται ὁ ἀνὴρ ὁ πρότερος	אֲשֶׁר־לְקָחָהּ לוֹ לְאִשָּׁה׃
ὁ ἐξαποστείλας αὐτὴν ἐπαναστρέψας λαβεῖν αὐτὴν ἑαυτῷ	4 לֹא־יוּכַל בַּעְלָהּ הָרִאשׁוֹן אֲשֶׁר־שִׁלְּחָהּ
γυναῖκα	לָשׁוּב לְקַחְתָּהּ לִהְיוֹת לוֹ לְאִשָּׁה
μετὰ τὸ μιανθῆναι αὐτήν,	
ὅτι βδέλυγμά ἐστιν ἐναντίον κυρίου τοῦ θεοῦ σου·	
καὶ οὐ μιανεῖτε τὴν γῆν, ἣν κύριος ὁ θεὸς ὑμῶν δίδωσίν σοι	
ἐν κλήρῳ.	

Appendix C2: Deuteronomy 24:1-4 in English translation	
Deut 24:1 (LXX)	Deut 24:1 (BHS)
Suppose a man takes a woman and marries her, but it happens she does not please him because he finds something shameful about her, and so he writes her a certificate of divorce, puts it in her hands, and sends her out of his house; she then leaves his house 2 and goes off to become another man's wife. 3 Then suppose the second man dislikes her, writes her a bill of divorce, puts it in her hands, and sends her out of his house (or the second man who married her dies); 4 her first husband, who sent her away, is not permitted to take her again to be his wife after she has been defiled; for that would be abhorrent to the LORD, and you shall not bring defile the land that the LORD your God is giving you as a possession	Suppose a man takes a woman and marries her, but it happens that she does not please him because he finds something objectionable about her, and so he writes her a certificate of divorce, puts it in her hand, and sends her out of his house; she then leaves his house 2 and goes off to become another man's wife. 3 Then suppose the second man dislikes her, writes her a bill of divorce, puts it in her hand, and sends her out of his house (or the second man who married her dies); 4 her first husband, who sent her away, is not permitted to take her again to be his wife after she has been defiled; for that would be abhorrent to the LORD, and you shall not bring guilt on the land that the LORD your God is giving you as a possession.

Appendix D1: Mark 10:1-9 and Deuteronomy 24:1-4 LXX and Genesis 1:27; 2:24 LXX	
Mark 10:2-9	Deut 24:1-4 (LXX)
2 Καὶ προσελθόντες Φαρισαῖοι ἐπηρώτων αὐτὸν εἰ ἔξεστιν ἀνδρὶ γυναῖκα ἀπολῦσαι, πειράζοντες αὐτόν. 3 ὁ δὲ ἀποκριθεὶς εἶπεν αὐτοῖς· τί ὑμῖν ἐνετείλατο Μωϋσῆς; 4 οἱ δὲ εἶπαν· ἐπέτρεψεν Μωϋσῆς βιβλίον ἀποστασίου γράψαι καὶ ἀπολῦσαι. 5 ὁ δὲ Ἰησοῦς εἶπεν αὐτοῖς· πρὸς τὴν σκληροκαρδίαν ὑμῶν ἔγραψεν ὑμῖν τὴν ἐντολὴν ταύτην. 6 ἀπὸ δὲ ἀρχῆς κτίσεως ἄρσεν καὶ θῆλυ ἐποίησεν αὐτούς· 7 ἕνεκεν τούτου καταλείψει ἄνθρωπος τὸν πατέρα αὐτοῦ καὶ τὴν μητέρα [καὶ προσκολληθήσεται πρὸς τὴν γυναῖκα αὐτοῦ], 8 καὶ ἔσονται οἱ δύο εἰς σάρκα μίαν· ὥστε οὐκέτι εἰσὶν δύο ἀλλὰ μία σάρξ. 9 ὃ οὖν ὁ θεὸς συνέζευξεν ἄνθρωπος μὴ χωριζέτω.	1 ἐὰν δέ τις λάβῃ γυναῖκα καὶ συνοικήσῃ αὐτῇ, καὶ ἔσται ἐὰν μὴ εὕρῃ χάριν ἐναντίον αὐτοῦ, ὅτι εὗρεν ἐν αὐτῇ ἄσχημον πρᾶγμα, καὶ γράψει αὐτῇ βιβλίον ἀποστασίου καὶ δώσει εἰς τὰς χεῖρας αὐτῆς καὶ ἐξαποστελεῖ αὐτὴν ἐκ τῆς οἰκίας αὐτοῦ, 2 καὶ ἀπελθοῦσα γένηται ἀνδρὶ ἑτέρῳ, 3 καὶ μισήσῃ αὐτὴν ὁ ἀνὴρ ὁ ἔσχατος καὶ γράψει αὐτῇ βιβλίον ἀποστασίου καὶ δώσει εἰς τὰς χεῖρας αὐτῆς καὶ ἐξαποστελεῖ αὐτὴν ἐκ τῆς οἰκίας αὐτοῦ, ἢ ἀποθάνῃ ὁ ἀνὴρ ὁ ἔσχατος, ὃς ἔλαβεν αὐτὴν ἑαυτῷ γυναῖκα, 4 οὐ δυνήσεται ὁ ἀνὴρ ὁ πρότερος ὁ ἐξαποστείλας αὐτὴν ἐπαναστρέψας λαβεῖν αὐτὴν ἑαυτῷ γυναῖκα μετὰ τὸ μιανθῆναι αὐτήν, ὅτι βδέλυγμά ἐστιν ἐναντίον κυρίου τοῦ θεοῦ σου· καὶ οὐ μιανεῖτε τὴν γῆν, ἣν κύριος ὁ θεὸς ὑμῶν δίδωσίν σοι ἐν κλήρῳ. Genesis 1:27 LXX καὶ ἐποίησεν ὁ θεὸς τὸν ἄνθρωπον, κατ' εἰκόνα θεοῦ ἐποίησεν αὐτόν, ἄρσεν καὶ θῆλυ ἐποίησεν αὐτούς. Genesis 2:24 LXX ἕνεκεν τούτου καταλείψει ἄνθρωπος τὸν πατέρα αὐτοῦ καὶ τὴν μητέρα καὶ προσκολληθήσεται πρὸς τὴν γυναῖκα αὐτοῦ, καὶ ἔσονται οἱ δύο εἰς σάρκα μίαν.

Appendix D2: Mark 10:1-9 and Deuteronomy 24:1-4 LXX and Genesis 1:27; 2:24 LXX in English translation

Mark 10:2-9	Deut 24:1
2 Some Pharisees came, and to test him they asked, "Is it lawful for a man to divorce his wife?" 4 They said, "What did Moses command you?" 4 They said, "Moses allowed a man to write a certificate of dismissal and to divorce her." 5 But Jesus said to them, "Because of your hardness of heart he wrote this commandment for you. 6 But from the beginning of creation, 'God made them male and female.' 7 'Therefore a man shall leave his father and mother and be joined to his wife, {Other ancient authorities lack [and be joined to his wife] } 8 and the two shall become one flesh.' So they are no longer two, but one flesh. 9 Therefore what God has joined together, let no one separate."	Suppose a man takes a woman and marries her, but it happens she does not please him because he finds something shameful about her, and so he writes her a certificate of divorce, puts it in her hand, and sends her out of his house; she then leaves his house 2 and goes off to become another man's wife. 3 Then suppose the second man dislikes her, writes her a bill of divorce, puts it in her hand, and sends her out of his house (or the second man who married her dies); 4 her first husband, who sent her away, is not permitted to take her again to be his wife after she has been defiled; for that would be abhorrent to the LORD, and you shall not bring defile the land that the LORD your God is giving you as a possession
	Genesis 1:27 LXX 27 So God created the humankind (*anthropon*), in the image of God he created him; male and female he created them.
	Genesis 2:24 LXX 24 Therefore a man (anthropos) leaves his father and his mother and is joined to his wife, and the two become one flesh.

Bibliography

Baer, Richard A. *Philo's Use of the Categories Male and Female* (ALGHJ III; Leiden: Brill, 1970)

Bal, M. *Lethal Love: Feminist Literary Readings of Biblical Love Stories* (Bloomington: Indiana Univ. Press, 1987)

Baltensweiler, Hans. *Die Ehe im Neuen Testament* (ATANT 52; Zurich: Zwingli, 1967)

Batten, Alicia. "An asceticism of resistance in James," in *Asceticism and the New Testament*, ed. Leif E. Vaage and Vincent L. Wimbusch (New York: Routledge, 1999) 355-70.

Batto, B. F. "The institution of marriage in Genesis 2 and in *Atrahasis*," *CBQ* 62 (2000) 621-31

Bauer, J. B. "ἀποστάσιον," *EWNT*, 1.339-340

Beduhn, J. D. "'Because of the angels': unveiling Paul's anthropology in 1 Corinthians 11," *JBL* 118 (1999) 295-320

Berger, Klaus. *Die Gesetzesauslegung Jesu: Ihr historischer Hintergrund im Judentum und im Alten Testament: Teil I: Markus und Parallelen* (WMANT 40; Neukirchen–Vluyn: Neukirchener Verlag, 1972)

Bergmeier, Roland. "Zur Septuaginta-Übersetzung von Gen. 3:16" *ZAW* 79 (1967) 77-79.

Bernhard, J. H. "The Connexion between the Fifth and Sixth Chapters of 1 Cor," *ExpT* 7 (1907) 433-43

Betz, Hans Dieter. *Galatians* (Hermeneia; Philadelphia: Fortress, 1979)

Blomberg, Craig L. "Marriage, Divorce, Remarriage, and Celibacy: An Exegesis of Matthew 19:3–12," *TrinJourn* 11 (1990) 161–96

Boyarin, Daniel. *A Radical Jew: Paul and the Politics of Identity* (Berkley, Los Angeles, London: University of California Press, 1994)

Brewer, David Instone. "Deuteronomy 24:1-4 and the Origin of the Jewish Divorce Certificate," *JJS* 49 (1998) 230-43

Brown, William P. *The Structure, Role, and Ideology in the Hebrew and Greek texts of Genesis 1:1 - 2:3* (SBLDiss 132; Atlanta: Scholars, 1993)

Brueggemann, Walter. "Of the same flesh and bone (GN 2,23a)," *CBQ* 32 (1970) 532-42

Büchsel, Friedrich. "ἐπιθυμέω / ἐπιθυμία," *TDNT*, 3.168-171

Bultmann, Rudolf. *Theology of the New Testament*, Vol 1 (London: SCM; New York: Scribner, 1951)

Cantarella, Eva. *Bisexuality in the Ancient World* (New Haven, London: Yale University Press, 1992)

Carmichael, C. *The Laws of Deuteronomy* (Ithaca: Cornell Univ. Press, 1974)

Catchpole, David R. "The Synoptic Divorce Material as a tradition historical problem," *BJRL* 57 (1974) 92-127

Clines, David J. A. *"What does Eve do to help?" and other Readerly Questions to the Old Testament* (JSOTSup 94; Sheffield: JSOTPress, 1990)

Collins, Raymond F. *First Corinthians* (SacPag 7; Collegeville: Liturgical, 1999)

Colson, F. H. and Whitaker, G. H. et al. (eds.) *Philo* (Loeb Classical Library, 10 vols, 2 suppl. vols, London: Heinemann; Cambridge, Ma; Harvard Univ. Press, 1961-)

Cook, Johann. "The Exegesis of the Greek Genesis," in *VI Congress of the International Organization for Septuagint and Cognate Studies, Jerusalem 1986*, ed. C. E. Cox (Septuagint and Cognate Studies 23; Atlanta: Scholars, 1986)

Cook, Johann. "Greek Philosophy and the Septuagint," *JNSL* 24 (1998) 177-91

Craigie, Peter C. *The Book of Deuteronomy* (Grand Rapids: Eerdmans, 1976)

Daube, David. *The New Testament and Rabbinic Judaism* (Peabody: Hendrickson, 1956)

Dautzenberg, Gerhard. "'Da ist nicht männlich und weiblich'," *Kairos* 24 (1982) 186-206

Dautzenberg, Gerhard. "'Φεύγετε τὴν πορνείαν' (1 Kor 6,18): Eine Fallstudie zur paulinischen Sexualethik in ihrem Verhältnis zur Sexualethik des Frühjudentums" in *Neues Testament und Ethik: Für Rudolf Schnackenburg* ed. H. Merklein (Freiburg: Herder, 1989) 271-98

Davies, William D. and Allison, Dale C. *A Critical and Exegetical Commentary on the Gospel according to Saint Matthew*, Vol I. I–VII, Vol II. VIII–XVIII, Vol III, XIX–XXVIII (ICC; Edinburgh: T&T Clark, 1988/1991/1997)

Davies, S. L. *The Gospel of Thomas and Christian Wisdom* (New York: Seabury, 1983)

Davies, William D. and Allison, Dale C. *A Critical and Exegetical Commentary on the Gospel according to Saint Matthew*, Vol I. I–VII, Vol II. VIII–XVIII, Vol III, XIX-XXVIII (ICC; Edinburgh: T&T Clark, 1988/1991/1997)

Delling Gerhard. *Paulus' Stellung zu Frau und Ehe* (BWANT 4/5; Stuttgart: Kohlhammer, 1931)

Deming, Will. "The Unity of 1 Corinthians 5-6," *JBL* 115 (1992) 289-312

Deming, Will. *Paul on marriage and celibacy* (SNTMS 83; Cambridge: CUP, 1995)

Dodd, Charles Harold. *The Bible and the Greeks* (London: Hodder and Stoughton, 1935)

Dogniez, Cécile, and Harl, Marguerite *La Bible D'Alexandrie: Le Deutéronome* (Paris: Cerf, 1992)

Dorival, Gilles, Harl, Marguerite, Munnich, Olivier *La Bible Grecque Des Septante. Du judaïsme hellénistique au christianisme ancien* (Éditions du Cerf/Éditions du C.N.R.S., 1994) url:

Elliger, K. and Rudolph, W. (eds.) *Biblia Hebraica Stuttgartensia* (Stuttgart: Württembergische Bibelgesellschaft, 1983)

Fabry, Heinz-Josef and Offerhaus, Ulrich (ed.) *Im Brennpunkt: Die Septuaginta: Studien zur Entstehung und Bedeutung der griechischen Bibel* (BWANT 153; Stuttgart: Kohlhammer, 2001)

Fernandez Marcos, N. *The Septuagint in Context: Introduction to the Greek Version of the Bible* (Leiden: Brill, 2000)

Fieger, M. *Das Thomasevangelium: Einleitung, Kommentar und Systematik* (NTAbh NF 22; Münster: Aschendorff, 1991)

Fitzmyer, Joseph A. "The Matthean Divorce Texts and some new Palestinian evidence," in *To Advance the Gospel: New Testament Studies* (2d ed., Grand Rapids: Eerdmans, 1988)

Foh, Susan. "What is the woman's desire?" *WTJ* 37 (1974/75) 376-383

Gordon, J. Dorcas *Sister or Wife? 1 Corinthians 7 and Cultural Anthropology* (JSNTSup 149; Sheffield: JSOTPress, 1997)

Goulder, Michael D. "Libertines? (1 Cor. 5-6)," *NovT* 41 (1999) 334-48

Gundry, Robert H. "The moral frustration of Paul before his conversion," in *Pauline Studies: FS for F. F. Bruce* ed. D. A. Hagner and M. J. Harris (Exeter: Paternoster, 1980) 228-45

Gundry, Robert H. *Mark: A Commentary on his Apology for the Cross* (Grand Rapids: Eerdmans, 1993)

Gundry, Robert H. *Sōma in Biblical Theology: With emphasis on Pauline anthropology* (Cambridge: CUP, 1976)

Gundry-Volf, Judith M. "Christ and Gender: A Study of Difference and Equality in Gal 3,28" in *Jesus Christus als Mitte der Schrift: Studien zur Hermeneutik des Evangeliums: FS für O. Hofius* ed. C. Landmesser, H. J. Eckstein and H. Lichtenberger (Berlin: de Gruyter, 1997) 439-79

Gundry-Volf, Judith M. "Male and Female in Creation and New Creation: Interpretations of Galatians 3:28c and 1 Corinthians 7" in *To Tell the Mystery: Essays on New Testament Eschatology in Honor of Robert H. Gundry*, ed. T. E. Schmidt and M. Silva (JSNTSup 100; Sheffield: JSOT, 1994) 95-121

Hagner, Donald A. *Matthew 14-28* (WBC 33B; Dallas: Word Books, 1995)

Hamilton, V. P. *The Book of Genesis Chapters 1-17* (Grand Rapids: Eerdmans, 1990)

Hanhart, R. "Textgeschichtliche Probleme der LXX von ihrer Entstehung bis Origenes," in M. Hengel and A. M. Schwemer (eds.) *Die Septuaginta zwischen Judentum und Christentum* (Tübingen: J. C. B. Mohr, 1994) 1-19

Harl, Marguerite *La Bible D'Alexandrie: L'Genèse* (Paris: Cerf, 1986)

Hays, R. B. *The Moral Vision of the New Testament: A contemporary introduction to New Testament Ethics* (Edinburgh: T&T Clark, 1996)

Hengel, Martin. and Schwemer, Anna Marie (eds.) *Die Septuaginta zwischen Judentum und Christentum* (Tübingen: J. C. B. Mohr, 1994)

Héring, Jean. *La Première Épitre de Saint Paul aux Corinthiens* (Neuchatel/Paris: Delachaux et Niestlé, 1949)

Higgins, A. J. M. "Anastasius Sinaita and the Superiority of Women," *JBL* 97 (1978) 253-56

Hock, Ronald F. "God's will at Thessalonica and Greco-Roman Asceticism," in *Asceticism and the New Testament*, ed. Leif E. Vaage and Vincent L. Wimbusch (New York: Routledge, 1999) 159-170

Hoek, A. van den "Endowed with Reason or Glued to the Senses: Philo's Thought on Adam and Eve," in *The Creation of Man and Woman: Interpretations of the Biblical Narratives in Jewish and Christian Traditions* ed. G. P. Luttikhuizen (Themes in Biblical Narrative: Jewish and Christian Traditions I; Leiden: Brill, 2000) 63-75

Holtz, Traugott. "'Ich aber sage euch': Bemerkungen zum Verhältnis Jesu zur Tora," in *Jesus und das jüdische Gesetz* ed. Ingo Broer (Stuttgart: Kohlhammer, 1992) 135-45

Holtz, Traugott. *Der erste Brief an die Thessalonicher* (EKKNT XIII; Zürich: Benziger Verlag; Neukirchen-Vluyn: Neukirchener Verlag, 1986)

Holtz, Traugott. *Die Pastoralbriefe* (THKNT 13; Berlin: Evangelische Verlagsanstalt, 1980)

Hooker, Morna. "Authority on her head: An examination of 1 Cor 11:10," *NTS* 10 (1964) 410-16

http://www.tradere.com/biblio/lxx/frame.htm.

Hübner, Hans. "ἐπιθυμέω," *EWNT*, 2.67-71

Hugenberger, Gordon Paul. *Marriage as a Covenant: A Study of Biblical Law & Ethics Governing Marriage, developed from the perspective of Malachi* (VTSup LII; Leiden: Brill, 1994).

Ilan, Tal. *Jewish Women in Greco-Roman Palestine* (Peabody: Hendrickson, 1996; Tübingen: J. C. B. Mohr, 1995)

Isaksson, A. *Marriage and Ministry in the New Temple: A Study with Special References to Mt 19:13-22 and 1 Cor 11:3*-16 (ASNU XXIV; Lund, 1965)

Janzen, David 'The Meaning of Porneia in Matthew 5:32 and 19:9: An Approach from the Study of Near Eastern Culture,' *JSNT* 80 (2000) 66-80

Jewett, Robert. *Paul's Anthropological Terms* (Leiden: Brill, 1971)

Jobes, Karen H. and Silva, Moises. *Invitation to the Septuagint* (Grand Rapids: Baker; Carlisle: Paternoster, 2000)

Kellermann, U. "Der Dekalog in den Schriften des Frühjudentums," in *Weisheit, Ethos und Gebot: Weisheits- und Dekalogtraditionen in der Bibel und im frühen Judentum*, ed. H. G. Reventlow (Neukirchen-Vluyn: Neukirchener Verlag, 2000) 147-226

Kirchhoff, Renate, *Die Sünde gegen den eigenen Leib: Studien zu πόρνη und πορνεία in 1 Kor 6,12-20 und dem sozio-kulturellen Kontext der paulinischen Adressaten* (SUNT 18; Göttingen: Vandenhoeck und Ruprecht, 1994)

Knight III, George W. *Commentary on the Pastoral Epistles*; (NIGTC; Grand Rapids: Eerdmans, Carlisle: Paternoster, 1992)

Koehler, L., Baumgartner W. and J. J. Stamm, *The Hebrew and Aramaic Lexicon of the Old Testament* (CD-Rom Edition; Leiden: Brill, 1994-2001)

Konradt, Matthias. "Εἰδέναι ἕκαστον ὑμῶν τὸ ἑαυτοῦ σκεῦος κτᾶσθαι... : Zu Paulus' sexualethischer Weisung in 1 Thess 4,4f," *ZNW* 92 (2001) 128-35

Lake, Kirsopp *Apostolic Fathers I* (LCL 24; Cambridge, Mass.: Harvard Univ. Press, 1970).

Lattke, Michael. "κεφαλή," *EWNT*, 2.701-708

Lefkowitz, M. R. and Fant, M. B. *Women's life in Greece and Rome* (London: Duckworth, 1982)

Lindemann, Andreas. *Die Clemensbriefe* (HNT 17; Die Apostolischen Väter 1; J. C. B. Mohr [Paul Siebeck]: Tübingen, 1992)

Loader, William. *Jesus' Attitude towards the Law: A study of the Gospels* (WUNT 2.97; Tübingen: Mohr Siebeck, 1997; Grand Rapids: Eerdmans, 2002)

Luz, U. *Das Evangelium nach Matthäus (Mt 1–7)* (EKKNT I/1; Zurich: Benziger Verlag; Neukirchen–Vluyn: Neukirchener Verlag, 1985). English: *A Commentary on Matthew: Vol I. 1–7* (Minneapolis: Augsburg, 1990)

MacDonald, Dennis R. *There is no male and female: The fate of a dominical saying in Paul and Gnosticism* (Philadelphia: Fortress, 1987).

MacDonald, Margaret Y. "Citizens of heaven and earth: Acseticism and social integration in Colossians and Ephesians, in *Asceticism and the New Testament*, ed. Leif E. Vaage and Vincent L. Wimbusch (New York: Routledge, 1999) 269-298

Marjanen, Antti "Women disciples in the *Gospel of Thomas*," in *Thomas at the Crossroads: Essays on the Gospel of Thomas* (Studies of the New Testament and its World; Edinburgh: T&T Clark, 1998) 89-106

Mayer, G. "אָוָה" in *TDOT*, 1.134-137

Meier, John P. *Law and History in Matthew's Gospel: A Redactional Study of Mt 5:17–48* (AnBib 71; Rome: PBIPress, 1976)

Merklein, Helmut *Der erste Brief an die Korinther: Kapitel 5,1 - 11,1* (Oek. TB zum NT 7/2; Gütersloh: Gütersloher Verlagshaus; Würzburg: Echter, 2000)

Metzger, Bruce M. *A Textual Commentary on the Greek New Testament* (2d ed., Stuttgart: Deutsche Bibelgesellschaft: New York: United Bible Societies, 1994)

Moloney, Francis J. "Matthew 19:3-12 and Celibacy," in *"A Hard Saying": The Gospel and Culture* (Collegeville: Liturgical, 2001) 35-52; earlier *JSNT* 2 (1979) 42-60

Moor, J. C. de "The duality in God and Man: Gen 1:26-27," in *Intertextuality in Ugarit and Israel: Papers read at the tenth Joint Meeting of the Society for Old Testament Study and Het Oudtestamentisch Werkgezelschap in Nederland en Belgie, held at Oxford, 1977* (OTS XL; Leiden: Brill, 1998) 112-25

Moritz, Thorsten *A Profound Mystery: The Use of the Old Testament in Ephesians* (SuppNovTest 85; Leiden: Brill, 1999)

Niederwimmer, Kurt. *Askese und Mysterium: Über Ehe, Ehescheidung und Eheverzicht in den Anfängen des christlichen Glaubens* (FRLANT 113; Göttingen: V+R, 1975)

Noort, Eduard.. "The creation of man and woman in biblical and ancient near eastern traditions" in *The Creation of Man and Woman: Interpretations of the Biblical Narratives in Jewish and Christian Traditions* ed. G. P. Luttikhuizen (Themes in Biblical Narrative: Jewish and Christian Traditions I; Leiden: Brill, 2000) 1-18

Nussbaum, Martha C. *The Therapy of Desire: Theory and Practice in Hellenistic Ethics* (Princeton, N.J.: Princeton Univ. Press, 1994).

Otto, E. "False weights in the Scales of Biblical Justice? Different Views of Women from Patriarchal Hierarchy to religious Equality in the Book of Deuteronomy" in *Gender and Law in the Hebrew Bible and the Ancient Near East* ed. Victor H. Matthews, Bernhard M. Levison and Tikva Frymer-Kensky (JSOTSup 262; Sheffield: Sheffield Academic, 1998) 128-47

Pagels, Elaine H. "Adam and Eve, Christ and the Church," in *The New Testament and Gnosis*; ed. A. H. B. Logan and A. J. M. Wedderburn (Edinburgh: T&T Clark, 1983) 146-75

Pagels, Elaine H. "Exegesis of Genesis 1 in the Gospels of Thomas and John," *JBL* 118 (1999) 477-96

Richardson, P. "Judgement in Sexual Matters in 1 Cor 6:1-11," *NovT* 25 (1983) 37-58

Roloff, Jürgen. *Der erste Brief an Timotheus* (EKKNT XV; Zurich: Benziger Verlag; Neukirchen-Vluyn: Neukirchener Verlag, 1988)

Rösel, Martin. *Übersetzung als Vollendung der Auslegung* (BZAW 223; Berlin: de Gruyter, 1994)

Rosner, Brian S. "Temple prostitution in 1 Corinthians 6:12-20," *NovT* 40 (1998) 336-51

Rosner, Brian S. *Paul, Scripture and Ethics: A Study of 1 Corinthians 5-7* (AGAJU 22; Leiden: Brill, 1994)

Ruef, J. *Paul's First Letter to Corinth* (Pelican NT Comm; Harmondsworth: Penguin, 1971)

Ruiten, Jacques T. A. G. M. van. "Eden and the temple: the rewriting of Genesis 2:4 - 3:24 in the *Book of Jubilees*," in *Paradise Interpreted: Representations of Biblical Paradise in Judaism and Christianity*, ed. G. P. Luttikhuizen (Themes in Biblical Narrative: Jewish and Christian Traditions II; Leiden: Brill, 1999) 63-94

Ruiten, Jacques T. A. G. M. van. "The Garden of Eden and Jubilees 3:1-31," *Bijdragen, tijdschrift voor filosofie en theologie* 57 (1996) 305-17

Runia, David. *Philo of Alexandria and the* Timaeus *of Plato* (Philosophia Antiqua 44; Leiden: Brill, 1986)

Sampley, John P. *'And the two shall become one flesh': A study of traditions in Ephesians 5:21-33* (SNTSMS 16; Cambridge: CUP, 1971)

Sänger, Dieter. "Torah für die Völker - Weisungen der Liebe: Zur Rezeption des Dekalogs im frühen Judentum und Neuen Testament," in *Weisheit, Ethos und Gebot: Weisheits- und Dekalogtraditionen in der Bibel und im frühen Judentum* ed. H. G. Reventlow (Neukirchen-Vluyn: Neukirchener Verlag, 2000) 97-146.

Schneemelcher, W. (ed.) *New Testament Apocrypha, Volume One: Gospels and Related Writings* (2d ed., Cambridge: James Clarke; Louisville: Westminster/ John Knox, 1991)

Schrage, W. *Der erste Brief an die Korinther (1 Kor 6,12 - 11,16)* (EKKNT VII/2; Zurich: Benziger Verlag; Neukirchen–Vluyn: Neukirchener Verlag, 1995)

Schüngel-Straumann, Helen "On the creation of man and woman in Genesis 1-3: the history and reception of the texts reconsidered," in *A Feminist Companion to Genesis* ed. A. Brenner (Sheffield: Sheffield Academic, 1993) 53-76

Siegert, Folker. *Zwischen Hebräischer Bibel und Altem Testament: Eine Einführung in die Septuaginta* (Münsteraner Judaistische Studien 9; Münster:: Lit-Verlag, 2001).

Sigal, P. *The Halakah of Jesus of Nazareth according to the Gospel of Matthew*, (Lanham: Univ. of America Press, 1986)

Sly, D. *Philo's Perception of Women* (BJS 209; Atlanta: Scholars, 1990)

Stegmann, Basil A. *Christ, The "Man from Heaven": A Study of I Cor. 15:45-47 in the Light of the Anthropology of Philo Judaeus* (Washington, 1927)

Steyn, Gert J. "Pretexts of the second table of the Decalogue and early Christian intertexts," *Neotestamentica* 30 (1966) 451-64

Stratton, B. J. *Out of Eden: Rhetoric and Ideology in Genesis 2-3* (JSOTSup 208; Sheffield: Sheffield Academic, 1995)

Teugels, L. "The creation of the human in rabbinic interpretation," in *The Creation of Man and Woman: Interpretations of the Biblical Narratives in Jewish and Christian Traditions;* ed. G. P. Luttikhuizen (Themes in Biblical Narrative: Jewish and Christian Traditions I; Leiden: Brill, 2000) 107-27

Thiselton, Anthony C. *The First Epistle to the Corinthians: A commentary on the Greek text* (NIGTC; Grand Rapids: Eerdmans; Carlisle: Paternoster, 2000)

Tobin, T. H. *The Creation of Man: Philo and the History of Interpretation* (CBQMS 14; Washington: CBA, 1983)

Tov, E. "The rabbinic tradition concerning the 'alterations' inserted into the Greek translation of the Torah and their relation to the original text of the Septuagint," in E. Tov, *The Greek and Hebrew Bible: Collected Essays on the Septuagint* (Leiden: Brill, 1999) 1-20

Tov, E. *The Greek and Hebrew Bible: Collected Essays on the Septuagint* (Leiden: Brill, 1999)

Trible, P. *God and the rhetoric of sexuality* (Philadelphia: Fortress, 1978)

Uro, Risto *Studies of the New Testament and its World* (Edinburgh: T&T Clark, 1998)

Uro, Risto "Is *Thomas* an encratite gospel?" in *Thomas at the Crossroads: Essays on the Gospel of Thomas* ed. Risto Uro (Studies of the New Testament and its World ; Edinburgh: T&T Clark, 1998) 140-62

Wallis, G. "חָמַד", *TDOT*, 4.452-461

Walton, John H. "The Place of the *hutqattel* within the D-stem Group and its Implications in Deuteronomy 24:4," *HS* 32 (1991) 7-17

Wanamaker, Charles A. *Commentary on 1 and 2 Thessalonians* (NIGTC; Grand Rapids/Exeter: Eerdmans/Paternoster, 1990)

Warren, Andrew. "Did Moses permit divorce? Modal *weqatal* as key to New Testament readings of Deuteronomy 24:1-4," *Tyn Bul* 49 (1998) 39-56

Watson, Francis. "The authority of the voice: A theological reading of 1 Cor 11.2-16," *NTS* 46 (2000) 520-36

Watson, Francis. "Strategies of recovery and resistance: Hermeneutical Reflections on Genesis 1-3 and its Pauline Reception," *JSNT* 45 (1992) 79-103

Watson, Francis. *Agape, Eros, Gender: Towards a Pauline Sexual Ethic* (Cambridge: Cambridge University Press, 2000)

Watson, Francis. *Paul, Judaism and the Gentiles* (SNTSMS 56; Cambridge: CUP, 1986)

Weinfeld, M. *Deuteronomy 1-11* (AB 5; New York: Doubleday, 1991)

Wenham, Gordon J. *Genesis 1-15* (WBC 1; Waco: Word, 1987) 29-30.

Westbrook, R. "Prohibition of Restoration of Marriage in Deuteronomy 24:1-4," in *Studies in Bible 1986: Scripta Hierosolymitana* 31 ed. S. Paphet (Jerusalem: Magnes, 1986) 387-405

Westermann, C. *Genesis 1-11. a Commentary* (London: SPCK, 1974)

Wevers, John William (ed). *Septuaginta: Vetus Testamentum Graecum* (Göttingen: Vandenhoeck und Ruprecht): I *Genesis* (1974); II,1 *Exodus* (1991); III,2 *Deuteronomium* (1977).

Wevers, John William. *Notes on the Greek Text of Deuteronomy* (Septuagint and Cognate Studies 39; Atlanta: Scholars, 1995)

Wevers, John William. *Notes on the Greek Text of Exodus* (Septuagint and Cognate Studies 30; Atlanta: Scholars, 1990)

Wevers, John William. *Notes on the Greek Text of Genesis* (Septuagint and Cognate Studies 35; Atlanta: Scholars, 1993)

White, S. A. "The all souls Deuteronomy and the decalogue," *JBL* 109 (1990) 193-206

Wire, Antionette C. *The Corinthian Women Prophets: A Reconstruction through Paul's Rhetoric* (Minneapolis 1990)

Witherington, Ben "Matthew 5.32 and 19.9 – Exception or Exceptional Situation," *NTS* 31 (1985) 571-76

Witherington, Ben *Women in the Ministry of Jesus* (Cambridge: CUP, 1984)

Ziesler, John A. "The role of the tenth commandment in Romans 7," *JSNT* 33 (1988) 41-56

Index of Modern Authors

Index of Ancient Sources